FROM THE HORSE'S MOUTH

AN ANALYSIS OF CERTAIN SIGNIFICANT ASPECTS IN THE DEVELOPMENT OF THE CALYPSO AND SOCIETY AS GLEANED FROM PERSONAL COMMUNICATION WITH SOME OUTSTANDING CALYPSONIANS

BY

Hollis Urban Liverpool, Ph.D.
Cultural Anthropologist & Assistant Professor of Social Sciences,
University of the Virgin Islands.

Know Your Author:

By

Ken Tannis, M.A. (Secondary School Language Teacher, Toronto, Canada.)

Hollis Liverpool is currently Assistant Professor of History at the University of the Virgin Islands, St. Thomas, USVI. He taught Primary and Secondary schools in his beloved Trinidad and Tobago over a period of thirty-five years, then served in the Ministry of Culture as Cultural Officer 111 and Director of Culture between the years 1993 to 1999 when he retired from the Public Service. He was educated at Patience Hill R. C. and Nelson Street Boys' primary schools, St. Mary's College, the Government Training College for Teachers (GTC), the University of the West Indies at St. Augustine and the University of Michigan at Ann Arbor, Michigan, U.S.A. Besides O and A levels, he holds a Trained Teacher's Certificate, a Post-Graduate Diploma in Education, a B.A. in History and Sociology, an M.A. in History, an M.A. in African History, a Certificate in Philosophy and a Ph.D. in History and Ethnomusicology. He has written over the years a multiplicity of papers and several books, including his masterpiece: **Rituals of Power and Rebellion** (Chicago: Frontline, 2001), and has addressed several world-wide conferences on Carnival and Culture generally. As calypsonian Chalkdust, he has recorded over 300 calypsoes (academic papers he calls them). In terms of calypso performance, he has won the Buy Local Competition in Trinidad five times, the King of the World Calypso Contest in St. Thomas on eight occasions, the World Calypso Monarch held in New York twice, and the Calypso Monarch of Trinidad and Tobago five times. He is at present working on the production of four more books namely: Calypso Backstage; The Colonial Media And Tubal Uriah Butler; A Biography of Lord Kitchener and The Age of Badjohnism.

Hollis 'Chalkdust' Liverpool
Author

CONTENTS

PREFACE

This monogram represents post doctoral research on the topic of culture and the calypso and follows on my doctoral dissertation now published entitled: "Rituals of Power and Rebellion, the Carnival Tradition in Trinidad and Tobago; 1763 -1962."

The Calypso is widely accepted today as the music of the British Caribbean chain of islands. In many ways, it mirrors the thoughts, feelings and aspirations of the inhabitants, exposing, through rhymed lyrics, the social ills which beset them, while at the same time it provides for many a form of entertainment in which their disturbed minds are soothed and their feelings of frustration are pacified. But for its importance, not many know of its history, its roots, its development, the motives of the singers and their contribution to Caribbean society. Few have studied the lives of the singers, the songs of the 18th and 19th centuries, the rich and beautiful lyrics of the bards, and the impact that certain events have had on the growth and development of the art form. The few articles that have appeared in sociological and ethno-musicological journals speak little of the life, loves and obstacles that calypsonians have faced in their struggle to eke out a living, and their commitment to give the calypso the status that they felt it deserved.

Accordingly, I interviewed ten (10) calypsonians to make the historical wrongs done to them right, to understand the art form better, to compare their views with written history, and, moreover, to understand their feelings, aims, obstacles, contributions and the motivational forces that propelled them into the calypso arena.

Historians very often can be wrong in their assumptions and conclusions. This is most so when history is written by persons who are not part of one's culture, but write as observers or from secondary and tertiary sources. It is therefore important that, in the Caribbean, we who are deluged by Euro-centric history and literature document our true history from the Horse's mouth. In this manner, archaeological data, travelers' accounts and written history will be reinforced. Truly, it is the task of the historian to collect all variants of a tradition, trace their transmission from the time of the

i

event to the present, sensitively translate and interpret the language of the tradition, and eliminate spurious and symbolic elements. The aim at all times is to search for historical truth.

In carrying out this research on the subject, I have selected a cross section of calypsonians; they differ in age, education, values and style of delivery. Many of them have since died; fortunately for me, I interviewed them in the 1970s when most of them were in the prime of their career. Those interviewed were: Lord Pretender, a calypsonian of the 1920s who unfortunately died in 2002; the Mighty Unknown, who, to use his own words, sang calypsoes "since the Rock of Gibraltar was a pebble" and who succumbed to death in 1979; Lord Beginner who campaigned mostly overseas and died in 1981; Lord Iere who departed this life in 1974; Lord Superior who has sung calypsoes for his living for his entire life; The Roaring Lion who roared until 1999; Ras Shorty I who passed away sadly in the year 2000; deceased Young Killer; and two then relatively young singers, Lord Drake and Smiley.

As such, I have sought to blend the young with the old and the not so young so as to gain objective viewpoints from a true sample of the population of calypsonians. Accordingly, I have covered an entire century of calypso's history and development. Their responses then represent, to a large extent, insights into our cultural heritage and our way of life. Many similar but timely and important aspects in the history and development of the calypso will come up time and again; I have continued throughout the text to comment on them in the interest of truth even though, at times, the commentary might seem to the reader to be repetitive.

In 1973, I presented the findings of some of the singers who I interviewed as my thesis in part fulfillment of the requirement for my undergrad degree in History and Sociology. I was awarded "Best Thesis" in that year for the Social Sciences, and was thus moved to research further with a view to producing the book. Few can imagine the joy I derived from speaking and communicating with these beautiful souls called calypsonians then and over the years.

I trust that from the calypsonians' moments of exultation and sadness, hopes and aspirations and unique points of view, you the reader will be enlivened with as much joy as I derived when I

reader will be enlivened with as much joy as I derived when I interviewed them.

ISBN 976-8194-13-8

Juba Publications
71, Opal Gardens,
Diego Martin, Trinidad. W.I.
doctordust@tstt.net.tt

Printed in Trinidad and Tobago by MASER LTD
Cover art by Dale dos Santos

Acknowledgements

The most enjoyable part of writing a book is thanking those friends and colleagues who helped make the long, solitary journey a pleasurable one. Winston Albert (calypsonian Alberto), Ralph Dyette, Dawn Amethyst-Sutton, Gil Figaro, Merle Albino-DeCoteau, Sylvan Murrell, Joseph "Bones" Thomas and Kenneth Tannis read parts of the typescript and made invaluable suggestions. Calypsonians Superior, Drake, Smiley, Young Killer, Ras Shorty I, Pretender, Iere, Unknown, Beginner and Lion allowed me the privilege of speaking to them on countless occasions, thereby adding valuable education to my storehouse. Without their help and willingness to provide me with data, this book could not have been compiled or written.

Michael Swann, Lance Heath and calypsonian Duke provided me with data that ensured historical truth. Gil Figaro, the producers of the film Calpyso Dreams and Irving Rauceo supplied me with photographs and data on the singers, and thus helped me to capture, as best as I could, the unique personalities of Killer, Unknown, Lion and Pretender especially. Carlyle Maitland was responsive to my many inquiries seeking information from the Carnival Institute. Ms. Mary Dickenson, Dr. Dion Phillips, Dr. Ededet Eniama and Dr. Adelle Belle from the University of the U.S. Virgin Islands gave me words of encouragement; their timely, useful quips motivated me in times of depression and steadied my hurried pace in times of anxiety. When I got stuck in writing or didn't know how best to express a particular point, I turned to my friend Dr. Reginald Griffith; he seemed to have a plaster for every sore and thus would readily supply me with a response.

My thanks are especially due to all the past researchers of calypso and other art forms in the Caribbean; their work and contribution have provided me with the basics and indeed the motivation to delve deeper into the oral traditions and social history of Trinidad and Tobago.

Carlton Scott, Rudy Pigott and Gordon Rohlehr impacted on my learning immensely and in many ways helped to nurture the intellectual seeds provided me by God. I owe thanks in abundance to the three of them. By teaching me the rudiments of music and the art of playing the cuatro, Scotty, as he is affectionately called, helped me not only to appreciate music, but above all, to recognize harmonious chord patterns and tuneful melodies in calypso. This musical background therefore served as a tool for drawing out from others in a special way, their contribution to the art form. Pigott with his mature, critical mind made me see insights into singers that, in my opinion, no one else has seen. On our way down to Couva where we both taught History in the 1970s, Rudy would literally tear Sparrow apart and criticize him negatively; on our way up to Port-of-Spain in the evening, Rudy would speak of Sparrow in glowing terms. Rohlehr saw the need to understand the history from the bottom upwards, that is, not from academics and researchers only, but from the calypsonians themselves.

Thanks are due in no small measure to my wife Ruth who understood the importance of having this volume written for the benefit of our people, especially the children, and who therefore never sulked or quarreled when I spent hours upon hours in my study typing painfully with my one finger on the computer, instead of giving her the companionship that she so richly deserves.

This project was partly funded by a few corporate friends namely: Angostura Limited, Maser Limited, Republic Bank Limited, Trinidad and Tobago National Petroleum Marketing Co. Limited, The Office Centre Limited of Dominica, The Ministry of Community Development and Gender Affairs, The Royal Bank of Trinidad and Tobago Limited, Rhand Credit Union Co-operative Society Limited and The National Lotteries Control Board. I wish to heartily thank them all for their donations.

Finally, but in the first place, thanks are due to God, who has made me for himself, and without whom I can do nothing.

DEDICATION

To

Carlton Kelvin Peter Scott

teacher, musician, thinker and friend, who taught me the
rudiments of music and watered the germinating seed of calypso
in me;

and to

Rudy Pigott

teacher, philosopher, historian, masquerader, Egyptian, Platoite
and friend, who by his deep insights and analyses of calypsoes
made me see titanic heroes in simple, angry, laughing men;

and to

Professor Gordon Rohlehr

of the University of the West Indies, who advised and
encouraged me in 1973 to research the theme.

Chapter 1

Julian Pierre -
"The Mighty Unknown"
(1914 -1979)
"Between capitalists, Union
and Government,
You can't tell who guilt or
who innocent."

(Unknown, Calypso Theatre, 1977).

His head bowed, his feet crossed, he sat whole night in a corner waiting to do his magic on stage. It was a serious job he had to perform, and like the true professional, he sat concentrating until his name was called. Then he would rise, yawn, stretch his hands into the air, kick his right leg as a horse rearing to go, and on stage in a minute, one would hear the fine art of rendition and the beauty of lyrics from the best in the calypso business. Yes siree, there were few men like Julian Pierre, a Mighty Unknown. There were few who remained as still as he did, few who could have concentrated regardless of all the fury about him, and few, like him, never meddling in the affairs of others. He kept to himself, and when he did speak in the tent, it was to correct a young calypsonian or to give advice.

Julian Pierre, a shoemaker by trade, began his professional singing career as a lad of twenty-two (22) in a tent at Queen Street, Port-of-Spain, singing with other stalwarts such as J.J. La Hori, Executor, Douglas, Butternut, Ras Casa, Young Hero, Pretender and King Albany who was the tent's leader. Before this, however, he was achantuelle[a] in the early 1920s with the band "Hit The Deck Sailor,"

---

[a] Chantuelle - These singers harangued stickfighters of long ago into action and composed ditties for masqueraders in days gone by. They were in demand and were treated with great respect because of their command of the word, and their ability to compose - often extemporaneously.

Dr. Hollis "Chalkdust" Liverpool

and remembers clearly that J.J. La Hori was also a chantuelle in other bands such as "Flanders Poppy" and "Quintal Chinese." Another popular band at the time too, was "Decker Millionaires."

Julian's story, as such, coincides with the traditional belief that most singers of that day were also chantuelles, and that calypso was derived from the chant/chantuel or war song of the Kalinda/Kalenda[b] bands. As a chantuelle (also spelt chantelle, shantwell), his task was not only to inspire the stickfighters into action, but to provide melodies for the carnival masqueraders to sing while displaying their mask costumes on the two days of Carnival. In fact, according to Lord Iere, singers preferred to sing for the upper class masqueraders as chantuelles, rather than sing calypso for commoners, for as chantuelles they were esteemed both by their song and the company to whom they sang.[1] Before Julian's day, however, he noted that chantuelles were associated with stick-playing, and their songs were of war or protest against the ruling White upper class. Daniel J. Crowley has supported this view in stating that the earliest chantuelles were French in character and were figures such as Soso, Papa Cochon, Possum, Sirisima the Carib, and Hannibal the Mulatto.[2] Famed folklorist J.D.Elder wrote: "chantuelles identified themselves with the heroes of war and named themselves The Iron Duke, Pharaoh, the Duke of Marlborough, Black Prince etc."[3]

Julian Pierre claimed that he started composing songs from the age of seventeen (17), but most of his early songs had to be given to other singers, for his parents being prominent Roman Catholics objected to his singing. In fact, the first time he chanted under the band "Hit The Deck Sailor" at 1, St. Paul Street, Port-of-Spain, he had "to borrow a pants to sing." This truth is shown clearly in Sparrow's calypso entitled "The Outcast." The chorus goes thus:

Calypsonians really ketch hell for a long time.
To associate yuhself with dem was a big crime.

---

[b] Kalenda - the name given to the stickfight ritual performed by Africans on the estate during and after enslavement.

Dr. Hollis "Chalkdust" Liverpool

If yuh sister talk to a steelband man,
The family want to break she hand,
Put she out; lick out every teeth in she mouth;
Past yuh outcast.[4]

Calypsonians were seen by many in the society(especially the Roman Catholics)as Satanists, doers of the devil's work, and this view is still held today, unfortunately by many, although one may argue that such persons are in the minority. The said Roman Catholics were solidly behind Cpt. Baker when in 1881, he tried to stop the kalenda."The Roman Catholics argued that the Negroes, as a pagan group, were desecrating a Christian festival."[5] An excerpt from the report of R.C.G. Hamilton[6] who investigated the riots [c] of 1881 stated: "It is common during Carnival for the vilest songs in which the names of the island's women are introduced to be sung in the streets."[7]

One can understand how even from earliest times up to the 1940s, calypsonians were associated with prostitution, lower class life and carnival jamettes.[d] It was considered sinful up to the 1970s to sing calypso in Lent, and children of the 1950s and 1960s often played the game called "cutting Lent," which meant that if one person A was caught singing calypso in Lent by B, and A and B had previously cut Lent, B was privileged to give A a clout behind his head. Gordon Rohlehr summed it up thus:

> The calypsonian, like the Blues singer, was regarded by the Christians in his society, as singing Devil music. Indeed, a friend of mine who was educated in a San Fernando convent from the late 1940s to the mid 50s told me that all convent girls had to attend a Special Retreat before Carnival to atone for all the sins that other people would be committing

---

[c] Rioting occurred in Port-of-Spain in 1881, between the stickfight masqueraders and the Police who were trying to stamp out the practice of stickfighting and the carrying of lighted torches (flambeaux).
[d] Jamettes - from French "Diametre;" the name given to all lower class persons who took part in the Kalenda.

Dr. Hollis "Chalkdust" Liverpool

during the season of license and festivities. Among these sins, of course, were the constant blasphemies of calypsonians against the name of God. Every calypso was another wound in Christ's side, and in the sacred heart of his mother.[8]

It was this stigma that caused many of Unknown's songs to be unknown; it was this stigma that made him give away many of his songs, a practice that still goes on today. It was this stigma that caused him to remain, to a large extent throughout his life, unknown. Many of his compositions he gave away to calypsonian Young Kitchener, including "Cleanliness is next to Godliness," and "Tina lost she Thermos Flask." To Lord Intruder, he gave two songs namely: "Walk Asche Walk" and "Donkey Radiator Bust."

By missing many seasons during the 1930s, by giving others his songs, and by singing at times in South Trinidad, Unknown became the victim of many stolen melodies. In short, others claimed his works. The chief or most outstanding sin committed against him was the theft of the song "Nettie Nettie" which, he said, he composed in the late 1920s, but which was claimed by the Roaring Lion.

In those days, it was fashionable for a man to produce an offspring, and a friend of mine having seduced a married woman, she was loathe to tell him that the resulting child was his, for fear of breaking up her marriage.

Unknown's friend, however, wanted the child; Unknown sang as a result:

Nettie! Nettie!
Give me the thing that yuh have in your belly.
Give me the thing that yuh have in your belly;
Ah want the baby to carry for mi mamie.

Lion's version, according to Unknown, clearly was stolen, for "it made no sense." Lion's interpretation went thus:

Christmas Eve night Ah nearly dead with laugh
Lying on mi bed with a high brown craft (repeat).
Ah heard a gin bottle with a wicked tone

The Tamboo Bamboo[e] nearly make me lose control.
It was Nettie! Nettie…

Julian Pierre patterned his singing, indeed his life, after a calypsonian termed "The Unknown Soldier" who also sang calypsoes in the 1920s. The Unknown Soldier was a volunteer in the Trinidad Regiment during World War 1, and used to "drop a song now and then and disappear." Indeed, many singers presently and in the 1960s have been known to do the same. Singers like Lord Laro,[f] Eisenhower and Creator fall in this bracket.

Julian Pierre spoke too, of the early calypso competitions which he stated were centred on local themes, usually the products of local businessmen. Calypsonian Attila the Hun testified to same, mentioning in the process a chocolate drink by the name of "Toddy" as being the topic for the night, while the Roaring Lion spoke of "Dancow milk" as the topic for an extempo[g] competition. Clearly then, it can be seen that calypso was used by the businessmen in the 1930s and early 1940s to advertise their goods in return for a few pieces of silver.

Julian vividly remembered a competition in 1929; the topic was "Gold Bond soap." That, he said, was his first competition. Other competitors that night were: King Frankie, King Mike, Sonny Claw and Old Man Chico. King Mike placed first while he, Unknown, obtained the second prize. He remembered too, that around 1931, calypsonians Radio, Attila, Pretender, Invader, Owl and himself spent a "night session from 1 p.m. to 8 a.m. in a house belonging to one Tom Keane, singing extempo songs on one another.

---

[e] Tamboo bamboo stands for French "Tambour bamboo" a method of playing music by striking lengths of bamboo on the ground. It replaced the drums which were banned in 1884.
[f] Laro and Creator are domiciled in Jamaica.
[g] Extempo from extemporaneous - meaning singing off the cuff i.e. singing while at the same time composing.

The session finished, they still left for the rum shop[h] . Like most of the singers then, said Unknown, "Ah coulda bust a good grog ."[i] I, however, never saw Unknown drink, for he gave up the practice in the late 1950s and became a teetotaler to the extent that he was given a job to help reform alcoholics at the St. Ann's Mental Hospital. In fact, he died while still gainfully employed in the post. He told me too, that his decision to stop drinking occurred one day while returning on a bus from Toco village where he and his fellow calypsonians had gone to entertain the villagers. So drunk was he-at least so he was told afterwards-that he held on to the driver and the steering wheel in an effort to drive the bus and almost killed everyone. After reminiscing on what he had done under the influence of alcohol, he decided that he had had enough. In fact, in one of his calypsoes, he was bitter on himself. He sang: "Rum make me lose mi job. Rum cause me to sleep in club. Rum make me lose mi wife; little bit again, Ah woulda lose mi life."

Sociologist Pete Simon has written of the "fly-by-night, wine women and song"[9] life of calypsonians who drank out all their earnings in rum, and Julian believed that that was true to a certain extent. Beginner once told me: "If you want to get rid of money, give it to Invader. He used to pull down a whole shelf of rum and have the whole house drinking."[10]

The extempo competitions which occurred in various tents were of a high standard, according to Unknown, and Lord Executor won most of them. One competition he remembered clearly took place in a tailor shop on George Street, Port-of-Spain, and when everyone felt that he was in the lead by far, Executor, in song, changed the subject. Being in a tailor shop, Executor gave listeners a dissertation of "How Thread Was Made," explaining, in his musical extempo presentation, the manufacturing process of thread from the weaning stage to the final product. Executor obviously won.

---

[h] Rum shop - a pub-type arrangement where alcohol was sold. Port-of-Spain had a number of these shops, mostly on street corners; they were usually run by Portuguese businessmen. They were conspicuous for their size, the painted facades of the outer building, the clatter of the inhabitants and the foul, rummy smell of the interior.

[i] A creolized term for a drink of rum.

Dr. Hollis "Chalkdust" Liverpool

The extempo story centred on competitions bears testimony to the alert mind and quickness of speech that characterized calypsonians of the late 1920s and 1930s. I was privileged to hear Unknown sing extempo on many occasions as we and other calypsonians "bust a grog" on George Street. Of this I am sure; few could have taken him on in the field of extempo. Fewer still could have beaten him in that dying art. In 1969, at the Naparima Bowl[j] backstage, whilst the semi-finalists were waiting to sing, Young Creole, Smiley, Psycho, Allrounder, Gibraltar, Tiny Terror, Killer and Yours Truly were all engaged in extempo singing. The 'contest' went on and on until someone threw a picong[k] at Jules. Unknown retaliated by composing right there and then in perfect timing, metre, rhyme and melody a ditty in which he called the names of every calypsonian present. The roar that emanated from the crowd caused the session to break up. Unknown's ditty went somewhat like this:

> Today at Naparima Bowl it's a pleasure
> To be liming with Creole, Smiley and Young Killer (repeat),
> Al Capacity, Black hat and Allrounder, Psycho, Chalkie and Gibraltar.
> So gentlemen, please leave me alone,
> I aint invite allyuh so leave the Unknown.

In 1968, as a member of the Calypso Theatre, Unknown was taken to Tobago by the Carnival Development Committee to entertain the people of Tobago. In those days, the C.D.C., as the Committee was called, selected the best of the calypsonians for road shows in Tobago, Mayaro, Toco and Chaguanas to cater for persons who for various reasons could not afford to hear the singers in the tents in Port-of-Spain. 1968 was Unknown's first trip under the auspices of the C.D.C., but it showed up the ability of Unknown in the field of extempo singing. While Unknown was singing at the Roxborough

---

[j] A concert hall in San Fernando, Trinidad.
[k] Picong from the French word "piquant" meaning sharp/biting. It reflects a humorous ditty or saying in Trinidad and Tobago.

Dr. Hollis "Chalkdust" Liverpool

Secondary school where one of the shows was held, Sparrow arrived to a huge roar from the crowd. The roar drowned out Unknown's song to the extent that no one listened or could hear him. When the tumult died down, Unknown immediately sang three extempo verses one of which I'll always remember. It went thus:

> We come here to entertain them free
> And they treating me as a nobody.
> Ah rather sing for the soldiers in Tokyo
> Than to sing free for the people of Tobago.

Julian Pierre remembered that the songs of the period were sung in eight lines and were called "double tone." The emphasis was on "big words and good grammar." Raymond Quevedo, calypsonian Attila, agreed with Julian's view. In his "History of Calypso" he described the style of singing in the early twentieth (20th) century as "the Oratorical Pattern," that is to say, the kaiso[1] songs were in the nature of "a rhetorical recitative in song,"[11] usually sung in the minor key, with eight (8) lines to the strophic stanza. The oratorical pattern was otherwise called the "Double Tone." Patrick Jones' calypso war with Executor in the early 1920s brings out the truth in Attila's statement.
The calypso goes thus:

> In the extension of this rebellion
> We hear the cries of assassination.
> The extermination of nation by nation
> Mimics your feeble expostulation.
> When babes cling to their mothers' breasts,
> The angel of heaven will confess.

---

[1] Kaiso - the root word for calypso. Many social historians believe that the word calypso is an offshoot of the word kaiso.

> For I am the terror of the land
> And I have no compassion, Sans Humanite.

Unknown gave an example of the type of calypso sung at the time, that is, the 1930s. He didn't recall the name of the singers, but was of the opinion that the said lines were used on many occasions by different singers.

> Judgement shall be tampered, never to be released
> Of (sic) you ignorant and temptational (sic) beast.
> Then shall be cast into my lion's den
> To release you poor fool I don't know when.
> Thou cursed pest! Thou shall be shocked
> Or else beheaded upon a rock.
> Yes, but when Ah wheel in general
> They call me master criminal - Sans humanite.[m]

The other singer answers:

> Mercury the first terror told me in my dream
> That the Modern Inventor will reign supreme.
> It was golden etceteras of so delight
> And in my devastation I'll gain my rights.
> Men know my orations are very strong;
> This simple composition cannot throw me down.
> Misse bah moi trois say masa clew moi vlai les pour tres
> yon lagahou - Sans humanite.

Unknown's memory of the songs gives testimony to many historical writings. First, there was indeed a calypsonian by the name of Modern Inventor and he indeed was adept at singing the "double tone' songs of the period. Second, many singers used the compositions of others in their bid to conquer their opponent at "war." Third, one sees the boast, the rhetoric of the stickfighters and midnight robbers that Daniel Crowley speaks of in his writings on

[m] Sans humanite - a creolized Patois phrase meaning "without mercy." The Picong songs usually ended with this phrase.

Dr. Hollis "Chalkdust" Liverpool

the period,[13] and the brilliant rhythmic improvisations that characterized the calypso of the early 1930s. Fourth, Creole Patois was the language used for calypsoes in the 19th century; by the early 20th century, singers used a combination of English and Patois.

Although University of the West Indies professor Gordon Rohlehr claimed that "in 1918, Executor was already regarded as an old-time calypsonian,"[14] Unknown hinted to me that "there was no barrier to age, for once your song was good, you would be allowed to sing." He, however, spoke of "pulling jacket" meaning that less known singers would beg the more popular ones to allow them to be heard by pulling their jackets. One discerns that in the 1930s, all singers had to perform in jackets; it was a symbol of esteem, affluence and even education according to folklorist Andrew Carr who was a constant visitor to the tents[n] then. Whilst "pulling jacket" is not common in modern day calypso tents, yet there are still ways in which the said act is done. Yesterday, it was "pulling jacket;" today it is bribery, nepotism, a pre-arranged audience that can at times act very arrogantly, and physical threats.

In looking at songs of the 1930s and 1940s, and comparing them with today's crop, Unknown condemned the "smutty and lewd" lines of today's calypsoes, pointing out that in the 1930s and 40s, "you must have a true story on the subject," couched in "high flown language made difficult for the ordinary man to easily understand." Listening to him speak, I got the impression that songs of the seventies (70s) such as "The Art of Making Love" by Ras Shorty I, "He Lick She" by Baron, and "My Connie" by Sparrow would never have been accepted in the 1940s. People must search for that which is considered lewd or offensive, and of course, the lyrics must make sense. The emphasis in the 1940s, according to Unknown, was on "grammar," and educated persons such as lawyer H.O.B.Wooding[o] were selected to judge the compositions. As such, even if songs were smutty, the "grammar

---

[n] Calypso was first sung in tents made of bamboo and thrash. Today the name is traditionally kept even though the calypso is sung in neon-lit halls.

[o] H.O.B.Wooding Attorney-at-law; he later became the Chief Justice of Trinidad and Tobago.

Dr. Hollis "Chalkdust" Liverpool

had to be good, the English must be well sung or otherwise well used." To a large extent, the emphasis was on sound, the sound of big words. In the 1990s, it would seem that people prefer the lewd rather than the jocular, the philosophical or the moral. As early as 1973, Chalkdust the calypsonian sang:

> If you want to win the Crown, sing about wine,
> women and song;
> Sing about your neighbour's wife; sing about
> your own sex life.
> Chalkie! Take it from we! kaiso and politics don't agree.
> So be aware, that up there, is sex bare they want to hear.

Unknown gave as an example of a smutty song of the early 1940s, one entitled "An ATS Girl." In it, he is being trained by this ATS[p] girl to perform certain body movements. Clearly, during world War 11, women were drafted in the Auxilliary Corps.[16] The song goes thus:

> Ah got in with an ATS girl named Melda
> She wanted to make me a Drill Inspector.
> She said your drilling practice starts at sharp nine
> So please don't make no mistake, but take your time.
> Believe Ah had to take all command from she
> Cause Ah wanted to join her Royal Navy.
> Chorus: She tell me: form fours; form two deep.
> Well Ah busy like a Lieutenant on mi feet,
> With about turn - advance barrage,
> Get ready for the command - Bayonet Charge.

Although the reader might find this calypso to be lewd, yet there is a story to it. Take again Lord Pretender in 1946 singing a calypso entitled "Lock and Key," in which he advised all men to secure their property well before leaving home. In the calypso, Pretender sought from technicians the technology needed to safeguard in a special manner a man's property from thieves and intruders.

---

[p] In Creole talk, ATS meant "Ah Turn Soldier." Thus many women became soldiers during the war.

Dr. Hollis "Chalkdust" Liverpool

12

Pretender sang:

> If somebody should invent a lock and key
> That a man could lock up his own property.
> Go where you like, you can boast and brag as man
> That - not a soul cannot trespass on your land.[17]

One of the best pieces of smut[q] I have heard came from Unknown in 1969 at the Old Fire Brigade building on Abercromby Street, Port-of-Spain. The building then housed the Calypso Theatre.[r] Unknown recalled the story of a dream he had, making love to a girl named Emeline on the train line, with the sound of the train making him realize that somebody or something was coming. The audience used to be in fits of laughter from the rhyming, symbolic words that Unknown used, and, of course, many pictured themselves making love on the train line, a popular pastime in the 1940s.[18] Unknown mused:

> Well Ah dream me and mi girlfriend Emeline
> Drop asleep one night on the train line
> Soon after, a little function,
> Whey Ah meet she - in Morvant[s] junction.
> I decide to tackle she. She say: you anxious, Unknown take yuh time.
> As Ah go to do whey Ah have in mind,
> Ah feeling a vibration on the train line.
> Chorus: Engine coming: Hoochew waya! hoochew waya! we still on the line.
>   Hoochew waya! hoochew waya! Engine again, well it coming this time.
>   But mamayo between wake and sleep
>   Engine going peep, peep, peep
>   Ah hearing hoochew waya! hoochew waya!
>   Engine comin' Well Ah say look Ah dead - this time.

---

[q] Smut - a name for a type of calypso where the lyrics depict sex and the story is generally considered to be obscene.
[r] Calyso Theatre - the name of a calypso tent run by the calypsonians with assistance from Government.
[s] Morvant - a district in North Trinidad.

Dr. Hollis "Chalkdust" Liverpool

The Road March[t] for Unknown must be a Road March, that is, it must be sung by the crowd and not played on a tenor pan. "The steelband cannot interpret the feeling generated or expressed by the lyrics of a song." Unknown may be correct, for it is no secret that calypsonians today aim at bringing out the musical ability of panmen by concentrating on chord progression and harmonious melodies. When we look back at past Road Marches of the 1940s and 1950s and recall Road Marches such as "Tantie Tea Shop Burning Down," "Fire Brigade Water The Road," "In a Calabash," and "Loomat Say He See Boysie,"[u] we can well understand what Unknown meant. One must understand, however, that because the band members of long ago were a more coherent and intimate group, they would naturally sing together. Moreover, the growing sophistication and commercialization of Carnival tend to destroy that oral tradition.

In the late 1930s and early 40s, there were many changes in the calypso, according to Julian Pierre. First, the "Double Tone" gave way to the "Single Tone,"[v] although Attila dates this change to the 1920s. Second, "as calypso scores were not written, you either sang in the minor key, the major key or a straight tune. A straight tune was a four line verse and a four line chorus. He gave as an example of a straight tune, the following:

Down the road, mama! down the road;
Tie up yuh dress and run down the road.
The children too harden,[w] so they have to feel.
In the prison channel - they going to yield.

Unknown was nurtured by the chantuelle tradition; hence he was of the opinion in 1973 that calypso bands needed singers to bring out the calypsonian's message at events such as Brassorama and Panorama.[x] He noted: "This is indeed necessary to keep calypso alive, so that unrecorded songs will be heard both locally and externally. Steelbands

---

[t] Road March - the song that is the most popular during the two days of Carnival.
[u] Boysie Singh was charged for murder of one fellow nicknamed "Bumper." Singh was a notorious tyrant who was eventually hanged for the murder of a socialite dancer named Thelma Haynes. Loomat was a crown witness in the case of Bumper.
[v] A name for the four line songs of the period.
[w] A creolized term for "being stubborn or obstinate."
[x] Carnival events involving brass and pan respectively.

Dr. Hollis "Chalkdust" Liverpool

14

should learn to accompany the singer." It would seem that, judging from the number of singers who today sing with brass bands-and in many cases steelbands-Unknown's dream has at last come true.

In 1973, I asked him to ponder on the future of the art form. He felt then that "a National Orchestra, more local recordings, a Calypso Dance to be exposed by the top guns in the Calypso world and more radio and television coverage" were necessary "if the art of calypso is to survive." He felt too, that not enough use was made of the calypsonian or the calypso in Trinidad, and pointed out the spiraling figure of road deaths while calypsoes like Magic's[y] "Obey the Highway Code" remains unplayed on the shelves of our radio stations. He was strongly of the opinion that the calypso "Portrait of Trinidad" by Sniper[z] "should open our day radio wise." In other words, Unknown was one of those few persons in our society who saw the calypso not merely for its entertainment value, but recognized that it was a mirror reflecting our colonial past, and a value-laden depository with messages for the future.

His strong forte in calypso was his ability to paint a story, using select words to clearly tell how he felt inside. For example, in "Prick for Judges," he attacked the Carnival Development Committee in 1977 for seemingly picking mediocre talent in 1976, and leaving out good calypsoes. Actually, he felt that calypsonians Terror and Short Pants should have been selected and not Mudada and Buzzing Bee[aa] . He sang:

Verse 1.
Jonah Regis, Tony Mitchell and Cumberbatch[bb]
It aint have dey match.[cc]

---

[y] Lord Magic - a singer from Marabella in South Trinidad; he campaigned mostly in Dutch St. Maarten.
[z] Sniper - Mervyn Hodge - deceased, another one of Trinidad's immortal calypsonians. The calypso itself was composed by the Mighty Penman-now a vagrant-but made popular by Sniper.
[aa] Buzzing Bee, daughter of pannist Hugh Borde; she reached the finals of the Calypso Monarch competition as a school girl, and was the youngest to have ever done so.
[bb] Mitchell and Regis were Calypso Monarch judges of the 1970s; Prince Cumberbatch was Secretary of the C.D.C. , the body that oversaw the carnival of Trinidad and Tobago.
[cc] Creole satire meaning: there's none to measure up to them.

Dr. Hollis "Chalkdust" Liverpool

If Ah had a ice pick, all ah dem would a get a prick
Last year when dey pick.
Because people come from the East, West, North and South
To hear calypsoes to talk about.
But history show the judges make a compro'
To kill our calypso.

Verse 2.
Is a long time ago
Judges trying to kill our calypso.
But this time Ah sharpening a stick;
Ah want to gi Tony Mitchell two prick.
Police could say Ah violating the law
But when Ah done prick Tony, man Ah go prick Padmore. [dd]
So dey better keep out
Cause Ah sure to prick Jonah Regis in e'mouth.
Chorus: You know why - as every one know
      Trinidad is the land of calypso.
      But St. Thomas have it under control
      Dem does crown the Calypso King o' de world.
      Nearly every country tiefing we art
      And de Director of Culture aint doing a fart. [ee]
      Just now we go have to go to Guyana,
      Antigua, Jamaica
      For calypsoes and Panorama.

Unknown again showed the class of genius when in 1975 in a calypso entitled "Too Much Government," he seemed to know exactly what was wrong with calypso and the reasons for it not taking its rightful place in the musical world in the Caribbean and overseas.

[dd] Marjorie Padmore, musician and female judge on the panel of Calypso Monarch judges. She is now deceased.
[ee] Creole for "aint doing nothing."

At the same time, he outlined what, in his opinion, should be the role and function of the modern-day calypsonian. The reader should note Unknown's ability to play with words and still convey meaning.

When they say calypsonians musn't mix with politics
Ah does watch dem fix.
Still dey want calypsonians to redden up dey finger[ff]
But that's only for kicks
You see every period before an election
You could hear them begging for vote from calypsonian
You see me so long'st I vote,[gg]
Ah go sing on dem political cut-throats.
Chorus: Because in this government have
    another government
    Undermining the real government
    And in that government have some
    other government
    Only retarding improvement.
    All dey mean is calypsonians must
    sing on bacchanal
    Or make roadmarch for them to go
    jump for carnival.
    But not me, ay, Ah fus Ah love mi country,
    So Ah go sing on everybody.
Dey does take calypsonians for a big pile of fools
Because we never went to High schools.
They even state how the culture is for undergraduate
And we language is inadequate.
You ent see dey woulden even send us on a course
Dey mean dat Tom, Dick and Harry must be
calypsonians' boss.
And the cultural department
Dem doesn't even pass through the calypso tent.
Chorus: In this government have some judges' government

[ff] Meaning to vote at an election.
[gg] Literally - So long as I have cast my vote.
Dr. Hollis "Chalkdust" Liverpool

Does sit down in calypso tent.
Some of dem doesn't know how much beat to a bar
Or when a singer over-run his metre.
All dey mean is calypsonians must
sing on bacchanal,
Or make roadmarch, like Kitchener,
for dem to jump for carnival.
But I've seen the ills of mi country
And mi belly burning me,
So Ah go sing on anybody.

Yes Siree! Unknown was one who used different words to get the message across, and like the true calypsonian of the early 20th century, through the skillful use of figures of speech, he punned on phrases and words, albeit at times, in a humorous vein.

One of the greatest events in his life occurred when a patron and former alcoholic rushed to him, and gave him, he said, a gift of fifteen dollars, as he belted out the calypso "How to Stop the Drinking Problem." Indeed, he was sympathetic to all alcoholics, he having been one.

When the Calypso Theatre opened its doors in 1966 to cater especially for singers who were unable to get into the bigger and more established tents, Unknown truly welcomed the initiative. In fact, from 1966 until his death, he stayed with the theatre, vowing during the winter of his life never to depart from his fellow singers there. In 1974, he sang "Dead people on The Pavement;" in 1975, it was "Too Much Government;" in 1976, it was "Tobago for Packro [hh] Tea;" in 1977, "Ah Vex" and in 1978, he thrilled the audience with "Rasta Family."

The Calypso Theatre, the reader should know, was the brainchild of Steelband leader George Goddard who in his day[ii] made a great contribution, not only to the steelband movement, but to culture in general, in Trinidad and Tobago.

[hh] A term for a cockroach-like mollusc found in the sea. Tobagonians use it as an aphrodisiac.
[ii] George Goddard, friend and fellow researcher died in January 1988. George was a pioneer in the formation of the Calypsonians' Assoc. in 1966.
Dr. Hollis "Chalkdust" Liverpool

Unknown felt very happy and proud to be a member of the cast at the theatre. It would be true to say that just as he believed in the Calypso Theatre, so too he had extreme confidence in the then Calypsonians' Association which he helped to found in 1966. In fact, he fought hard and tirelessly to make the Association strong by his songs, his oral contributions at meetings and his willingness to contribute financially to the organization.

Politically, Unknown favoured no one. He once condemned laissez-faire teachers whom he said were driving taxis, selling sweepstakes, owned dressing salons, while his "children got only 'calpet'[jj] in schools."

> Dem teachers too bad, bad, bad;
> Dey worse than the jamette in concrete yard.
> Dey does only work five hours a day
> And they want the Colonial Secretary's pay.

Unknown pulled no punches nor held back any left hooks lyrically. In the calypso "Ah Vex" in which he castigates Derek Walcott[kk] for suggesting that Trinidad is the land of only carnival and sex, not only does Unknown speak firmly to Derek, calling a spade a spade, but he uses beautiful metaphors to cover things he believes he ought not to say in keeping with the tradition of calypso. According to Unknown, one "couldn't say in calypso the terms that refer to the parts of the body that we keep covered." In addition, you couldn't try to cover them up by using any sophisticated terms such as "boomsee, bumsee, bamsee, or even bottom." Hence Unknown sang:

[jj] Calpet - a local term for a slap with the hand on the back of somebody's head. It was normally done to little boys who had recently received a haircut.
[kk] St. Lucian-born Trinidadian author and playwright who won the Nobel Prize for literature in 1992.

In Barbados, big man and woman
Does be naked on the beach say dey sifting sand.
And when you see the sand get between dey cry
Dey does stoop down in the water and wash dey eye.
And if you only bend down to lace yuh shoe,
Barbadian like Jack Spaniard on top o'you.
And if you don't tie up yuh lacin'fas'
Dey does jump on yuh back and bawl: Gee Jackass.
Chorus: So Ah vex! Ah vex! Derek Walcott say
       Trinidad is carnival and sex.
       Ah vex! Derek suffering from one big complex.
       Derek! Go back to St. Lucia yuh mother country[ll]
       There you'll see all kinda vice and sexology:
       Man marrying man and is Tee la lee la.
       And Derek woulden say a thing about St. Lucia.

In 1972, in calling upon calypsonians to control their own affairs, he again pulled no punches. In a calypso entitled "Co-Operation," he belted out:

Sparrow, Kitchener and Lord Blakie,[mm]
Sylvester Taylor, and Sam Bodie[nn]
All ah dem is big time manager.
Now dey draft in a next fella.
Now when you see dem make all dey lump sum
Dey does spit you out like bubble gum.
You come like a pest
Going to John Public crying distress.
Chorus: Everybody going co-operation

[ll] Pronunced "mother cont - tree" as if he were about to be obscene.
[mm] Famous calypsonians.
[nn] Calypso tent managers.

Dr. Hollis "Chalkdust" Liverpool

And they getting through.
It's high time that we calypsonians
Should go co-operative too.
Put down a few cents in the season
To build dey own tent.
Then and only then
We would be responsible businessmen.

If TUCO (Trinbago United Calypsonians'Organization)[oo] had heeded the words of Unknown, today the association would certainly have been in a more favourable financial footing and would not have to depend on Government to finance its many competitions, as is the custom nowadays.

Unknown, called Jules by his close friends, sang on varied topics. In the early seventies (70s) it was "To Diego Martin We Walking," recalling the hard times of people who had to walk for miles long ago to purchase food or to carry out their civil duties. In the seventies he warned me also in a clever satirical manner: "Chalkie! Big people business go land you in custody."

Unknown won the second "Buy Local"[pp] calypso competition in Trinidad and Tobago in 1966 beating the author into third place, was a semi-finalist in the Calypso Monarch contest in 1977, and was honoured posthumously in 1980 by the Carnival Development Committee, for his contribution to calypso and carnival.

It is perhaps significant and ironic that he who warned the authorities in 1974 that they had the weapons "to avoid malnutrition and starvation, else poor people would die on the pavement," should himself drop dead on a pavement on George street on December 15, 1979, while the apples he was taking home for his three little darlings-his young daughters-rolled into the canal

---

[oo] Calypsonians formed the Trinidad and Tobago Assn. of Calypsonians and Calypso Composers in 1965; the Calypsonians Assoc. in 1966 and Tuco in the 1990s.

[pp] Buy Local - a competition managed and produced by the PNM the then governing political party to advertise locally produced goods. The author, Chalkdust won it on six occasions, three consecutively and now holds the Texaco trophy for his achievement. The competition ceased in the mid 1970s.

Dr. Hollis "Chalkdust" Liverpool

at his cold feet. Ironically in 1974 he had sung: "So Ah begging them to come to some settlement, or is a heap o' dead people on the pavement."

Hail Unknown, a great, talented and serious calypsonian, who came into this world in1914 and departed for his eternal reward in 1979; he devoted forty (40) years of his life to calypso and influenced many, including yours truly. May he rest in peace.

ENDNOTES

[1] Thomas, Randolph (Iere). January 1972. Personal Interview. Port-of-Spain. Trinidad.

[2] Crowley, Daniel. "Towards a Definition of Calypso," in Ethnomusicology 3, No.2 (May 1959): 57 -66; No.3, (Sept. 1959): 117 -24.

[3] Elder, J.D. "Colour, Music and Conflict in Trinidad." In Ethnomusicology 8, No. 2, (1964): p.4.

[4] Francisco, Slinger. "The Slave." In Sparrow's Greatest Hits, Solid Gold: S 134, 1969. [7.07 min.]

[5] Elder, J.D. op.cit.

[6] R.G.C. Hamilton - was sent in 1881 to investigate the riots which occurred in port-of-Spain during Carnival that year between the police and the revelers. His report was dispatched to the Secretary of State for the Colonies on June 13, 1881.

[7] Hamilton, R.C.G. 1881 Canboulay Riots. Published as "The Hamilton Report" in Vanguard. Feb.8, 1969. P.5.

[8] Rohlehr, Gordon. "The Development of the Calypso 1900 - 1940." T.S. (Jan. & May 1972). P. 8. Also published in 3 Issues of Tapia as "Forty Years of Calypso."

[9] Simon, Peter. "Calypso." In Art and Man. (Feb. 1969): 33

[10] Moore, Egbert (Beginner). August 1972. Personal Interview. Belmont. Trinidad.

[11] Quevedo, Raymond (Attila). "History of Calypso." In This Country of Ours. Trinidad. 1962. P. 89.

[12] Rohlehr, Gordon. "The Development of the Calypso." 1972. P.16.

[13] Crowley, Daniel J. "The Midnight Robbers." In Caribbean Quarterly 10, Nos. 3&4. (1956): 263 -274.

[14] Rohlehr, Gordon. Op. cit. P. 14.

[15] Liverpool, Hollis. "Juba Dubai" in Yours Regally. Original Regal Tent, 1973. P. 17.

[16] McFarlane, Mervyn. Personal Communication. Nelson St. Boys'R.C. School. P.O.S., 1967.

[17] Hill, Errol. "Calypso Drama." In Caribbean Quarterly 15, Nos.2&3. (June - Sept. 1958).

[18] McFarlane, Mervyn. Personal Communication. Nelson St. Boys'R.C. School. P.O.S., 1970.

The Tramcar in the 1920s – Courtesy W. Besson

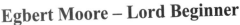

Chapter 2

Egbert Moore – Lord Beginner

Darling! doo doo!
Please don't make me blue – O
lord!
Every time ah turn in the night
Ah take mi pillow for you.

(Lord Beginner – "Louise"
from the Author's
Record Collection.)

In an age when calypsonians took unto themselves ferocious names such as the Growling Tiger, the Roaring Lion, Killer, Executor and Hero, it is indeed surprising to hear of Egbert 'Bertie' Moore calling himself "Beginner." But he assured me that he was actually named by his fans for he began to sing at the tender age of fifteen (15) and right away, as his rich, beautiful voice echoed and chanted among the masqueraders preparing for Carnival, he was hailed as "The Lord of Beginners" whence he received his name. It so happened that from the moment the senior bards heard him chant, they were enthralled with his voice, he said, and all acclaimed that his entrance into the world of chantuelles signified the beginning of an era. Accordingly, Egbert Moore, affectionately called Bertie by his close friends, came to be called and known in the calypso world, Lord Beginner.

Young Bertie was extremely lucky to have had the experience of being a chantuelle from 1920 to 1926, for this experience, he said, served him in good stead later on. It not only "trained" him for the world of calypso; it gave him the "tonic, motivation and skill to make many tunes later on in the call and response vein." His early life therefore proves firstly that calypsonians of the 1920s, in most cases, started off their careers as chantuelles, a musical task they preferred to calypso singing. Secondly, many early songs were sung in the "Call and Response" pattern.

Dr. Hollis "Chalkdust" Liverpool

Dena Epstein who researched the origins of African music in the Caribbean noted that as early as 1656, monks such as Jean Baptiste Du Tertre and travellers like Johann Schoepf had observed the African in the Caribbean "alternating in song between a solo performer and a chorus," in other words, singing in the "Call and Response" style.[1]

Although Beginner had a sweet voice and was respected by the bards, he yet felt insecure among the "big guns" in Chinnette Alley, North Trinidad, where the powerful singers gathered. As such, he retreated to the South to join the "Demonites Devil band" and there he rubbed shoulders with other chantuelles such as Houdini, Trafalgar, Muncy Daley, Modern Inventor and William Pasty who was "the boss of them all" in terms of singing competitions. In 1925, after five years of singing, he defeated the king William Pasty and ascended the chantuelle throne in the Southland.

His chantuelle life can be summed up by Errol Hill's writings thus:

> Chantuelles met in bands by the turn of the century, and as in times before Carnival, they did battle composing extempo[a] songs, and improvising songs of criticism and songs of praise.[2]

Beginner's experience, then, is proof that long before the official Calypso King competition started in 1939, chantuelles held tent competitions among themselves and crowned their monarchs in the 1920s. It would seem too, that in preparation for Carnival the calypso tent, which was seen for the first time around 1921 following the input of Railway Douglas, attracted both chantuelle and calypsonian.[3] In any case, many calypsonians were chantuelles, and many chantuelles were calypsonians. The difference, according to Beginner, lay in the audience. Singing for the upper class masqueraders and rich Whites at their headquarters in preparation for Carnival made one a chantuelle; singing for the poor at street corners, rumshops, barbershops[b] and in calypso tents made one a calypsonian. Of the tents in those days, Beginner stated:

---

[a] Extempo - to sing off the cuff that is, to compose on the spot.
[b] In rumshops where rum was sold and barbershops where men cut their hair, calypsonians used to hang out daily. There, heated arguments and discussions took place. These allowed the singers to obtain many themes/topics for future calypsoes.

Dr. Hollis "Chalkdust" Liverpool

No tent had a particular system, or any particular singer. When you sang, the whole band would throw back the chorus.[c] You didn't want much music, and the musicians played for free.

In speaking to Beginner, one gets the impression then, that as early as the 1920s, singers had no special loyalty to any tent; rather they sang where the financial returns kept them motivated or where they had special friends or interests. This trend of changing from tent to tent indeed continued throughout the 1930s and 1940s until it slowed somewhat, but never stopped, in the 1990s.[4]

How different from a chantuelle tent the modern, neon-lit, spacious halls that house today's singers are? Today, one has to employ a chorus to accompany the lead singer and also pay the musicians whose salaries ranged from $70 to $200 weekly in the 1970s, to approximately $1000 to $2000 weekly in the 1990s. Bandleaders today in the tents can command up to $3000 weekly. A typical example of a chantuelle song of the 1920s, according to Beginner, went thus:

Ma! Maracaibo, that's the place to go.
Ma! Maracaibo, that's the place to go.
When the fever get in your bone
You got to lie down and groan.
So you better feel glad and remain in Trinidad, every one
and all.

The term "every one and all," stated Beginner, sometimes replaced "sans humanite," especially when the singer wanted his chorus to "throw back," in short, to repeat the verse he had just sung. In looking at the term "sans humanite" which ended the songs of the period, especially the songs of picong,[d] and the satirical odes of the 1920s, Errol Hill pointed out that "it is the same as the Hausa word kaiso, but it is a Creole translation meaning - without pity."[5] In any

---

[c] Throwing back the chorus shows the Call and Response pattern of singing.
[d] Picong from French 'Piquant' meaning sharp, biting. In Trinidadian Creole, these were songs whereby singers humoured one another.

case the term "sans humanite," according to stickfighter Tarzan Walla, was a way of informing the audience of the singer's might in battle, of his sense of importance in the band, of his violent self-effrontery and rhetorical force, and of his pompous nature and boast.[6] Beginner pointed out too, that the chantuelle songs of the 1920s were mostly sung in English using the "single tone" technique of four lines. He gave as an example:

> Last year Carnival
> Midnight that was bacchanal,
> When Ah nearly lost mi life,
> When Ah went home with the Police wife.
> Altogether - Last year ... (repeat).

The reader should note that even from way back in the 1920s, the Police were looked upon as evildoers and as people who joined the rich Whites to put pressure on the poor. Long before that in the 1870s, in keeping with a trend that began after Emancipation,[e] the constabulary was mostly English-Speaking black Barbadians and Vincentians, while several of the officers were white Irishmen. These policemen had to deal with a Patois-Speaking population, bitterly opposed to the invasion of English-Speaking immigrants from the northern islands of the British Caribbean chain. Despite the hostility showed to them, immigrants from the smaller islands continued to pour into Trinidad in search of better conditions of living.[7] Between 1871 and 1911, 65,000 immigrants arrived.[8] Two factors heightened the conflict between immigrants from the islands and native-born Trinidadians: the immigrants refused to work full-time on sugar estates, and preferred to compete with other African labourers-immigrants as well as natives-for jobs in the city.[9] The Barbadians were given jobs as Police Constables, thus placing them into positions of authority over locals. As early as

---

[e] Emancipation in the British Caribbean - 1838.

1849, the Governor gave as his reason for allowing Barbadians into the Force [f] the fact that:

> No native of Trinidad has ever entered the Force; in fact threats have been held out that anyone so doing would be denounced…I found on my arrival here a sort of system carried on by men who went from one island to the other, and, when tired of one, or having misconducted (sic) themselves, they passed on to another, and were almost certain to be received, as there was no great desire to enter the Force; this I have stopped, by requiring characters from the other islands, and I hope soon to improve the Force, by remodeling the system.[10]

Worse yet, in the years following Emancipation, the majority of Africans, immigrants as well as freed wage-labourers, refused to sign contracts on estates and preferred jobs in the city. In a dispatch to the Secretary of State, Governor Keate in 1849 gave as their reason the following:

> The adult African under indenture,[g] and in good hands, works remarkably well till the close of the year when required to renew his contract; this he does most unwillingly, not that he objects to remaining five years or longer, under the same master, but that he is firmly impressed with the idea, that touching pen and paper consigns him to perpetual slavery, from which the only escape is by absconding.[11]

Immigration was such a big factor in the heightening of urban conflict and social divisiveness that the calypso singers in Trinidad towards the end of the century blamed Barbadians for every economic

---

[f] The Police Force - so called because it was to serve as a military unit that could assist in times of war or an emergency.

[g] Approx.12,000 Free Africans worked as Indentured citizens in the British Caribbean. About 6, 581 of these came to Trinidad. In addition, between 1839 and 1849, an estimated 10,278 West Indians arrived

Dr. Hollis "Chalkdust" Liverpool

problem on the island. The calypsonian sang:

> Oh not a cent, not a cent,
> Not a cent to buy rice (repeat).
> When the Barbadians come to this country
> They think nobody like them (repeat).[12]

Beginner himself, in providing me with examples of single tone-type[h] calypsoes, again noted the low esteem in which policemen were held. He sang:

> Ah went on a spree - one morning.
> Ah went to see Dorothy - Foreday morning.[i]
> Ah met in a collision;
> It was me and a policeman.

From listening to Beginner's example of a single tone calypso, it is to be noted that at midnight after Carnival was bacchanal, in that most men resorted to seducing women, especially the ones they had just met for Carnival. From the 1920s to the present, there have been composed hundreds of calypsoes all speaking of the sex feast that is now part of Trinidad's Carnival, especially on Carnival Tuesday night. Sparrow in 1957, singing about that Tuesday night stated: "when you get yuh chance, don't play too cool. Ho Ho! Don't be a fool."[13] Again in 1966, in a calypso entitled "Rosalind," he told his newly-found girl: "we going home tonight." Others have sung: "Tuesday night when the music blast, we go rock and roll and play mas." Even calypsonian Blakie in 1973 stated: "Ah go take she home just as well. Ah don't care if mi two eye swell."[14]

Beginner spoke of the competitions held in the era 1920 to 1930 and said that:

> People were prejudiced to go in the tent, but they filled the theatres, and so we used to have big competitions at the Palace and New theatres in San Fernando, especially when North and South matches were arranged.

Singing against stalwarts of the period such as Executor, Muncy Daley, Attila, Chinese Patrick, Trafalgar and Controller who all

---

[h] Single Tone - marked by four lines and sweet melodies.
[i] Pronounced 'Fo day' - Creole for early morning before the dawn.

Dr. Hollis "Chalkdust" Liverpool

represented the North, Beginner, Confuser, the Duke of Normandy and Fitzi Banride representing South proved to be formidable opponents whenever they met. One draws from Beginner's memories the fact that calypsonians travelled far and wide throughout the length and breadth of the country spurring on, music-wise, the carnival bands to action, fighting against kings of villages orally with the villagers "feteing them" afterwards, improvising lines as they changed their verses to the applause of the calypso-loving, cheerful crowd.

The rich elites and big businessmen such as East Indian Ranny Phillip who owned and managed the Rose Bowl club in Belmont Valley Road, Port-of-Spain, Sultan Khan a jewel shop owner in San Fernando, and one Mr. Williams (father of Ronnie Williams, a deceased chairman of the C.D.C.), used to arrange and produce the competitions, while academics such as Mr. Kitchener Thorpe a judge of the Supreme court, and Mr. Rupert Archibald of legal fame then, judged them. It should be understood that calypsonians of the 1920s and 1930s permitted people from the professional middle class world of "respectability" to judge a grass root art form.[15] In the view of Beginner, calypsonians as members of the lower classes looked up to those Africans who through education had achieved something, even though they just as often attacked the norms of "decent" society.

Egbert Moore remembered clearly and vividly an outstanding competition held at Dragon tent at the corner of Prince and George Street in 1927, in which he and Attila were the heroes. Attila sang a calypso entitled "Day by Day, all the Young Girls Breaking Away." Beginner sang about "Rudolph Valentino" a great American actor, lover, playboy, and social fighter of the period who had unfortunately died. Beginner's song went thus:

> Rudolph Valentino
> Was the best star on the Movie show. (repeat)
> But he found movies couldn't pay,
> So with the angels he gone and stay;
> He form a complo, and he join with Caruso.
> Slick Valentino.

He actually won the competition, he said, but the judges gave the

Dr. Hollis "Chalkdust" Liverpool

first prize to Attila, stating that the word "complo" was not English but Patois, even though it meant a pact or agreement. "In those days, said Beginner, "English was the thing."

In the early years of the twentieth century, young colonials of the period strove to master the English language. This fight to gain mastery of the language was noted by J.H. Collens, Chief Education Officer who pointed out in 1886 that the "struggle for language was particularly painful," and he had to "check the disposition of (his) pupils in Trinidad to use long-winded words and high flown phrases."[16] It's the same emphasis on English that Raymond Quevedo spoke of as "the oratorical pattern recitative in song" pointing out that: "It is possible that this period of the Kaiso was influenced by the great public speakers and inspiring orations of the epoch of Sir Henry Alcazar, M'zumbo Lazare, Maresse-Smith and Bishop Hayes." [j][17]

Professor Gordon Rohlehr, after his research into calypso's history, wrote that the majority of calypsonians at the time still lacked formal education. They were still the dispossessed of the streets, and, as such, they showed their vocabulary power by trying to appropriate and master the language of the schoolmaster and of the traditional English bards

> Attila's surmise that calypsonians derived some of their rhetoric from the great orators of the period is certainly borne out by the roles which calypsonians singing in the oratorical style sometimes assumed. Their vocabulary is taken from war, astronomy, the courts of law, the schools. They assumed the roles of all who wielded power over the word: the priest, the lawyer, the judge in particular, and the pedantic (and often brutal) schoolmaster castigating pupils. Calypsonians never saw themselves as merchants or planters,the people who are really wielding power in the society. It was the rhetoric of the time which fascinated them more than any other thing: powerful sounding words,

---

[j] Members of the rising Black middle class in Trinidad and Tobago: Edgar in the agitation that led up to the Water Riots of 1903; Henry Alcazar became a member of the Legislative Council in 1894.

rather than real power.[18]

One can understand therefore why Beginner came second to Attila. Executor and Attila were secondary school boys-they went to St. Mary's College-and the other singers feared them for their use of words. Here, for example, is Executor throwing picong at Attila.

> I admire your ambition you'd like to sing
> But you'll never be a Kaiso king.
> To reach such a height without blemish or spot,
> You must study Shakespeare, Byron, Milton and Scott.
> But I'm afraid I'm casting pearls before swine,
> For you'll never inculcate such thoughts divine.
> You really got a good intention but poor education, sans humanite.[19]

Hearing Beginner speak, one marvels at his memory, and the details of his life as a calypsonian. For example, he remembered that "Radio[k] began singing in 1928, and Caresser, Tiger and Destroyer in 1935." He recalled leaving South Trinidad "in 1929, and proceeded North where I became head of the band 'Silky Millionaires,' and from then on I stayed in the North." He was on target when he said that:

> After the 1930s we formed ourselves into teams and sang for money in tents. There were three major teams: (a) Douglas who by himself and a few helpers used to pack up the place; (b) myself, Radio and Executor; and (c) Lion, Attila and Inveigler.

This arrangement was the forerunner of the various brigades[1] and tents that have now become a part of the history of the calypso in Trinidad and Tobago and indeed in the Caribbean, including the U.S. Virgin islands. Beginner is definitely on target, for Attila, in his writings, recalled that he too chanted as a chantuelle for Salada Millionaires; Chieftain Douglas and King Radio chanted for Silky Millionaires; Senior Inventor chanted for the Chinese Mandarin

---

[k] Norman Spann - calypsonian King Radio.
[l] Some calypso tents were known as 'brigades.' There was the 'Old Brigade' and afterwards the 'Young Brigade.'

Dr. Hollis "Chalkdust" Liverpool

Syndicate while Reggie Ross chanted for the Mystery Syndicate. In those days each band of carnival masqueraders had a tent which was called a Syndicate. From the Salada Millionaires who advertised Salada tea came the Toddy Syndicate and featured in 1929 singers such as Executor, Modern Inventor, Trafalgar, Attila, Mentor and Persecutor. The Silky Millionaires, who were in existence up to about 1933 and consisted of Radio, Beginner, Railway Douglas and Inveigler, shifted later to the Railroad Millionaires at 47, Nelson Street, under the tutelage of the same singers with the addition of Executor.

An interesting point that both Beginner and Attila noted was that in those days there were distinctions in terms of race and colour, so that white Norman Le Blanc was chantuelle to a group of Whites known as the Shamrock Syndicate; the Duke of Marlborough who was of mixed race, chanted for the Mulattoes who formed the Crescent band; and Julien White Rose, a White Creole, chanted for the White Rose band of middle class Creole Whites. Attila himself was a Mulatto, the son of a Trinidadian mother and a Venezuelan father. He attended St. Mary's College[m] and so his colour, education and affluence gained from his parents enabled him to become a chantuelle. Beginner, though an African, was fair in face, and this must have worked in his favour, when he sought the job of chantuelle. Many calypsonians, as Lord Iere pointed out to me, aspired to be chantuelles, but many could not achieve that high standing because of their low social status, the job being the domain of mostly the "fairer-skinned fellows."[20]

From the chantuelles came the calypsonians and from the Syndicates came the professional tents in the 1920s where calypsonians were now regarded as paid, seasoned entertainers. Beginner recalled that "Fernandes[n] and them built the first real tent at where the Telephone Company is now on Henry Street, and it was called the White Star tent."

---

[m] The top Roman Catholic Secondary School on the island.
[n] J.B. Fernandes & Co. Ltd. - rum distillers in Trinidad.

This recollection of Beginner as to the first real professional tent somewhat confuses the picture for calypsonian Houdini (Wilmoth Hendricks) who resided in the U.S. before he died, claimed in an article written in 1968 by Errol Hill in the <u>Trinidad Guardian</u>, that he erected the first tent in 1920 in a Prince Street back yard,[o] and called it "the Chinese Junk Yard."[21] The same Errol Hill in his book The <u>Trinidad Carnival: Mandate for a National Theatre</u> points out that from personal communication with Railway Douglas, the first professional tent was set up by the said Douglas in 1921, following his sojourn to Europe as a soldier during World War 1.[22] The tent was called "The Railroad Millionaires Tent" and it was situated at 26, Duncan Street, in Port-of-Spain. To further confuse the picture, both J.D. Elder and Errol Hill record that Norman Le Blanc organized a tent early in the 20th century, charging a small entrance fee. What all this adds up to is that between 1900 and 1930, the tent was a makeshift building of bamboo, coconut branches, carat leaves and flambeaux[p] lighting. Douglas used surplus tarpaulin obtained from the Trinidad Government Railway (TGR) where he worked, to erect a more weather-proof structure in 1921. Hence he has been given the fame as having invented the Calypso Tent Movement. In any case, were not the Syndicates tents? The difference between syndicates and tents, according to Beginner, is that in calypso tents, in contrast to syndicates, there was better organization and professionalism: seating arrangement, paid musicians, superior lighting, a chorus group, well-dressed, salaried singers in jackets and ties, a Master of Ceremonies and a planned programme for the evening. I however share the opinion of Professor Gordon Rohlehr who, in seeking to clear up the confusion, observed that "what all this seems to prove was that the calypso was in a stage of transition, and that then, as well as now, each generation attached great importance to what used to be popular in its days."[23]

---

[o] Yards in Port-of-Spain served as meeting places for artists and masqueraders. They were the Peoples' theatres.

[p] A Creolized Patois term for the lighted torches at the time.

Dr. Hollis "Chalkdust" Liverpool

Returning to Beginner's memory pad, he noted that:Tents were extremely popular in the 1930s; barrack yards in the city were used as tents; many singers changed tents because of dissatisfaction with the tent management; in Nelson Street near to the Dry River was a tent; Douglas' tent was opposite Goat Street bordering on Nelson Street; the Duke of Albany's tent was by Royal Theatre on Charlotte Street, Port-of-Spain.

However, what I consider to be not only a great piece of information but a milestone in the development of the calypso is the fact that Beginner recalled that:

People were afraid to come to the tents in the late 1920s and even in the early 1930s. We used to have a lot of hooligans in the area, particularly in nearby Royal Theatre. Besides, the poor people there couldn't pay, so we moved from the vagabond area.

Thus the area bordering Park, St. Vincent and Edward Streets in Port-of-Spain became the hub of activity for calypso in the mid 1930s and 1940s for it represented not only middle and upper class clientele and an area where people and residents were not pestered by hooligans, but it represented a center for commuters on tramcars and trolley buses traveling to and from Port-of-Spain, Newtown, St. James, Belmont, St. Clair, and Woodbrook. In addition, although, according to Beginner, prices of admission were twenty-five (25) and fifty (50) cents-those close to the stage paid the higher price-"people in the George and Nelson Street area couldn't pay the admission price," and "Whites never frequented that hooligan area." The calypsonians therefore aimed at making money from the rich upper class people, who were not like the "hooligans who used to peep through the bamboo."[q] In contrast, Whites came and sat on the bamboo seats inside.

It is no wonder then that Railway Douglas, as early as 1921, in trying to attract the middle and upper classes "did not allow stick

---

[q] Bamboo stalks were used to cover the sides of the construction.

Dr. Hollis "Chalkdust" Liverpool

fighting (kalenda) music to be performed in his tent." Douglas never used the "Vera" or stick fight drum, according to Beginner. "The Vera was a long enclosed thing like a grater. It was packed with stones and played with a piece of wire." Douglas' musical instruments used to uplift, in his view, the image of calypso were a flute, clarinet, cuatro, guitar and bass. These would be somewhat like Parang[r] instruments. The drum was the traditional African instrument." According to Errol Hill, Douglas used French and Spanish-Creole instruments, in order to make the calypso accompaniment more sophisticated. Douglas had the tent well lit to attract patrons. This shows too, the suspicion in which people viewed the tents during the late 1920s and early 1930s. Hill went on to say that "Douglas never allowed any Dame Lorraine[s] or Calenda (sic) practice in the tent so as to attract the respectable class."[24]

Tents set up in that elite area around St. Vincent and Edward Streets, according to Beginner, included one at 95, Edward Street. in 1946; the "Commandoes Calypso tent" run by one Chesterfield Bravo where Kimling Restaurant was once situated; one run by Mr. Johny Khan (who later carried Lion and Attila to the USA) on Edward Street; and still another on Park Street run by one Mr. Hezekiah who owned a bakery near to the corner of St. Vincent and Park Streets.

After studying Beginner's life as a calypsonian, one realizes that he was one of the most travelled singers. His first trip overseas was to Guyana in 1935, after which, he toured the United States on three occasions to make recordings. He sang in night clubs in Curacao, Aruba, Jamaica, Holland, Spain, France, Germany and Scotland, before finally settling down in England where he lived from 1947 to 1961. In fact, it was he, he said, who was responsible for Lord Kitchener's sojourn to Britain in 1947 and the Growling Tiger's trip to the United States in 1935.

---

[r] Music representing Trinidad's Hispanic heritage played mostly at Christmas time.
[s] French for 'Fashionable Lady,' it was a ritual that was carried out by Africans at Carnival time.

Dr. Hollis "Chalkdust" Liverpool

In England, Beginner began to follow closely the rise of West Indian cricket, and commented naturally in song on almost every important game. Beginner realized early that the West Indians were, through the medium of cricket, conquering the menace that was colonialism, and were proving to Englishmen that they had intellect and administrative ability to run their own affairs. Cricket then was the symbol of their fighting spirit and thus it was a great achievement to beat England at their own game. For C.L.R. James[t] in 1963, cricket was more than a game. In fact, he himself said: "it plunged me into politics long before I was aware of it." It was politics; it was art. C.L.R. James wrote: "What is art? -but only when we learn to integrate our vision of Walcott[u] on the back foot through the covers with the outstretched arm of the Olympic Apollo."[25]

Beginner's songs on cricket give us much knowledge concerning the figures and statistics of the matches between England, Australia and the West Indies. He himself said: "when I sing about a cricket match, you didn't have to read the newspapers again." On hearing the lyrics of Beginner's songs, the reader must understand the true saying that calypsonians are chroniclers of past social and political events. Here, for example, is Beginner's version of the M.C.C. versus the West Indies clash in 1933/34.

West Indies and M.C.C. met once more.
Ah never see cricket so nice before,
For Mr. Grant[v] was really excellent;
Wyatt was magnificent.
Sealey[w] and Headley[x] were superfine
But the heroes were Hylton and Constantine.

The best excitement that you ever had
In the history of cricket in Trinidad,

---

[t] C.L.R. James, cricketer, author, philosopher and historian.
[u] Sir Clyde Walcott, famous West Indies batsman.
[v] Mr. Rolph Grant, Captain of the West Indies team.
[w] Ben Sealey, well-known West Indies batsman.
[x] George Headley, a great West Indian batsman.

Dr. Hollis "Chalkdust" Liverpool

To see the last over, the second to last ball
The last minute and the last man to fall.
Anxiety made Layes resign
Shouting: give us it Constantine.
And the batsman put his foot in front a fast one
L.B.W. and West Indies won.

One feels the mood, the anxious moments in the match, and one can hear the deafening roar as West Indies won. In another calypso entitled "Cricket Champions," he sang:

You can't beat the West Indies at all
Trueman you can bowl the ball.
You can't beat the West Indies at all.

Of the Australia versus the West Indies clash in 1952, he mused:

West Indies and Australia fought vigourously
In a cricket fight for supremacy.
Somehow Australia has won the game;
West Indies lost but we love we name.
Our boys were sublime;
All Ah going to say is: better luck next time.

One of Beginner's heroes in England was the late, great cricketer Sir Learie Constantine, for Beginner saw him as the hope of the oppressed, the man to help Africans in London out of economic despair and the racial discrimination practiced against them.

Learie Constantine, that old pal of mine!
Learie Constantine, that old pal of mine.
Though the selection was very bad
We had a good man from Trinidad.
Who he was? - Learie Constantine.

Hear Beginner in the late 1940s singing of the West Indies tour of England in 1939, while still praising the skills of Constantine.

Dr. Hollis "Chalkdust" Liverpool

The crowd didn't play; the brass band play
At Lords that beautiful day.
The king and queen had left their throne
To visit the match but they had to groan.
Oh the cripple and the blind
All hail for Constantine - sans humanite (or) every one and
all.

No wonder Constantine was knighted for his contribution to cricket and given a state funeral on his death in 1970 by his nation.

With regard to the selection of West Indian cricketers for England, Beginner sang:

They left out Mr. White; they carried Ray.
They left out George John and let Bartlett play
With Pascall, the manicou man from Maraval,
Every one and all.
It was a bad selection
When West Indies cricket went to England.

Many West Indian cricket enthusiasts have over the years castigated the selectors for their choice of cricketers whenever teams are chosen for test matches, especially for overseas tours. Calypsonian Cypher noted as late as the 1960s that "the game is played according to colour."[26] Many too spoke of insularism and poverty. C.L.R. James spoke too of bad selection methods, noting that, in order to qualify for the West Indies team from Trinidad, one had to be a member of either Queen's Park Club or Shamrock. The former had wealthy members who were mixed in terms of race, while the latter was "almost exclusively White." James went on to say that he "would have been more easily elected to the M.C.C. than to either."[27]

Beginner was indeed a chronicler of sport. So adept at soccer was he that as early as 1939, he penned a song about a famous football match between Demerara[y] and Trinidad at the Queen's Park Savannah in Port-of-Spain.

Ten thousand was at the Savannah

---

[y] A district found along the estuary of the Demerara River in Guyana.

When we lost to Demerara.
Ten thousand walk out the Savannah
When we lost to Demerara.
The Guyanese had the ball under control;
Leonard kick it over the goal.
Now I wonder how they feel
To know we lost the Martinay shield.

Indeed it was his love for sport that rewarded him financially and enabled him to return to Trinidad in the 1960s and start life all over again. His composition "Cricket, Lovely Cricket" sold thousands of records, while "the B.B.C. used it to introduce many programmes, particularly programmes on West Indian life and cricket." The calypso was based on the 1950 West Indies tour of England, a tour that heralded the West Indies as the conqueror of England, and brought to the fore the famous "spin twins" Ramadhin and Valentine,[z] as well as the three batting heroes who became known as the "three Ws:" - Everton Weekes, Frank Worrell and Clyde Walcott.

Cricket, lovely cricket!
At Lords where I saw it (repeat).
Yardley tried his best
But Goddard won the test.
We gave the crowd plenty fun
Second test the West Indies won.
Chorus: With these little pals of mine
Ramadhin and Valentine.

Sport wasn't the only specialty of Beginner. Perhaps having served as a soldier in the Trinidad Army Corps; perhaps because of his colonial education; perhaps because VJ[aa] day found him and five other calypsonians in the United States; and perhaps because he

---

[z] Sonny Ramadhin from Trinidad and Alfred Valentine from Jamaica.
[aa] Victory over Japan - was celebrated in most countries who supported the Allies.

lived in Britain since 1947, Beginner sang many songs praising Britain for the part she played during World War 11, and for her brand of colonial administration. One such song he sang in 1942 at 95, Edward Street,[bb] made the then Governor,[cc] ambassadors, the Colonial Secretary and several other dignitaries pay public tribute to him. In fact, the Governor even summoned him to a private audience, and he may well have been the first calypsonian to have been so honoured. The fact is that from 1900, many calypsonians were loyalists. Some sang glorifying Britain's history and her empire. That trend continued and blended strangely with a slow, steady growth of nationalism. Beginner's song went thus:

Verse 1.

Two bullies up in Europe who haven't any shame;
See how they are going on with a kind of cruel game (repeat).
But when they all finish with this war entirely,
There won't be any Italy, or either Germany.
Chorus: But there'll always be an England.
    And England shall be free,
    If England means as much to you
    As England means to me.

Verse 2.

The world has developed so funny I can say
That anything you have, it can be taken away.
As long as you are powerful, mighty, big and strong,
You can leave all the right and go in for the wrong.
But soon the smaller nations will live without no fear,
There won't be any Germany to go and interfere.
Chorus: But there'll always be an England ...

Verse3.

Mr. Ernest Bevin[dd] said to work like hell to make it grand.
Force is the only language that the Nazis understand.

[bb] One of the buildings that housed the calypso tent after it was shifted from the 'vagabond' area.
[cc] Sir Hubert Young paid tribute publicly to Beginner.
[dd] Ernest Bevin - Minister of Labour in Churchill's War Cabinet.
Dr. Hollis "Chalkdust" Liverpool

He said: boom for boom;[ee] don't matter what they try and what they do;
Anytime they drop a boom, we must go and drop two.
There mighn't be a Hitler, Mussolini and the rest;
There mightn't be a Churchill to remain to stand the test.

Verse 4.

The battle of the Atlantic is raging as you see
And many ships all sinking daily on the open sea.
But the bullies up in Europe haven't no regard;
They may try to spread the war and come and fight in Trinidad.
There mightn't be a Beginner to sing a sweet refrain;
There mightn't be a Radio or Attila here again.
Chorus: But there'll always be an England …

Chorus: But there'll always be an England …

Continuing his staunch support for Britain even after the war, he sang his "Ode to Churchill."

Chorus: Ministers may reign
But we'll never find a brain
Like Winston Churchill again.
Sir Winston Churchill reached to eighty and resign.
Like him another we will never find.
He done his duties so brave and bold;
He saved his country and he saved the world.
He was the greatest Prime Minister,
A genius and a pal of America.

With Beginner preaching such nationalism and inspiring Trinidadians to stand solidly behind the mother country, it was no wonder that the Governor of the colony then paid public tribute to him in 1942.

The reader, however, should not believe that all calypsonians congratulated Britain, nor were they all loyalists.[ff]

[ee] 'Boom' meaning 'Bomb.'
[ff] Singers like Tiger, Attila and Radio showed their resentment of Britain in song.

England was at the same time bitterly resented in song by many, while trade unionists such as Arthur Cipriani, Tubal Uriah Butler, Adrian Cola Rienzi and a host of others objected to British democracy and the human misery that followed the Crown Colony system. Moreover, they in turn called for political reform, with Cipriani calling for Independence. Many too, showed their resentment of Britain during the Water riots,[gg] the Butler Riots,[hh] and the fight for Adult suffrage and recognition of trade unionism. Attila himself relentlessly attacked the Colonial system throughout the 1940s. He attacked governors, ministers, councils; hardly anyone escaped his fury. What may have caused the calypsonians to sing songs praising Britain was the fact that much literature and news from the media flourished then. In addition, the occupation of many West Indian islands by American servicemen together with the Eurocentric education spread by Britain inevitably affected many.

I asked Beginner whether he ever disassociated himself with the oppressive colonial system of the Caribbean. Responding, he was quick to point out that there were certain laws like the banning of calypsoes that he didn't like. He assured me that whenever there were any riots or upheavals, he was always on the side of the people. In fact, he remembered a song which he took great pride in singing. It was sung in 1906, and was extremely popular during his boyhood days. It went thus:

> Response: Ah no more Cola[ii] again!
> Call: Zandolee[jj] find your hole
> Response: Ah no more Cola again!
> Call: He was a very bad man.

Cola in fact was a policeman who during the Water Riots used to oppress the poor. "He used to pass by the prostitutes and say: 'zandolee find yuh hole!' and had them running." A few years afterwards, he was dismissed from his post; hence the song was made to mimic and laugh at his misfortune.

[gg] Riots in Trinidad between the people fueled by the Ratepayers Assn. and the Colonial Govt. in which 16 persons died, 43 were wounded and the Red House burnt down.
[hh] Riots in Trinidad in 1937 with Butler, the labour leader, as the central figure.
[ii] Sergeant Joseph Alexander Cola, an astute police officer of the era.
[jj] A type of ground lizard.

Dr. Hollis "Chalkdust" Liverpool

Cola was up to 1909 a Sergeant in the Police Force, so that the song must have been composed about 1912 - 1914.

Showing how much he cared for little people, he gave as an example the imprisonment of one Mr. Tansley.

> Tell me why Tansley didn't stay
> When he stole the college money and he ran away (repeat0.
> He played the part of rascality
> Stealing the money from the colony.
> And as he couldn't prevail,
> He got six months in the Royal jail.
>
> Oh Tansley my boy your days are done.
> Quite in Barbados he tried to run.
> But Captain Cipriani told the Government: No!
>
> You must remember that we can't take things so.
> If our boys can be charged with embezzlement,
> Tansley must bear the same punishment.
> And as he couldn't prevail,
> He got six months in the Royal Jail.

The song explains itself. Thus the reader can see that while Beginner sang loyalist songs, he was critical of Englishmen who broke the territory's laws, and thus he sided with Cipriani in denouncing discrimination. Beginner also sang a calypso in the mid 1940s called "Sons and daughters of Africa"[kk] in which he assessed the world situation at the end of World War 11. In it he predicted a new day for the African and exhorted them to "give more consideration for your rising coloured generation."

Another important development of the calypso which Beginner stressed was the use of the same tune by many singers in the 1930s and 1940s. "Singers," he said, "hardly ever composed new tunes, but simply added lyrics to the known melodies of the day." This explains why calypsonians were able to travel from tent to tent singing their double and single tones without much difficulty from the musicians, with regard to musical arrangement and accompaniment.

[kk] Attila also sang a calypso entitled the 'Emancipation Centenary' in 1938; it also began with the lines 'Sons and daughters of Africa.'

Dr. Hollis "Chalkdust" Liverpool

But Beginner was no exception to the "same tune" rule; I found a few of his tunes sharing the same melody. "Tansley," for instance, has the same melody as "Rudolph Valentino." Being a "tunesmith,"[ll] he said, "many singers stole his tunes." His "Louise" was stolen and used by Attila in the calypso "King George V Coronation" of 1935. "Attila," Beginner claimed "was the biggest thief, for he hardly ever composed melodies." According to Beginner, "The Graf Zeppelin composed by Attila, was the same tune as 'The Night When the Boat House Tumble Down,' and King Radio used the same tune in 1947 when he sang A Mother's Love." Continuing the point, he noted that the melody to King Fanto's song "No More Iona" was used by Attila when the latter sang "Bye Sweet man."

Beginner may be correct in his assumption of Attila, for Attila's song on "Toddy" was originally a melody composed by Mentor. However, this use of melodies by singers of the day ought not to be construed as stealing. Like the Blues, the calypso was a traditional art form, an urban-folk, African custom, a communal practice from which tunes were handed down. Obviously, a music founded on the principle of improvisation requires set formulae and choruses. To emphasize the point, the parodies (which incidentally to Beginner are not calypsoes, but folk songs which originally were sung in other Caribbean islands) gave rise to many songs using the same melodies. For example, Beginner stated:

> The 'Sly Mongoose' tune caused Invader to sing 'Bring Back the Old Time Cat-O-Nine,' and there was even a circus in Trinidad in 1944 that used the same tune as its theme which was called 'Blow Kangaroo.' Most islands, even Guadeloupe, claimed the tune 'Sly Mongoose.'

Beginner went on to show that the song "Not a Cent to Buy Rice" has the same melody as "Oh What a Night." The tune for "Rum and Coca-Cola" popularized by Invader [mm] came from a song entitled "L'Annee Pasee" originally composed in Martinique. He stated:

[ll]   A singer and composer of tunes, according to Beginner.
[mm] Rupert Grant - Lord Invader.

Dr. Hollis "Chalkdust" Liverpool

Even Radio used the same tune, though not the chorus, in 'Man smart, Woman Smarter,'and although the tune was claimed by Lanky Belasco[nn] as the true composer, a fact which Trinidad musicians at the time supported, a calypsonian named Macbeth[oo] sang it in New York. Radio demanded payment for it and was paid one hundred and fifty thousand ($150,000.00) dollars while in the United States.

To crown it all, Beginner, observant as he was, noted that the Mighty Sparrow through Reginald 'Piggy' Joseph[pp] copied the words and melody of the song "I've Discovered a New Philosophy, How to Make Women Happy" from Attila. But Attila himself "never a maker" copied the tune from an old folk song which he (Beginner) "born and meet in Trinidad" called "When the Baby Born, Half is Mine." What all this indicates is the traditional handed-down nature of the original Kaiso, and the nature of immigration in the nineteenth century which must have made Trinidad the repository of the natural music of the Spanish, English, Dutch and French archipelago. Beginner therefore brought out an important pillar in the structural development of the art form. Many other examples of "thief" he gave, but the few stated here will suffice to demonstrate that in those days, emphasis was placed more on the lyrics than on the melody of the calypso. The singers simply added lyrics to known melodies most of the time. Beginner was different; he liked good lyrics, but stressed original melodies. If he stole, he stole from himself.

Espinet and Pitts in a booklet on the "Development of the Calypso" published in 1944, in explaining how tunes were composed by calypsonians wrote thus: "When creating a new

---

[nn] Lionel 'Lanky'Belasco, musician, claimed that he composed the tune in 1906.
[oo] Macbeth sang calypsoes in Harlem and was the father of Ralph McDonald, N.Y. Jazz Percussionist who won a Grammy Award with the tune 'Just the two of us.'
[pp] Reginald 'Piggy' Joseph, notable calypso composer.

Dr. Hollis "Chalkdust" Liverpool

calypso he commonly uses and sometimes reworks a popular calypso melody of the past."[29]   Attila himself made the point at a lecture delivered at the Public Library in the 1950s. Among other things, he stated: "it is often alleged that for decades preceding the 1920s and 1930s, calypsos were composed around a certain fixed number of established tunes that were used repeatedly with subtle variations." Attila went on to state that "there were only twelve basic calypso rhythms."[30]   It means therefore that many of the tunes for which the public credits singers are not in fact theirs. Many knowledgeable persons know that calypsonians often reintroduce old melodies or even melodies from Latin America or from the European, classical period, and then add their lyrics to them. I personally know many tunes the melodies of which were stolen and are yet held as outstanding calypsoes by the public at large.

From my experience as a composer, I can safely say that it is very difficult to compose a calypso or song that is free from former melodies and folk songs. At times after having completed the composition, and after paying careful attention to the melody contained, I would yet find that the melody in one or a few lines strongly resembles either a school song, a past calypso, a popular song on the radio or some piece of classical or operatic music. Beginner called such things "impediments." In my opinion, the "impediments" illustrate the traditional nature of the art form, for each innovation is carried out against the background of a controlling tradition.

Beginner spoke at length on the calypsonians' image that has been associated with jamettes,[qq] prostitution, smut[rr] and the uneducated, dispossessed classes. People used to

---

[qq] From French 'diametre' meaning diameter. Those who behaved beneath the diameter of responsibility were so termed in the 19th century. Later, in the late 19th and 20th centuries, the term was associated with loose, vulgar behaviour, especially among women.

[rr] Smut - calypsoes centred around the sex act.

wonder why he joined that gang of uncouth men. He however believed that the stigma attached to calypso and calypsonians was brought on by the very life the singers lived. "If you wanted to get rid of money, give it to Invader," he exclaimed. In fact, delving into calypso's history, the reader is sure to hear that Lord Invader won a large sum of money from a lawsuit with the Andrews Sisters[ss] and drank it all in rum.[31] Beginner noted:

> Invader like to full up a car with girls, pull down a shelf of rum, and drink it out. He even opened a night club, but drank out the entire place till he bust. Radio was the same sort of fellow but a little less, for he too drank out the money paid him for 'Man Smart, Woman Smarter' in a club on Seventh (7th) Avenue, New York.

In terms of deportment, Beginner continued:

> People use to say to them in the streets: All yuh, look dem dirty calypsonians! Many of us kept back our own selves, for some use to dress badly, gamble and drink. I, however was a bit different because of the few pennies I made; I could of (sic) afford to buy a few suits.

And dress he did, up to the time of his death in 1981. To simply purchase foodstuff in Port-of-Spain, Beginner would put on his coat. Moreover, he would never come into the Regal Calypso tent, even if he was merely coming to see me, without his coat and tie. Sociologist and School Principal Pete Simon had this to say in 1969:

> Day-to-day, now-for-now living was the calypsonians' way of life - the life of the chartered libertine. He had no roots and was proud of it. He spent money as soon as it came to hand. 'Easy come! Easy go' was the rule. Drinking, gambling

---

[ss] The Andrews Sisters recorded it for Decca records on October 18th, 1944. Hence the lawsuit.

and womanizing were his main pursuits. A home as such was not in his scheme of things. He was more often than not, quite content with his batchy.[tt] Many are the times he would wake up on the counter of some bar or clubroom, drunk like a fish and ask for an eye-opener, then stumble out to face an uncompromising world.[32]

What Pete Simon didn't realize was that calypsonians were not the only type of persons who behaved thus; stick fighters, masqueraders, steelbandsmen, jamettes and prostitutes all tuned into that way of life from 1900 up to the 1970s. What else could people, downtrodden, living in abject poverty do? What else could a man with poor education and little or no means to obtain same do? What else could the lower class, given no education in management, finance or banking do? What else can one, robbed of his rich cultural heritage, prevented on so many occasions from practicing his native culture, subjected to imperialistic and colonial ideas, principles and values do? What do we expect an unemployed and at times unemployable, hungry and frustrated man to do in times like those? I leave the answers to the reader.

I asked Beginner one day whether he felt the calypsonian had made a genuine contribution to contemporary society. He answered as though he was shocked at the question.

"Of course." Then he proceeded to say:

Demerara in 1931 had no singer, no calypso. Barbados was worse. Barbadians used to ask us: 'what kind of chupidness all you singing?' Calypso made Trinidad famous not only in the United States and Britain, where people use to ask me if I'm singing Spirituals or African songs, but in Barbados, British Guiana, and St. Vincent. I, Attila and Tiger went through the Caribbean on our way to the States, and Attila

---

[tt] Creole term for a small apartment.

even get locked up in Grenada for using obscene language. Lion and Radio visited those islands in the late 1930s.

Speaking to Beginner about calypsonians then, the name Houdini came about. However, from Beginner's description of Houdini's character, he (Beginner) seemed to have disliked or hated him. I had learnt from King Radio that Houdini had left Trinidad in 1929 to go to the United States to do recordings. In fact, he was the very first calypsonian to have gone there for that purpose.[33] I therefore pressed Beginner for more information with regard to Houdini's character, and found out that Houdini was disliked by most calypsonians, just as Sir Galba who died in 1957, was hated by the singers in the first half of the 1950s.

Beginner informed me that on their first trip to the United States, Attila, Tiger and himself were held on their arrival by immigration authorities and placed on Ellis Island, a place reserved for illegal immigrants and stowaways. He was later informed by immigration authorities that this was done because there already were people of their occupation in the United States. According to Beginner, "the law at the time was that you couldn't enter the States to do a job, if some one else could have done the job and was already there." Beginner therefore felt strongly that since they were going to sing in night clubs and make records in New York, and since Houdini was already there, he (Houdini) had informed the authorities about their trespassing on his soil. The reader would therefore understand why Beginner disliked Houdini.

Professor Gordon Rohlehr, in trying to show the "Robber Talk"[uu] or the transposition of the "Robber Talk" into the lyrics of the calypso referred to a calypso war between Caresser, Attila, Lion, and Executor. It went thus:

For it's all propaganda, deceit and pretence.
He hasn't got a shadow of intelligence.
The money that was spent on his slate[vv] and books
Has not improved his manners and looks.
He has a good inclination, but foreign education, sans humanite.

ATTILA
From the very first day that I was born
Men like Houdini started to mourn;
Monarchs wept and princes cried
When they saw this new star up in the sky.
Astronomers in my horoscope state:
He'll be proud, illustrious and great.
And they named me Attila, the terror, the brutal conqueror, master mi minor.

LION
The earth is a trembling and a tumbling
And the heavens are falling; and all
Because the Lion is roaring.
My tongue is like the blast of a gun. When Ah frown
Monarchs have to bow down to the ground.
Devastation, destruction, desolation and damnation,
All these - I'll inflict on Insubordination,
For the Lion in his power is like the Rock of
Gibraltar, sans humanite.[34]

The excerpts which were taken from the calypso war between Executor, Caresser, Attila and Lion, transcribed from The Real Calypso 1927 - 1946, compiled and annotated by Samuel Charters -

---

[vv] Up to the mid 1940s, primary school children in Trinidad and Tobago wrote on slates: tablets made out of fine-grain rock, compressed clay, shale and coal.

Dr. Hollis "Chalkdust" Liverpool

RBF - (13 rpm), do not carry Executor's contribution which went thus:

> At last the hour of vengeance is at hand;
> I am in the land (repeat).
> The Lord Executor's word of command,
> With my glittering sword in hand.
> Tell Houdini, this is the hour of destiny
> In this colony.

The calypso war tells the story of the singers' dislike for Houdini. The reasons for such a dislike Gordon Rohlehr perhaps overlooked. Attila and Executor, more so than Caresser, felt that they were educated and deserved to be more popular than Houdini, yet Houdini was given the opportunity to travel to the United States and sing before large audiences, whilst they continued to labour in Trinidad for "ka ka dan." ww Moreover, Houdini used to attack them in songs while in the United States, even recording his hatred of them, while they had no opportunity to reply. As such, when Houdini returned on holiday in the early 1930s, they threw picong at him. Houdini, in return, despised and looked down on them as persons with no ambition, ill-dressed and unkempt. Obviously, Houdini's travels and his American dollars made him feel superior to the Trinidad-based calypsonians. Thus did Beginner sum up the reasons why Houdini was disliked: "Houdini was a big-minded fellow. When he came to Trinidad, he used to walk with a parrot on his shoulder and a walking stick in his hand. The Americans used to call West Indians - 'monkey chasers,' and when we went to America, Houdini used to call us monkey chasers too."

In looking back at the years 1940 to 1947, Beginner refuted a statement by the Roaring Lion-who in 1971 made a series of Radio programmes for Radio Trinidad entitled "The Story/History of Calypso and the Men Who Made It"-that calypsonians were paid"huge sums of money" ranging from one hundred ($100) to two hundred ($200) dollars a night on the average. [35]

---

ww A creolized term for 'little;' peanuts compared to millions.

Dr. Hollis "Chalkdust" Liverpool

Beginner, in contrast, said that the tent then made an average35 of one hundred dollars ($100) a night and "though I started at two dollars ($2) a night, when I became a big-boy I was paid, like the rest, approximately six dollars." He recalled that the tent had few expenses to meet and

> Musicians use to get six dollars ($6.00) for the whole band in the years 1920 to 1930. In the early 40s, the salary of the band was about twenty dollars ($20.00) nightly, but in 1947, just before I left to settle in England, top calypsonians made as much as forty-eight
>
> dollars ($48.00) a night, with the small fries getting about eighteen dollars ($18.00).

These figures show the change in the salaries of the working population as a whole and give the reader an indication of the G.D.P. and general economic development of the people of Trinidad and Tobago. In 1968, for instance, when I joined the calypso fraternity, my biggest purse, which was obtained during the last week of the tent, was eighteen dollars ($18.00). In 1973, the Regal Calypso tent paid its band of musicians the sum of eighteen hundred dollars ($1800.00) weekly. One must remember that in the 1940s, calypso tents opened on weekends and on a few days during the week. On Sundays they were closed. Even so, the band in the 1940s comprised fewer musicians than the 1970s. Regal was also the first tent to pay its singers, musicians and staff by cheques.

Beginner continued to give further insights into the organization of the tents in the 1940s pointing out that on weekends, besides the tent, they would hold shows in cinemas. He exclaimed: "Long ago, the managers showed us all the money that the show made, but Ah hear today the fellas don't know how much the show make." That might be true, but at the Regal tent in the 1970s, all revenue was declared and a system of payment based on rank, experience and the ability to attract patrons was instituted.

About his fellow calypsonians in his day, Beginner declared:

> Executor was the strongest I ever met, but he wasn't my type. I used to dance about, and had a better voice and

Dr. Hollis "Chalkdust" Liverpool

rendition, while Executor used to stand up one place and fumble with his hat. Radio too had a lot of bounce, and used to get on like what Sparrow does now. Attila was a strong composer, but he had no calypso voice; he used to drag. Lion was more of a song man. He used to take Bing Crosby and them songs, and put words to it. His was a kind of mix-up song and kaiso.

Should the reader play some of the old songs of Lion, Executor, Radio and Attila, he or she would certainly come to the conclusion that Beginner's summation cannot be taken lightly, but indeed had some truth in it.

When I left this great and talented warlord who gave us hits like "Anacona," "Louise," and "Cricket, Lovely Cricket," I felt sadder but wiser. Though his last days were spent in abject poverty, yet he was proud, proud of his contribution, proud of his many sweet refrains, proud of his voice, proud of kaiso. That pride he exhibited daily in his dress. He "dressed to kill" with an empty pocket in his trousers. Even in the era nearing his dying day, he remained humble, feared none, respected all, his voice strong and sweet as ever; his voice box straining eager to tell me and the world that it was he who, above all, had made melodies and tuneful refrains an important aspect of calypso.

In his last days, I grew to love him very much and we spent many an hour talking, reminiscing, singing and praying. Because of his contribution to calypso and to human development, the National Joint Action Committee (NJAC) and a few loyal friends took the initiative to bury him and to pay for his funeral expenses. In the winter of his life, he would come to the Regal Calypso tent and seek a salary from us even though he was not a member of the cast; I readily paid him, adding sometimes to the purse, a drink. At times when I gave him a drink, or when he demanded one of me, I would ask him why with his sweet voice he would desire to spoil it with rum? To that he answered: "I learnt to drink through Kaiso. Ah must take a drink before Ah face dem hooligans in Royal Theatre.You is a Kaisonian too Chalkie - leh we fire one." And fire one we did - sometimes two, three and four.

May he rest in peace.

Dr. Hollis "Chalkdust" Liverpool

53

ENDNOTES

1 Epstein, Dena. Sinful Tunes and Spirituals. (Chicago: University of Illinois Press, 1977), pp. 25 & 36.

2 Hill, Errol. The Trinidad Carnival: Mandate For A National Theatre. (Texas: University of Texas Press, 1972), 24.

3 Hill, Errol. The Trinidad Carnival op. cit. 1972, P. 65

4 Liverpool, Hollis. Calypsonians to Remember. (P.O.S. : Juba Publications, 1987), pp.42 - 43.

5 Hill, Errol. op.cit. p.76

6 Walla, Tarzan. Personal Communication. Todds Road. August 1968.

7 Carr, Andrew. Personal Communication. Port-of-Spain. August 1965.

8 Trotman, David. Crime in Trinidad. (Knoxville: Univ. of Tennessee Press, 1986), 151.

9 Liverpool, Hollis. Rituals of Power and Rebellion. (Chicago: Frontline, 2001), 255.

10 Harris to Grey, "Correspondence relating to the General Conditions of Government of the Colony," in Parliamentary Papers. 1849, 37: 563, Public Record Office. (PRO).

11 Copy of a Despatch from Gov. Keate to Rt. Hon. Henry LaBouchere, M.P., July 6, 1857, in Parliamentary Papers, 1859. 20: 1, (PRO).

12 Jones, Patrick. Calypso, Lore and Legend, An Afternoon with Patrick Jones. Cook Long Play Album 5016, 1957, Personal Collection.

13 Francisco, Slinger (Sparrow). Creole Bacchanal. Personal Collection of Calypso lyrics.

14 Personal Collection of Calypso Lyrics: Blakie, Sparrow et al.

15 Carr, Andrew. Personal Communication. P.O.S., August 1965.

16 Collens, J.H. A Guide to Trinidad. (London: Elliott Stock, 1886), 39.

17 Quevedo, Raymond. "History of Calypso," in This Country of Ours. (Trinidad: PNM Publishing, 1962).

18 Rohlehr, Gordon. "The Development of the Calypso, 1900 - 1940. TS. Jan. & May, 1972. p. 13.

19 Trinidad Guardian, Dec. 9th 1968.

20 Thomas, Randolph (Iere). Personal Interview. P.O.S., 1972.

21 Trinidad Guardian. 11th February, 1968.

22 Hill, Errol, op.cit., p.65.

23 Rohlehr, Gordon. "The Development of Calypso." op.cit. P.65.

24 Hill, Errol. op. cit. P.66.

25 James, C.L.R. Beyond a Boundary. (London: Hutchinson & Co., 1963) P. 71; P 206.

26 Scott, Dillary (Cypher). Personal Collection of Calypso Records.

27 James, C.L.R. Beyond a Boundary. op.cit. P. 56.

28 Carr, op. cit. August, 1965.

29 Espinet, C.S, & Pitts, H. Land of the Calypso: The Origin and Development of Trinidad's Folksong. (P.O.S.: the author, 1944), P.25.

30 Hill, Errol, op. cit., P.75

31 Nizer, Louis. My Life in Court. (Doubleday & Co. Ltd., 1961), pp. 265 -327.

32 Simon, Pete. Art and Man. (Feb. 1969): P.25

33 Spann, Norman (Radio). Personal Communication. P.O.S., August 1965.

34 Rohlehr, op. cit. pp.16-18.

35 Roaring Lion " The Story of Calypso and the Men who made it," Radio Trinidad, Nov 8th & 15th, 1970

Dr. Hollis "Chalkdust" Liverpool

In the Virgin Islands with the Governor

George Mc Sween 'Sir Galba'

Chapter 3

Rafael De Leon -
The Roaring Lion
(June 15, 1908 - July 11, 1999)
If you want to be happy
and live a king's life,
Never make a pretty woman your wife.
All you have to do is hear what I say
And you'll be happy, merry and gay.
So from a logical point of view,
Marry a woman uglier than you.

(Lion - "Ugly Woman" 1934 - Author's Collection).

Hubert Raphael Charles was known in his lifetime by many names: The Walking Encyclopedia; Lion Flaps; The Candle Man; The Metro Lion. A tall African, he was always nattily dressed especially when he appeared on calypso shows; then he would wear his bowler hat, three-piece suit with matching waistcoat, shoes, socks, coat handkerchief and tie, while with a hand-carved walking stick, he strutted rhythmically, with his head held high. All who came to know him personally, however, knew straight away that he was a lion, for he had the temperament of a lion. Indeed, he called himself the "Roaring Lion" so as to drive fear into the hearts of his enemies especially those who had the nerve to challenge him in "war."[a] In his lifetime, he strove to document the history of the calypso, by his books, his newspaper articles and his many radio programmes, particularly one done in 1971 entitled: "The History of Calypso and the Men who made it."

I had the pleasure of speaking to Lion on countless occasions,

---

[a] An extempo duel between two or more singers involving big words and high-sounding phrases. It usually occurred in the yards of Port-of-Spain before it moved into the tents.

Dr. Hollis "Chalkdust" Liverpool

55

but the times when he spoke best of calypso's history and development were when he could be persuaded to sit and have a drink. He enjoyed a drink but was never a drinker; he enjoyed better the "old talk" that most times the drink triggered off. \
While drinking with him especially after a fruitful meeting of the Calypsonians' Association[b] or an audition of the Calypso Theatre, the talk would inevitably center on the growth and development of the calypso.

Speaking to Lion always involved having to compare and contrast his thoughts with other sources, and subject his sayings to the survey of traditional historical documentation. We had many an argument as to the origin of calypso, especially because he denied the African roots of the art form and even wrote a book entitled: "Calypso from France to Trinidad."[1] According to Lion,

> Calypso was never really started by the African slaves. It is a crime to even think that this is so. I know that there are quite a few people who set themselves up as experts on the question of calypso and folk dances of Trinidad, but the plain or painful truth is that they absolutely know nothing about the calypso.

I recall that the very name calypso caused us to have many an argument on George Street, Port-of-Spain. Listen to Lion:

> Calypso is religiously and ceremoniously the folk song of the Caribs who inhabited this country long, long ago. The word 'calypso' succeeded the word 'kayso' and 'kaiso' succeeded the word 'cariso,' which ought to have been spelt 'cairiso.' 'Cairi' was the name the Caribbean Indians gave Trinidad. It means the land of the Humming Bird. The Spaniards who were the first to conquer the island referred to the songs of the Caribs as 'cairi Songs,' but the French who came after, not as conquerors, shortened the word to 'cairiso.'

---

[b] Lion served as the President of the Assn. in the early 1970s with the author as Secretary.

Dr. Hollis "Chalkdust" Liverpool

I asked Lion how did the word 'cairiso' become 'cariso' leading to the term 'kaiso.' He informed me that:

> After the British occupation[c] which came much later, the name 'kaiso' or 'cairiso' gradually changed to 'calypsoe.' It was spelt then with an 'e' at the end. Incidently (sic), calypso in Greek mythology is the name of a Goddess or rather a witch who enchanted men into swines (sic). There is also a very lovely story about this witch named 'Calypsoe' sometimes called 'Circe.' She, it is said, is really responsible either directly or indirectly for the origin of the folk song of this country which is now known as the calypso.

Famed writer of folk stories Mitto Sampson agreed with Lion that the word "calypso came from 'carrieto' which is a Carib term for a joyous song." [2]Indeed, there has always been a veil of confusion surrounding not only the term calypso, but the origin of the art form as well. While it's the consensus of most academics that it originated from Africans brought to the Caribbean as enslaved men and women, Professor Gordon Rohlehr states that the term 'calypso' seems to have been an English corruption of a term which may have been African, French, Spanish or even Carib.[3] Rohlehr also links the calypso with the Post-Emancipation era pointing out that the freed men used the art form to criticize their powerful masters and later the rising Mulattoes and the middle class.[4] At a meeting of the Calypsonians' Association, in supporting an item on the agenda being discussed, King Radio, who died in 1971, explained that: "calypso is a way to air your views. It was during slavery a way to rebuke the master without him being conscious of it."[5] Unknown agreed with King Radio and added that the ridicule of the master was known as: "'Fiornay' or 'Fiorne' which the master never understood. Later on, instead of using it on the boss, they threw picong at their friends and on themselves." Errol Hill's[d] theory is very interesting: "The word

---

[c] Britain conquered Trinidad in 1797.
[d] Professor Errol Hill, author, dramatist and Carnival historian.

'kaiso' came from 'kaito' (West African) pronounced 'kaitso' or 'kaicho,' meaning an expression of great feeling." Famed folklorist and singer, Edric Connor, in linking the calypso with enslavement in the Caribbean, noted that "kaiso is an African word meaning 'bravo.'[6] "Errol Hill went on to say that the "antecedents of calypso were the praise songs of derision of West African natives captured as slaves and brought to the West Indies."[7] Hill's theory relative to the origin of calypso ties in with my own research findings with regard to the griots of West Africa who performed at the courts of kings and at important social functions in the village.[8] Famed Egyptologist and historian Ben Jochanan mentioned in an Emancipation lecture that he too found the word "kaiso" in Africa, particularly in Egypt, and that it signaled an expression of praise.[9] Lion's friend and fellow calypsonian Attila went to great lengths to explain that not only is the calypso African and was first associated with enslavement, but that the very "first" word he heard to describe the art form was 'kaiso.' "It was used to describe the song when sung, as well as a means of expressing ecstatic satisfaction over, what was in the opinion of the audience, a particularly excellent calypso.[10]

Errol Hill confused the picture a little when he said that the direct antecedent of the modern calypso was the 'belair.'[e] As proof, he went on to quote the Port-of-Spain Gazette of 1838, the editorial of which speaks of a gentleman who, believing that the Africans were about to murder all the free people in the island, "used to commit to writing the 'belairs' as their half-licentious, half-meaning songs are called." To further emphasize his theory, Hill says that the editor of the same newspaper referred to the 'belair' as the native song of Trinidad, and wrote: "Certain women of the planter class danced the 'belair' to African drums."[11] Hill may be correct, but in any case the "belair," according to McDaniel, Honeychurch et al, is undoubtedly African music, though it can be described as creolized

---

[e] Belair sometimes spelt Bele; A creolized African song and dance.

Dr. Hollis "Chalkdust" Liverpool

African music.[12]   Hill's theory is not only supported by many intellectuals and folklorists, including A.P.T. Ambard, ex-editor of the Port-of-Spain Gazette, but also by an editorial in a newspaper of 1950 that stated in part: "calypso is the disgustingly debased form of the old and very pretty belair."[13]

Many writers too, including J.D.Elder, associate the calypso with the 'kalenda' songs of the early twentieth century.[14]   In any case too, the kalenda was African music played at stick fight rituals and in the African carnivals of the 18th and 19th century.[15]   To stabilize the issue, Bryan Edwards, a historian writing in the 18th century noted:

> Their songs are commonly impromptu, and there are among them individuals who remember the improvisatori or extempore bards of Italy, but I cannot say much for their poetry. Their tunes in general are characteristic of their natural manners; those of the Eboes being soft and languishing; of the Koromantyns heroick and martial. At the same time there is observable in most of them a predominant melancholy which to a man of feeling is sometimes very affecting. At their meetings and midnight festivals, they are not without ballads of another kind, adapted to such occasions, and here they give full scope to a talent for ridicule which is exercised not only against each other but also, not unfrequently, at the expense of their owner or employer. (Quoted in "Rituals of Power and Rebellion," p. 187)

Although the evidence strongly suggests that the calypso is African in form and function, Dom Basil Matthews, a teacher, priest, sociologist and ex-principal of St. Benedict's College of La Romain, Trinidad, is of the opinion that " calypso is a French word meaning 'carouse' or 'debauch,' from which the Creole words 'cariso,' 'calyso,' and 'cayiso' derive. It came from the French 'carrouseaux.' "[16] Another suggested theory states that the calypso descended from old Spanish-Speaking Peons[f] in Trinidad, and that "the word 'caliso' is an old Venezuelan-Spanish term for a topical local song in the highlands along the Spanish Main.[17] There is also the belief that the word 'cariso' comes from the Spanish 'carrijo' meaning a reed or cane, and, according to Attila, "was the term of approval for an appropriately effective song."[18] For me, Professor Krehbiel[g] was on target when he wrote: Regardless of the origins of the word calypso, there can be little doubt that the aspects of topicality, allusion and improvisation in calypso derive from Africa."[19]

Another predominantly African area upon which Lion commented was the 'bongo.' To all and sundry, the 'bongo' is African music and dance performed mainly at 'wakes'[h] throughout the Caribbean. For Lion, however, the 'bongo' came from the Caribs. "It is," he said, "one of the four phrases to the calypso." In fact, he linked not only calypso to the Caribs, but other folk music as well. Listen to Lion:

> There are four phrases (sic) to the calypso namely: the 'bongo' song or song of the dead; the 'kalueda' or song of war; the 'limbo' or harvest song; and songs that were sung during the telling of fairy tales. These were called 'cairi' songs by the Spaniards.

The reader can draw his or her own conclusions, but in doing so, he or she must remember that Trinidad and Tobago passed under several European nations, and, moreover, different tribes, races and nationalities settled on the island from time to time. It would indeed be difficult to escape the influence of the conquering nation states, or the culture of the conquered inhabitants.

---

[f] Early migrants from Venezuela and descendants of Peninsula Spaniards.
[g] Henry Edward Krehbiel, author of Afro-American Folk Songs, (N.Y.: Frederick Ungar Publishing Co., 1962).
[h] African ceremonies kept in honour and remembrance of the dead. They feature prayers, singing, dancing, hand-clapping, drinking and eating.

Dr. Hollis "Chalkdust" Liverpool

I once asked Lion what he thought of the writings of Gordon Rohlehr, Errol Hill, Mitto Sampson and J.D. Elder who had all written ideas completely opposite to his thoughts. He replied:

> We are now living in a modern age, and the people of this age are too intelligent to continue to subscribe to some of these useless proverbs and theories of the past. Therefore it is high time that we face facts and take care of our own, rather than make a fuss of that which is not ours.

For Lion, calypso has made a great contribution to our society in that it has made us better known overseas. He saw the calypso as the art form that should be the driving force behind tourism, and pointed out that calypso is now a household word throughout most of the English-Speaking and Spanish lands where it has been translated. To prove his point, one of his songs, he stated, is considered a national song in Nigeria. The composition, he said, was sent there by him with the hope of getting the two major political groups, headed by Drs. Awolo and Azikiwe then, to join hands before that country's independence. The song, recorded in 1952, was published by the Jewie Recording Co. To further his point, he boasted that the Queen sent him a letter of thanks when her father died, as he had written a calypso on the occasion of the death of King George VI, at the request of the B.B.C. Never one to miss out composing on an important occasion or a historical visit, Lion sang on the visit of the Pope, John Paul 11, to Trinidad just before he (Lion) died; needless to say, he was heralded by the Pope for his special song and even received, in return, the papal blessing. One particular verse went thus:

> His Holiness John Paul, the Pilgrim Pope
> Came just when we have lost courage and hope.
> We've sunken low spiritually
> And lost all sense of Christianity.

There is so much maliciousness, wickedness and selfishness;
Our nation is plagued by sheer lawlessness.
It seems the world is gone mad,
So we need his blessings in Trinidad.

Chorus: So let's get together and welcome the Pilgrim Pope,
For he has brought us blessings, expectations and hope.
Chant the glad tidings and sing hallelujah.
Our Lord is gone up, but left us his Vicar here.

Few of us can dispute the fact that the calypso reached the ears of inhabitants and lands that we in our lifetime may perhaps never reach. Few can dispute the fact that tourists are lectured on the calypso and its greatness by tourist officials in London, New York and Toronto-to name a few places-with the aim of increasing their tourist markets to Trinidad in particular, and to the Caribbean in general. In fact, as we travel on planes throughout the Caribbean, calypso music comes over the airwaves, with the hope that the tourists, before they disembark on Caribbean lands, will be put in an atmosphere of gaiety, fun and laughter.

With regards to the role of businessmen in the promotion of the calypso, Lion noted that in the 1930s and 1940s, not only did businessmen promote competitions among calypsonians, but they used the calypso for advertisement purposes. He singled out the song by J.J. La Hori that went thus:

All the young girls who have no clothes
Take a walk to Murphy and Mose.

It was, he said, one of those songs that went a long way in promoting the products of businessmen. Well do we remember in the 1950s too, Lord Melody advertising Nagib Elias and Sons, a firm reputed for its "hardware, iron, cement, etcetera," and Sparrow singing: "Guiness is a man's best friend." These advertising jingles turned out to be household songs in that they were known and sung by the entire populace, thereby bringing huge profits to the firms.

From 1965 to about 1978, the PNM[i] organized a calypso competition and jamboree based on the theme 'buy local.' It was instituted to galvanize the public to support local industry at a time when most persons preferred foreign goods to locally produced ones. The PNM preached then that political independence must be accompanied by economic independence, if the people of Trinidad and Tobago are to be truly independent and independent and free from the trappings of colonialism; hence, they produced the show allowing singers to compete for the Texaco[j] trophy. The Mighty Striker won the first competition in 1965. Other winners were Lord Relator, Mighty Unknown (1966), Mighty Prowler and the author who, having won it thrice consecutively from 1976 to 1978, was given it permanently. Not only was the calypso used for advertisement purposes long ago, but businessmen would give to calypsonians in the 1940s and 1950s large quantities of rum, whisky, jerseys (T shirts), raw cloth and other samples of their manufactured goods with the hope that the calypsonian would mention the name of the firm or the name of the product in a calypso. This generosity on the part of businessmen was confirmed by the Growling Tiger, who became so close to businessmen that during the greater part of his life, he lived by collecting advertisements from firms for erecting advertising banners in the calypso tent.[20]

Although Lion knew the hardships suffered by the calypsonians and the other lower classes in the 1920s at the hands of the privileged classes, he still recalled that it was the said upper class which assisted them financially and supported them in the tent. He recalled the names of men like Amral Sultan Khan who first staged calypso shows at the Palace Cinema, one Mr. Strasser who did the same at the Olympic Cinema in Belmont, Eduardo Sa Gomes who sent them to the U.S. to carry out recordings, one Sarran Teelucksingh who also promoted calypso shows, Captain Arthur Andrew Cipriani to whom they went for advice and lawyers Gaston Johnson and L.C. Hannays who assisted them legally and

---

[i] People's National Movement, the party founded by Eric Williams, John Donaldson, Andrew Carr, DeWilton Rogers et al. under the banner of which the country gained its Independence in 1962.
[j] The Oil Company operating in Trinidad then.

Dr. Hollis "Chalkdust" Liverpool

financially. Of those days he observed: "You couldn't play calypso records near to another man's shop, neither could you sing calypso in Lent." He recalled too, that one Papa Bodie used to assist the calypsonians in the early decades of the twentieth century and all calypsonians had loved him. Papa Bodie was truly a patron of the art for Attila noted that one night, Bodie visited the tent and it would seem that a young singer was called upon to thank him in song for his contribution. The young singer must have failed to do so in the manner expected by the senior singers, causing Inventor (Henry Forbes) to sing:

> I intended to give you a castigation,
> But instead you will get my compassion.
> You have demonstrated your inability
> And you have failed miserably.
> You can't sing on Papa Bodie whom we all know
> The friend and patron of caliso.
> You can't give satisfaction; you are a mock kaisonian! Sans humanite.[21]

According to Lion, the Governor started to come to the calypso tent in the early 1920s. Such visits esteemed the tent, helped to remove the stigma that a calypso ought not to be sung in Lent, and caused other upper class persons to attend calypso concerts especially those held in middle and upper class areas. With regard to the English governors of the territory, Attila and himself were the first persons, Lion claimed, to entertain them and their families at Government house. "The first Governor I entertained there was Sir Murchison Fletcher and the last was Lord Athlone." Lion and Attila were not, however, the only calypsonians to entertain governors; Lord Beginner claimed to have entertained Sir Solomon Hochoy in his country manor at Blanchisseuse in the 1960s.

The history of the art of calypso singing demonstrates change. Over the years, because of laws, regulations, events and change in societal values, the structure and function of the art form has changed considerably. Just as Executor in 1950 found that the calypsoes of the period 1900 - 1920 were much different from those of the 1940s,[22] so too Lion was of the opinion that calypsoes of the 1970s, 1980s and even the 1990s were different from yesteryear. Mitto Sampson, for example, described the Young Brigade[k] of the 1940s thus:

> With the ...upsurge of the Young Brigade, we witnessed a complete metamorphosis of tunes and tonics. Pandering to the U.S.A., soldiers' tastes and salacious details, the young cavalcade unleashed a cavalcade of torrid and harmonious pornography. Many of their innuendos were so thinly veiled, they repelled; others were raw, flat, lewd, but always catchy and spicy. People from every stratum of society jam-crammed the tents to hear the youths sing on 'lesbianism,' conjugal discord as a result of Yankee infiltration, queen perversions, barrack yard episodes, and the predilection of local belles for American lads.[23]

The quote indeed shows the influence of American soldiers on Trinidadian society, particularly in the area of female prostitution where "both mother and daughter (were) working for the Yankee dollar."[24] It would seem too, that that characteristic of the Young Brigade described by Mitto Sampson persisted throughout the 1940s, 1950s, 1960s and 1970s, for journalist Keith Smith, in an article in 1973, summarized the programme offered at the Young Brigade as all centred around "the pussy pun." Lion therefore was of the opinion that there was too much vulgarity in calypsoes of the 1970s and 80s, and that ninety nine per cent (99%) of calypso then was not calypso. "Moreover," in describing the singers of the 1970 to 1990 era, he went on to say, "ten (10) out of fifteen (15) so-called calypsonians do not compose, but are mere calypso singers."

Continuing his views on the differences between the calypso of the 1970 to 1990 era and those of a bygone age, Lion was of the firm opinion that the calypso is dead after carnival, whereas in his heyday calypsonians sang in cinemas throughout the year. Turning to the type of songs sung in the 1990 era, he felt that the Calypso

---

[k] The Young Brigade - the name of a calypso tent.

Dr. Hollis "Chalkdust" Liverpool

Monarch competition had exhibited a drop in standards, as compared to the 1940s and 1950s. "In the Calypso King Competition, people looked forward to something intelligent, purposeful, and not the stupid humour of the tent." In other words, according to Lion, there was a difference between calypsoes for the Competition and calypsoes for the tent. The tent called for light songs sung in a humourous vein, whereas the songs for the Monarch Competition were almost always serious, political or social commentaries, the lyrics of which, above all, made sense. In fact, Beginner mentioned that singers were forced in the 1920/1930 era to compose different songs to suit the different audiences whom calypsonians faced in the Savannah,[1] the cinema and the tent.[25]

Calypso kings in the 1930s and 1940s, according to Lion, were, first of all, outstanding singers in their villages and towns. After dominating the competition in their individual villages, then could the singer seek laurels in the city of Port-of-Spain. Beginner agreed with Lion on this score pointing out that he was only accepted in Port-of-Spain because he had held his own among the outstanding singers in San Fernando. [26]This characteristic of the king as described by Lion was certainly true, for Kitchener himself was the master of his tent in Arima before he sought fame and fortune in Port-of-Spain.[27] Similarly, singers such as Black Stalin, Duke, Composer, Tallish, Maestro, Ras Shorty I and Bitterbush all made a name for themselves in Southern areas before they were accepted as calypsonians in their own right in Port-of-Spain.

"Besides kings like Radio and King Fanto," according to Lion, "lesser known fellows were called dukes. For example, there was the Duke of Marlborough." I asked Lion whether these kings ever lost their titles. He replied:

> The title was more or less an award. As such, kings of villages from 1900 - 1930 used to meet different kings of other villages in war. During the battle, grog flowed, after which all monies collected used to be given to the visiting warlord.

---

[1] The Queen's Park Savannah - the venue of the Calypso Monarch Competitions.

Lion continued to see outstanding differences between calypsonians of the 1930s and 40s and those of the 1970s and 1980s. For instance, he said, better fees were paid to calypsonians in the 1940s in comparison to the 1970 era. He himself remembered paying King Radio five hundred dollars ($500), Small Island Pride two hundred and forty dollars ($240) and Pretender one hundred and fifty dollars ($150) nightly. These were large sums for, in the 1970 era, top calypsonians made approximately five hundred dollars ($500) weekly. Although one might be quick to say that Lion was wrong, the reader must remember that when a show was promoted at a cinema in the 1930 to 1940 era, approximately seventy percent (70%) of the revenue amounting to about eight hundred dollars ($800) was given to the calypsonians to be divided among them. One must remember too, that there were not as many singers on the cast then as in the 1970s. In addition, the band of musicians in the past was smaller in number. Lion however claimed to have paid out such large sums from shows carried out in his calypso tent. Where in the 1970s too, young calypsonians, according to Lion, had a tendency to look at their elder counterparts as 'has-beens,' 'once-good,' and 'old-timers,' Lion remarked that in his heyday, younger singers had respect for seasoned campaigners and felt happy to be around them. This point was made also by Kitchener and Superior in discussions I had with them.

Lion went on to say:

> Long ago, we were a much more united force. We stood up for one another. We never stole or deprived another of his share. If a person sang your song at a show, next day he would bring you a raise. Another thing, calypsonians always appeared on shows at short notice. They never absented themselves. Nowadays it's a common thing to advertise someone and he never appears.

If Lion spoke the truth, and indeed he seemed truthful, calypsonians in the 1940s were definitely more united. The reader must bear in mind, however, the increased number of singers in the1970 - 2002 era with their differing personalities, and the fact that they belong to a less intimate and coherent group, perhaps because of the increased commercialization of the tents. The reader must realize too, that before one sings at a show today, music scores have to be written and rehearsals have to be carried out, so that one is not expected to sing at every nook and cranny at short notice as in Lion's heyday.

Speaking about competitions in the tent in the 1930s, Lion described to me one which he said stood out in his mind "like a rock in the ocean." At Victory tent in 1934, the manager Mr. Reynold Wilkinson arranged an extempo competition with a businessman to market a new brand of condensed milk known as 'Dancow milk.' King Iere, Attila and Radio sang their extempo verses to thunderous applause from the audience. While he Lion was singing on the theme afterwards and seemed to be in the lead, judging from the audience's reaction, Lord Executor walked in. The crowd called for Executor who exclaimed: "What is the topic? Ah don't even know the topic!" He was told the topic and, according to Lion, "Executor 'mash up' the place and won." Lion placed second. One of Executor's verses went thus:

> Doctors and analysts all declare
> That Dancow milk must be sold everywhere (repeat).
> For these are not the days of fable,
> So look for the cow on the label.
> Say what you may and take it anyhow
> But give the fame to Dancow.

On another occasion at the Riband Bleu Club in New York, the crowd was calling topics and Executor and he (Lion) were responding to them in song. The duo was part of a team of four [m] who had gone to New York to make recordings for the Decca Gramophone recording Company in 1937. That night, Executor was telling the crowd that he could extempo on any topic on earth. Suddenly, a patron asked them to sing on a 'circle.' Executor in perfect metre and rhyme responded in song:

> I'm just a simple kaisonian;
> I am no geometrician.

---

[m] The team comprised Rufus Callender (Caresser), Raymond Quevedo (Attila the Hun), Felix Garcia (Executor), and Lion.

Dr. Hollis "Chalkdust" Liverpool

> What is a circle? I for one don't care
> But of one thing I'm sure; it isn't a square.

Interestingly, Lion, Unknown and Beginner all hailed Executor as the greatest extempo artist of all times.

Lion spoke too of the kind of smut sung in the 80s and 90s. To him, it was "nastiness." It had no "art" as in the 1940s and 1950s. His example of smut with "art" was his song on Dorothy:

> Miss Dorothy went to bathe
> And a catfish made a raid
> And Dorothy bawl: Ah me!
> Look a cat fish gone with mi lignum vitae.

It was indeed art for when Lion in 1940 sang about homosexuality among the upper class calling it "soldering" and "polishing," Albert Gomes[n] complimented him for his art stating that he had turned a topic that was "distasteful" into a "highly entertaining" one.

As late as 1974, Lion was still complaining about the "vulgar, artless" songs being sung.

> There is a ton load of vulgar songs every year
> And not a verse of interest to the cultured ear (repeat).
> Lots of them are disgraceful, deprave and rude,
> Senseless, shocking and extremely crude.
> To sing such songs one has to be insane,
> Otherwise totally devoid of shame.
>
> Chorus: they wouldn't sing about Shakespeare, Pushkin, Dumas and Dickens,
> H.G. Wells, Madame Blavatsky, Horatio and Kipling.
> Voltaire, Molere and Dennis Didero,
> Instead of the muck they call calypso.

In 1956, Sparrow ruled the roost of calypso with a song called "Jean and Dinah." The calypso described the fact that the prostitutes in Port-of-Spain had to revert to the local men since the American soldiers had left the scene. "The Yankees gone and Sparrow take over now."[28]

---

[n] The leading politician of the early 1950 era, and a supporter of the calypsonian in his struggle with the elite classes.

Dr. Hollis "Chalkdust" Liverpool

Sparrow won the Calypso King Competition that year and the song has since been acclaimed as one of the all-time best by calypso aficionados. Lion however stated that his calypso sung a few years earlier (around 1941 when the American soldiers were being sent to Europe for the Great Offensive) on the topic is what gave Sparrow the idea to compose "Jean and Dinah." Lion's song was called "Pam Palaam," and it was described by Attila as "a fine piece of local double entendre."[29] Lion addressed Pam Palaam thus:

> Pam Palaam you too smart
> But note I'm no rubbish cart.
> And if you enter my bachelor
> You'll be paid a penny in silver paper.
>
> For the sake of a couple dollars
> They had turned their backs on their own lovers.
> Denying their own people their favours
> For the Yankees who had the dollars.
>
> No more cruising about in the city.
> No more pretty dress matinee.°
> They can no longer go Docksite dancing;
> They have to walk; there is no more jeep driving.
>
> And all at once they are only throwing crop.
> Bit by bit their jewels are in the pawn shop.
> But I'm not sorry for them, not a bit.
> For like a dog they must return to their vomit.

The metaphorical idea of the dog returning to its vomit, according to Lion, is the same as that used by Sparrow in "Jean and Dinah," where the prostitutes are shown as persons who rejected the locals when the Americans were around. When the Americans left, they were forced to return to Sparrow and his kind.

One of the men whom Lion admired was the famous trade unionist and political leader, Captain Cipriani. Hardly a discussion between him and me would go by without him referring to "the Cap" as Cipriani was called. Cipriani to Lion was "the friend of the

---

° A Cinema show that usually started at 12.30 p.m.

bare foot man." Lion said that "he would never refuse a poor man a penny; he would always find something to give him." Cipriani who became the president of the Trinidad Working Men's Association in 1923, fought against racism as practiced in the British army toward local West Indian soldiers, defended workers' interests and attacked the Colonial Government in his quest for better conditions and an increased standard of living for the underprivileged. As leader of the Trinidad Labour Party which he formed in 1934, Cipriani was in the forefront of the battle waged to improve the "constitutional backwardness"[30] that characterized Trinidad and Tobago in the 1940s. Cipriani used to assist and defend the calypsonians especially when the upper classes accused them of singing smut or attacking the elite class. He died in 1945. Lion immortalized him in song thus:

> It is the creed of the creation
> That there should be a leader in every land (repeat).
> Just as Hitler is to Germany
> And as Mussolini dictates Italy,
> So there is a saviour in La Trinity
> In the person of the Captain Cipriani.

Finally, Lion informed me that the reason why singers of old were able to attack "big topics" and use "high-flown language," was because they read widely, and used the Public Library to full advantage.

> Before Executor sang on the 'Reign of the Georges,' he studied that period in British history. Today, instead of using the library, they flock to the race pools to learn who is living with whom, or who is horning who.

Lion is quite correct on the point that calypsonians used to visit the library before making a calypso, for I recalled as a boy seeing the Growling Tiger and him in the Trinidad Public Library in Port-of-Spain doing research. At the same time, it is important to note that calypsonians frequented race pools, sports meetings and other social gatherings in order to get topics for songs for the ensuing season, according to calypsonian Lord Kitchener.[31] Kitchener, indeed, was to be always found at all sports meetings in the country, be they horse racing, football or athletics. There, when the crowd spoke, Kitch listened and the topic flowed.

Lion narrated to me a number of 'firsts' in his career.

a. He was the first to sing at the Governor's house before a Governor.

b. He was the first to sing to a "real American public:" the elite on Broadway. The show was sponsored by Rudy Valley and the Decca Recording Co. Attila also appeared on the show. There, he met Bing Crosby and Bill Robinson, two famous stars of that era. In fact, when Bing Crosby came to Trinidad years later, Bing brought him a bottle of whisky, he remarked.

c. He composed the first song to be banned in Trinidad. It was called: "Nettie Nettie." Unknown however said that the song was his and not Lion's composition.

d. He was the first to appear at Country Club in Boissiere, Trinidad, at a time when only White folks frequented there. This was certified by Attila who pointed out that Lion made the "break through the taboos and restrictions of the exclusive 'Country Club' where he appeared one night in tails, topper, gloves and even sporting a monocle."[32]

e. He was the first singer to go on tour with a steelband - TASPO in 1951.

f. He was the first to be sent away officially; in 1933 he led a group on tour of Barbados and St. Vincent.

g. He was the first to sing in clubs on Broadway. According to Attila, "Lion appeared with distinction in New York nightclubs like 'The Village Vanguard,' 'Sunks' and others."[33]

h. He claimed to be the first Trinidadian artist to entertain tourists on ships, namely: the SS Uruguay and the SS Argentine.

i. He was the first to open his miniature "Tourist Bureau:" a restaurant, store and handicraft boutique catering for the needs of tourists. It was called "Quarryville." It is a well-known fact that Lion always had an eye for the entrepreneur world. In the 1960s, he opened a candle factory in Morvant, Trinidad. Before that, however, he ran a cosmetic concern while in England, and up to the time of his death in 1999, he was involved in the sale of lottery tickets and other commercial paraphernalia.

j. He made the first motion picture, that is, he was a part of the film cast. The picture was called "Holiday in Trinidad" and a check revealed that the said picture was produced by the "Amazon Picture Incorporated Co. Ltd."

k. According to Lion, calypso reached its zenith in 1941, for in that year a motion picture was filmed incorporating for the first time a calypso entitled "Ugly Woman." Needless to say, Lion was the composer and the film was called "Happy Go Lucky." Attila confirms this, stating that the film was produced by Paramount Films. [34]

l. Lion claimed to be the first person to record a steelband. This statement was confirmed by some ex-Casablanca Steelband members, with whom I had the pleasure of speaking. The recordings were done in the late 1946 and early 1947.

m. He was the first to entertain soldiers in the U.S. army.

It is said in some circles, however, that Lion was born Hubert Raphael Charles but changed his name to Raphael De Leon to escape the stigma placed on him by the court where he was found guilty of committing a crime. [35] In fact, some of his early recordings bear the name 'Hubert Charles' and others noted 'Raphael Charles De Leon' and 'Raphael Arias Cairi Llama De Leon' as the composer. [36] His many names, however, take away little from an outstanding composer, singer and trendy dress setter who was voted the 'Best Dressed Singer' as late as 1969 at the Calypso Theatre by his fellow calypsonians. [37] To understand his contribution and the power of his mere presence in the calypso world, the reader should analyze the summation of his character by Kitchener. Kitch said of

73

Long ago when people went to the cinema to hear calypso, few went inside early. The majority remained outside the cinema waiting to see if Lion would appear. When this well dressed bard appeared they would then flock to the paying booths, pushing, rushing and yelling for Lion. 'Look him! Look him! They shouted. Only when they saw him in person, they would make an attempt to go to the show inside. No other singer has reached the heights and glory he attained.

ENDNOTES

[1] DeLeon, Raphael, (Roaring Lion). Calypso From France to Trinidad: 800 Years of History. (P.O.S.1988).

[2] Crowley, Daniel. "Towards a Definition of Calypso." Journal of the Society for Ethnomusicology,Vol.3, No. 2, (May 1959): 57 -66.

[3] Rohlehr, Gordon. "The Development of the Calypso 1900 - 1940." T.S. (May 1972): 1.

[4] Rohlehr, op. cit., pp.1 - 3.

[5] Spann, Norman, (King Radio). Meeting of The Calypsonians' Association, November 1970.

[6] Hill, Errol. The Trinidad Carnival: Mandate for A National Theatre. (Texas: University of Texas Press,1972), p.144.

[7] Ibid. pp. 135 - 140.

[8] Liverpool, Hollis. Rituals of Power and Rebellion: The Carnival Tradition in Trinidad and Tobago, 1763-1962 (Chicago: Frontline Books, 2001), pp.185- 196.

[9] Ben Jochanan, Yosef. "The Glory that was Africa." Emancipation Lecture, NJAC, P.O.S., August 1982.

[10] Quevedo, Raymond. Attila's Kaiso - A Short History of Trinidad's Calypso. (P.O.S.: UWI, 1983), pp. 2 - 7.

[11] Hill, Errol. op.cit.

[12] Mcdaniel, Lorna A. "Memory Songs: Community, Conflict and Flight in the Big Drum Ceremony of Carriacou, Grenada."Ph.D. diss., Univ. of Maryland, 1986.

[13] Hill, op. cit.

[14] Elder, Jacob, D. "Evolution of the Traditional Calypso of Trinidad and Tobago:A Socio-Historical Analysis of Song Change." Ph.D. diss., Univ. of Pennsylvania, 1966.

[15] Walla, Tarzan. Personal Communication. Todds Road. August 1968.

[16] Crowley, Daniel. "Towards a Definition of Calypso," Journal of the Society for Ethnomusicology, Vol. 3, No. 2, (May 1959): 57 - 66.

[17] Crowley, Daniel. Ibid.

[18] Ibid.

Dr. Hollis "Chalkdust" Liverpool

19 Hill, op. cit., p.143.
20 Marcano, Neville (Growling Tiger). Personal Communication. P.O.S. Feb. 15, 1989.
21 Quevedo, Raymond (Attila). Attila's Kaiso. op. cit. pp. 20 - 21.
22 Rohlehr, op.cit., p.30.
23 Best, J.R. in The Trinidad Guardian. February 24th, 1950.
24 Grant, Rupert (Lord Invader). "Rum and Coca Cola." Author's Personal Collection of Calypso lyrics.
25 Moore, Egbert. Personal Communication. P.O.S., August 1970.
26 Ibid.
27 Roberts, Aldwyn (Kitchener). Personal Interview. St. Thomas. April, 1977.
28 Francisco, Slinger (Sparrow). "Jean and Dinah." In Sparrow's Great Hits. Tropico: TSI 1067.
29 Quevedo, Raymond (Attila). Attila's Kaiso. op. cit., p. 80.
30 Williams, Eric. "Speech at Woodford Square." 1956. Author's Collection.
31 Roberts, Aldwyn (Kitchener). Personal Communication. Rainorama Palace, Diego Martin. Jan. 1998.
32 Quevedo, Raymond (Attila). Attila's Kaiso. op. cit., p. 105.
33 Ibid.
34 Ibid.
35 Thomas, Randolph (Iere). Personal Communication. UWI, St. Augustine. August 1970.
36 Rohlehr, Gordon. Calypso and Society in Pre-Independence Trinidad. (P,O,S.: The Author, 1990), p. 590.
37 The Management Committee of the Calypso Theatre, of which the author was a member, gave out special prizes for punctuality, regularity, best dressed attire and the singer getting the most encores.
38 Roberts, Aldwyn (Lord Kitchener). Personal Communication. P.O.S., March 1973.

The Lord Kitchener—Courtesy Irving Rauceo

Chapter 4

LORD IERE

Lord Iere - Randolph Thomas
Ah went down Donkey city (to)
Circumcise mi body.
Ah meet a donkey karaying
with a mule.
And the mule said to the donkey:
Saga boy, don't karay behind me;
Donkey woe! Don't tear up
mi Junior Commando.
(Lord Iere - Donkey City -
Author's Collection).

Randolph Thomas, known in the calypso world as Lord Iere, was born on the 31st of August, 1909, and received unto himself the sobriquet Iere, the 31st of August being the day the island of Trinidad was supposedly discovered by Columbus who, it is said by some historians, found the Arawak Indians there and their name for the land was Iere. He was a medium-sized heavily built African man with a crooner's voice and was persistent that I should interview him and get "the true story of calypso." At first, ignorant of his worth and his contribution, and allowing my first impression to get the better of me, I used to dodge and hide from him. His persistence, however, paid off in the long run, for he would come to see me at the St. Augustine Campus of the University of the West Indies where I was a student, and then I could no longer hide. We became close friends afterwards, to the extent that I stopped hiding from him, and I came to regard him as a true exponent of the art. He had a passion for story telling, and when he spoke, he relived the events of the past as if the eventualities were actually happening once more, so that in speaking to me, he sometimes groaned, then he sighed; often he wept, wiped his eyes dry with a sweet-smelling handkerchief and then laughed when reality stepped in once more. We would purchase a flask of rum, sip and chat and he would pour out, along with the rum, such details of the social history of Trinidad and Tobago as could easily fill the pages of at least three books for secondary and tertiary students.

Iere entered the world of entertainment as a boy aged twelve, singing, dancing and masquerading as a comedian with a troupe led by one Vernon Porter. He became an adult masquerader with a band in 1926, played "beast" for the band called "Hell's Population" in 1927, and continued to play "mas" up to 1970 with various leading bands. In addition, he sang as a chantuelle for many bands from 1927 to 1935, participated in many stickfight contests in the Southland, entertained hundreds of tourists and soldiers during the period 1931 to 1939, and sang classical music at concerts, music halls and festivals all over Trinidad and Tobago. The reader then can well understand that Iere, like Lion, was a walking encyclopedia on carnival, calypso and steelband, as well as the arts in general.

In terms of his stint as a chantuelle, Iere, like Beginner, claimed that not every calypsonian was a chantuelle, and not every chantuelle was a calypsonian, whilst some singers were both chantuelles and calypsonians. The difference between the two roles has already been clarified by calypsonian Beginner. Iere therefore underscored the fact that chantuelles were mostly employed by the upper class to sing in middle and upper class environments. Iere pointed out: "A chantuelle in those days was more important than a calypsonian. A calypsonian was a dog, so I preferred to sing as a chantuelle." This was presumably what Errol Hill, speaking of chantuelles, meant when he said:

> By 1898, Shantwells (sic) were more literate; some went to secondary schools where they studied European history and felt patriotic. They extolled the might of Britain and the loyalty of the country. [1]

Iere gave an example of a typical Chantuelle song in the early 1920s. It was sung by King Fanto, "a great calypsonian and chantuelle of the early twentieth century."

Dr. Hollis "Chalkdust" Liverpool

From afar, you can hear
King Fanto's voice in the atmosphere (repeat).
Not one soul to be saved on the day of carnival
When Dragon appear (repeat).

The reader can actually see the dragons sweeping all their capes before the crowd, the chorus of voices of the masqueraders singing behind, while the gaily dressed chantuelle chanted his rich voice to high heaven. Iere continued to show me why he never sang calypsoes until 1939, and turned down a request by King Iere[a] to appear on a calypso show in 1935.

> I preferred to sing and chant on carnival and play stick in the South especially. But I would sing calypso now and then, mostly at Crown Lion Hall, Mucurapo Road, next to the market in San Fernando, where there was a calypso tent. I sang there professionally with singers like Bluebird and Molester, and was paid thirty six (36) cents and up to six (6) shillings for a night's task. Calypso wasn't really for me then, for I was never a strong composer. Moreover, as a chantuelle, the band gave me clothes and food, whereas the calypsonian had to go from tent to tent in search of a job.

It is a truth that Iere possessed a rich strong tenor-like voice and he was paid as a chantuelle mostly to chant and lead the masqueraders in song. It is to be noted, from the quote by Iere, the nomadic life of the calypsonian in the early 1920s and 1930s. Iere himself claimed that he too went from tent to tent singing calypsoes between 1939 and 1942. Perhaps what Iere meant or better yet, his reason for not singing calypsoes until 1939 was summed up by Pete Simon thus:

> Unkept, unshaven and sometimes unwashed, he had a most uncompromising image but he had his talents. Decent people had no part of him. That is why he took such fiendish delight in punching holes in the armour of those in their ivory towers; in ridiculing, lampooning and satirizing those who won't tolerate and patronize him.

---

[a] Blind Iere was sometimes called King Iere or the Blind Sensation. He was a calypsonian of the early part of the twentieth century.

Dr. Hollis "Chalkdust" Liverpool

He took his love whenever he found it, siring a string of unwanted children in the process. His women were generally the prostitutes and denizens of the demi-monde[b]– promiscuous, hard-drinking, hard-swearing women of easy virtue. More often than not, he prided himself on being a 'sweet-man' or 'gigolo,' and it was social suicide for any decent girl to be seen even speaking with him.[2]

This description of the life of the early calypsonian truly explains why the society of the middle and upper classes looked down on the calypsonians, stickfighters and masqueraders and termed them all jamettes. The reader must however understand that the lower classes, including the calypsonians, often had no other alternative, given the unsanitary conditions of the barrack yard where the majority lived, the lack of basic social amenities that was a normal way of life, and the fact that most of them were unemployed, and, with little or no education, unemployable.[3] Small wonder then that as late as 1963, calypsonian Sparrow, in looking at the way calypsonians were treated by the society at large, uttered:

> Calypsonians really ketch hell for a long time.
> To associate yourself with them was a big crime.
> If yuh sister talk to a steelbandman,
> The family want to break she hand;
> Put she out; lick out every teeth in she mouth;
> Pass yuh outcast.[4]

Small wonder too, that in 1968, when news, that the author was a calypsonian by night and a teacher by day, reached the ears of the officials of the Ministry of Education, he was promptly charged under the nation's laws for engaging in activities that brought him extra "emoluments under the Crown." The truth was that the society did not value calypsonians and steelbandsmen then, and considered them to be socially unacceptable persons. Moreover, the life led by the calypsonians did little to lift them out of the muck and mire where society had dumped them all. Teachers were more favoured

---

[b] French for "half-world." The world or class of women who have become socially declassed, or of douthful reptation and standing, as intermediate between those of unquestioned respectability and the courtesan class

and therefore could not belittle themselves by associating with calypso and calypsonians.

As a stickfighter, Iere recalled an incident when he played "Wild Indian" one year in San Fernando in or around 1936 or 1937. That year, he observed the thrill of a mounted stick. He recalled reaching with his band of Wild Indians near the Library. At the same time, another band-Sampson's band-playing the same theme, "Wild Indians, came up to them and their members yelled out: "War Declare!" Sampson wanted to play sword fight with Iere. Stickfighting being an illegal activity, the police sent them into a narrow lane, each man with a stick and a shield to kill each other if they so desired. One of Iere's men named Gussy asked for the fight instead. To Sampson, Gussy declared: "You advantaged me last year, but Ah well prepared this year." Gussy "made a wood[c] at Sampson, who break the wood but the stick bend like a snake and hit Sampson behind his head." Sampson then accused Iere of hitting him from behind, but what Sampson did not know was that Gussy used a "mounted" stick. That year Iere won the Broadway Competition for masquerading (playing Wild Indians). On his return to Library Corner later in the day, Sampson attacked him again, but retreated when Iere's queen of the band pulled out a razor. According to Iere, it was "the longest razor I have ever seen." Not being able to beat Iere, Sampson went to a nearby corner rumshop and beat some innocent young boys who had gone there to hide-possibly from the wrath of Sampson himself. Iere said he cornered Sampson in the rumshop, "and there and then I turned the true spirit of a beast. I had a piece of steel at the end of a wooden spear, drank a rum and chanted: koee wambay rackeboney! Bring Sampson!" Sampson, seeing Iere's mood, fled, possibly through a back door. Iere said he searched for him, found him at about 7 p.m., but Sampson again escaped.

Iere's exploits that day in San Fernando provide for us a good indication of what carnival, masquerading, and stickfighting was like, in days of long ago. Moreover, it is a fact that Wild Indians, Jab Jabs and Warriors used to have real fights on carnival days.

---

[b] He threw a blow at Sampson.

Dr. Hollis "Chalkdust" Liverpool

In addition, one notes that many stickfighters used to "mount" their sticks by taking them to the cemetery and infusing them with African spirits. The same was done in Haiti and the same practice continues today.

It is important for the reader to know that the stickfight and calypso singing are traditions that were practiced by the enslaved and freed men and women during the 18th and 19th centuries. Moreover, according to J.D. Elder, both traditions bear a closeness in that the calypsonian as chantuelle chanted for the stickfighter, his chants providing the motivation and spirit that would enable the stickfighter to fight with zeal and power.

Besides playing "Wild Indian" masquerades, Iere played a comedian in many carnival bands. In 1934, he tried his hand at singing "sentimentals." He came up with a song entitled the "Dawn of Love." "The song took the country by storm, and people thought it was an American composition." At that time too, Lord Iere decided to sing calypsoes outside of the harbours of Port-of-Spain and San Fernando for tourists and other upper class persons so as to get away from the stigma that was attached to calypsonians. According to him, even when he tried to do so, he was unlucky, for his songs never went down well with the audience. He sang for tourists from 1931 to 1939, during which time he made the most money in his life, he remarked. His fortunes, however, came to an end when World War 11 stepped in and the tourist traffic slowed considerably.

Accordingly, he came into Port-of-Spain to seek a living and one Tecki heard his voice and introduced him to the Blind Sensation, King Iere. King Iere was asked by Tecki to coach him. He was supposed to sing with King Iere in 1935 but he got cold feet and absconded. In 1939, he begged Tiger to put him on a show at the Royal Theatre and for this, King Iere supplied him with two songs: "Robust Man" and "Mih Little Sister Make me Shame." The first verse of the latter went thus:

> Ah got a little sister make me shame;
> Lord she went to make her name

She went by the U.S.O.
And bring back a petit popo.
But the thing that hurting me
I, her brother, must pay the price of an unknown soldier.

Growling Tiger contracted him to sing at 100, St. Vincent Street in 1942, under the management of one Mr. Chester Bravo, an architect. The site at 100, St. Vincent Street, the reader should know, was an important landmark in the history of the calypso; it housed mainly the Old Brigade singers and Victory Calypso Tent up to the early 1950s. As a memorial of the part it played in the growth of calypso, when the Calypso Theatre led by George Goddard under the auspices of the Calypsonians' Association opened its doors in 1966, it was sited at 100, St. Vincent Street. While Iere was contracted to Growling Tiger, he was paid a princely sum ranging from fifteen (15) to thirty (30) dollars nightly. Iere agreed with Lion that "in the 1930s, the big boys carried home up to one hundred (100) dollars a night, even though the price of admission was fifty cents, seventy-five cents and a dollar." He remarked:

> On an average, there were about one hundred persons in the tent, but the big boys-Lion, Attila, Growler, and Radio-shared most of the money. Later on, the price of admission used to be one dollar with reserved seats two dollars.

One notes the general increase in the price of admission to calypso tents. The Roaring Lion explained that:

> By 1933, prices rose to 12c, 24c and 36c. This, however, quickly went up to 24c and 48c. In 1934, after our trip to the USA to record our songs, it rose to 24c, 48c and $1. It remained that way until 1941; and between that time and 1945, it rose until it stood at $1, $2, and $3; and reserved seats $4 and $5. [5]

When I started my calypso career at the Calypso Theatre in 1967, the admission fees were $1, $2 and $3.00 respectively. At the Regal calypso tent in the 1970s, fees were raised to $2, $3 and $4.00. By the end of the 1980s at Spektakula Forum, prices of admission were $10, $15 and $20.00, and at the end of the 1990s patrons paid $20 and $30 to enter the hallowed halls of calypso.

Lord Iere was honest enough to state that he "didn't make" as a calypsonian. In short, he did not receive the intensity and type of ovations that were given some of the more gifted composers. It was this failure to achieve, as others of his time did, that caused him to bring in his wife to sing chorus with him and later to team up as a duet. Moreover, it was as Lord and Lady Iere that his fame and fortune spread. Lady Iere began to sing in 1942, her first song being "A Warning to Mothers." "Most of Lady Iere's songs," according to Iere, "had that motherly-love feeling, and good wife image." A verse of her first song went thus:

> A warning to mothers!
> Keep your eyes on your daughters.
> From the age of seven now, they are wise;
> Immorality they try to equalize.
> Don't let them out of your sight;
> These force-ripe men we have are too bright.

The circumstances that caused Lord and Lady Iere to team up, and to afterwards give the nation so many beautiful songs as they harmoniously blended their voices to usher in something new in the art form, ought to be known. It was 1943; Iere had left the "United Nations Tent" because of "unfair treatment in competition" and had gone over to "Victory." At Victory tent, he sang a calypso entitled "Old Time Calypso." He was hailed in the press; "from then on, all the big boys prepared to fight me."

The Victory tent under Mr. Johny Khan, usually held on certain days a "Grand Change of Programme" in order to attract a crowd. It was on a Sunday night at Arima that Iere learnt from Growler that the new "Change of Programme" was scheduled for the following Monday. While waiting for transportation that Sunday night in Arima, and possessing nothing new for the "Change of Programme," Iere and his wife at the bus stop practiced a new song called "Ice Cream Block." Let Iere tell the story:

> We got no sleep nor transport that night, so we sang to keep ourselves awake. Next morning, we came down by train. Monday night was a night of nights; it was competition time and every singer was encored. Radio sang: 'Madam bring back yuh Basket;' Invader hit them 'Ah don't want Glasses to see;' Tiger - 'Grenadian Heavyweight;' Attila - 'Ode to Russia;' Growler - 'Farmer and the Breadfruit Tree;' and Lion sang - 'Man dancing with Man."

When therefore Iere heard such a repertoire of good songs all being encored, he decided that he alone was no match for them. Accordingly, he announced that he and Lady Iere would sing a duet. That night, the singing duo of Lord and Lady Iere was born. Let Iere tell the story:

> The ovation I received was as if the galvanize[d] was coming down on my head. Straight away, Mr. Espinet of The Trinidad Guardian together with the manager and Ted Joseph organized a carnival on stage since officially there was no carnival. 'Ice Cream Block' became the 'Road March.'[e]

The reader should note that as early as 1943, Iere was speaking of 'road marches.' Although Kitchener told me that he invented the term in 1946,[6] the truth is that from the turn of the century the 'road march' was in existence. It was however called then the 'leggo of the day,' for certainly the masqueraders let themselves go, that is, they surrendered their spirits and their bodies to the power of the music.

The calypso entitled "Ice Cream Block" thus made Iere very famous, and caused him to appear "at night spots all over the island, and at USO building[f] and Crow's Nest."[g] Iere also hailed the tune as representative of a change in the structure of the calypso,

[d] Tents in those days were covered with galvanized sheets.
[e] The tune played the most times on Carnival day.
[f] USO stood for United States Overseas. The building stood at Wrightson Road, Port-of-Spain.
[g] Crow's Nest was the home of the commander of the U.S. Naval Base at Chaguaramas.

Dr. Hollis "Chalkdust" Liverpool

that of a longer chorus: four (4) line verse and eight (8) line chorus. He stated that there never was that type of calypso before, the four line single tone being the dominant form then. The opening strophic verse went thus:

> Of all the singing vendors we got in town
> This particular one stands renown.
> With Gold Bond soap he was very sweet
> Now he got a bracket that is hard to beat.
> Chorus: Is Ice Cream Block! Thelma Mason!
> When you buy it, tear the paper, but do-re-me!
> > Mama de man look he passing;
> > Hear how he passing and singing.
> > Papa bring the money;
> > Ah want a block to cool down mih body.

From Iere's song it can be gleaned that first, ice cream blocks (frozen ice cream on a short palette or stick) were something new to Trinidad and all and sundry were filling themselves with them on the streets. When in 1967 too, the "Snow Cone"[h] was introduced to the streets of Port-of-Spain, Calypsonian Gibraltar made a hit with a composition termed "Snow Cone," the lyrics of which explained how "man, woman and child (were) going home (while) sucking their snow .cone."[7] Second, many street vendors in the city used to sing out loudly as they sought to sell their products. In 1960, for example, Lord Melody sang the popular calypso "Ice Man" in which he narrated a number of the cries used by street vendors. The calypso, composed by Pat Castagne,[i] identifies "plantain to boil and fry;" "bottles, bottles, bottles;" and "peewah, peewah, peewah, get yuh nice, nice, peewah" as being some of the street cries that "does amaze" him.[8]

Iere, whose heyday was from 1939 to 1948, described to me a competition held in 1943 at the "United Nations" tent on Duke Street and from the themes on which the calypsonians sang, one is made aware of the loyalty of Trinidadians to Britain that characterized the period. The reader must understand, however, that the said loyalty displayed by so many citizens then was more a feeling of joy that the

---

[h] Shaven ice coated with coloured syrup sold in a plastic cup.
[i] One of Trinidad's outstanding musical composers. He in fact composed the nation's national anthem.

war was finally about to end, rather than one of patriotism to Britain. In the competition, according to Iere, Caresser sang "Rule Brittania," a calypso which "he already sang in 1942;" Beginner sang: "There'll always be an England;" he sang on the "World War;" whilst Lady Iere's topic was the "Jollification of the United Nations." A verse of Lady Iere's song went thus:

> After the War is over,
> There will be no more dread for dictator.
> A peaceful and loving world this would be
> Better conditions universally.
> Chorus: With Britain, Russia and America
> United as they are.
> It takes one hundred Germans and Japanese
> To attack democracy.

In the competition, "Caresser won, Beginner placed second while Iere was third. Lady Iere received a special prize for her feminine effort, for in those days, she was one of only two female calypsonians on the scene, Lady Trinidad being the other." That the first three singers all praised Britain for her part in the war, and that Caresser won though he sang "an old song," showed clearly the thinking of the society towards World War 11, then. It must be remembered that there were many other songs of the period all cast in the same vein, for example:

> Run yuh run, Kaiser William run yuh run.
> Run yuh run, Kaiser William run yuh run.
> You hear what Chamberlain say:
> Cheer boys cheer;
> Surety, with security,
> We go conquer Germany.

Then there was Destroyer's song of 1941:

> Adolph Hitler! Adolph Hitler!
> How you looking at the British Empire (repeat).

Dr. Hollis "Chalkdust" Liverpool

> You planned an invasion;
> You must be take Great Britain for Poland.
> But you must remember
> Britain is supported by America. [9]

According to Iere, and indeed it was true, the news media encouraged such loyalist feelings, but people themselves longed for the end of the War, hoping that a better way of life would ensue. It must be understood too, that the calypsonians returned after the War to complain in song of post-war depression, British tyranny and the need for political reform. To show their joy at the end of the War, the first "road march" of the post war carnival of 1946 contained the following words sung to the tune "Mariann:"

> Five years and eight months we aint play no mas,
> But we burn Hitler moustache, he too dam fast. [10]

Two of Iere's better known calypsos were "Donkey City" and "Mariann" which he composed in 1945. "Unfortunately," according to Iere, "the world has learnt of 'Mariann' through King Radio who has been credited in Trinidad and Tobago and in foreign circles as being the composer." Iere gave an interesting story as to how the song was composed. He said:

> Carlton Gooding and I were drinking at Brittania Bar at the corner of Prince and Duncan Streets when a girl friend of mine was making fares[j] in a gate way next door. There and then news of the Allied victory came through. It was about 11.00 p.m.; hearing the news, the girl worked harder. I asked her if she wasn't tired. She said, 'no.' There and then, I made the song. The verse went:

> What a day the 7th of May,
> Everybody merry and gay;
> People gathered by the corner
> When they hear Germany surrender.
> With flags in their hands on parade

---

[j] A Creole term meaning to have sex with a prostitute or, as a prostitute, to solicit men for sex.

Joyfully playing their masquerade.
Hear mi leggo:
Chorus: All day, all night Miss Mariann
      Down by the seaside you taking man.
      The water in your backbone could sail a boat.
      The strings on your banjo could choke a goat.

Iere's song and story make sense, for Mariann, his girl friend, appeared to him on that night to be highly oversexed. He said, however, that he changed some of the lyrics so as to be able to sing it in the tent, it being too smutty. His chorus went:

    Four years and eight months we aint play no 'mas'
    But we burst down Hitler's moustache, he too dam 'fas.'

According to Iere, Radio's version was different, and Iere believed that he having recorded it at W.V.D.I. Radio Station at Chaguaramas, the Americans carried it to the U.S.A., where it became popular; hence Radio stole it. Radio's version was:

    V.J. was a holiday.
    Mariann was the breakaway.
    Ah sorry Mr. Roosevelt didn't live to see
    Himself and Mr. Churchill's victory.
    Chorus: The leggo was: All day, all night Miss Mariann ...etc.

The second line of Radio's verse as well as the first line of his chorus demonstrate that King Radio was obviously not the composer, yet the world attributes the song to him. What all of this adds up to is that in the 1940s, owing to the lack of recording equipment, the presence of few recording companies and the non-existence of copyright, it was almost impossible to prevent one singer from stealing the works of another. Thus Unknown claimed that Lion stole "Nettie Nettie" from him, and Spitfire in 1970 cried bitterly while complaining to me that "Blakie tief mih song." Spitfire was referring to: "Kokee-oh-ko" which Blakie recorded.

The reader would note that Iere was afraid to sing his song for fear that it might be branded as too smutty. The reason for this was undoubtedly because the art of singing "smut" was especially looked upon as a class act which few men mastered. The song had to be well composed and must be one of "double entente."[k] It couldn't be lewd or offensive to patrons, especially women and young adults. If by its smutty lyrics it offended the patrons, then there was a man standing on the side portals of the stage with a "crooked stick" to pull the singer off. This act usually brought thunderous laughter from the paying patrons, especially when the singer, thinking that he was not that smutty, at times sought to dodge and shield himself from the stick.

In 1945 and 1946, Iere sang his other famous hit "Donkey City." It was in reply to Radio's version of his "Mariann." Iere's first verse went thus:

> V.J.[l] was a holiday; Mariann was the breakaway.
> Friends believe we aint no sap
> The United Nations clean bowl the Jap.
> You'll agree with me, My leggo is Donkey city.
> Chorus: So Ah went down Donkey City
> To circumcise mih body.
> Ah meet a donkey karaying with a mule - way pa.
> But the mule said to the donkey:
> Saga boy, don't karay behind me.
> Donkey woe-back mule!
> Don't tear up mih Junior Commando

To the uninitiated, it sounds like smut. In fact, for many, it is one of the best pieces of smut ever composed, but Iere gave me the assurance that it was not smut. It was meant to "mamaguy"[m] Radio for stealing his song. He assured me that Donkey City meant the Japs; the mule was the big boy Yankee and Junior Commando referred to the Yankees' English comrades. The reader should therefore get a clear picture of the meaning of the term "double entente"[n] in calypso.

[k] Satire occasioned by figures of speech to give the calypso a double meaning.
[l] Victory over Japan.
[m] Creole term meaning: to make a fool of someone.
[n] Satire that makes for double meaning.

Dr. Hollis "Chalkdust" Liverpool

In 1947, Iere's popularity landed him a tour of Guyana with the Red Army Steelband. He left the troupe, however, on account of the "bad behaviour of the members." In Guyana, he sang with the Mootoo Brothers, a popular band then, and teamed up with other artists such as Bill Rogers and his troupe. He described his tour as a "success." In 1948, he and Lady Iere toured Barbados with Kitchener[o] and Killer; he described that tour as "the greatest time in mih life." My research showed, however, that Kitchener did not go on tour with Iere, but must have passed through Barbados on his way from Aruba and Curacao to Jamaica and Britain. Iere, like Lion, claimed a number of "firsts" in the calypso world.

a. He was the first singer to appear at the exclusive Aquatic Club in Barbados in 1948. The reader must understand that the club was opened exclusively for Whites up to the 1960s, and as such, it was indeed a breakthrough for Iere and for calypso in general. In Barbados, he sang in part: "Lovely Barbadose, headquarters in the West Indies to repose."

b. He was the first singer to appear at the Calypso Theatre when that tent swung open its doors for the first time in 1966. Iere also spoke of a number of other "firsts" in the development of the calypso. For example,

c. Railway Douglas' tent was at No. 6, Prince Street, and he was the first to use gas lamps instead of the commonly used flambeaux.[p]

d. Railway Douglas was the first to open a "real calypso tent;" He borrowed some tarpaulins from the Railway and covered the tent. Hence the construction was called a tent, and today, despite the use of neon-lit spacious halls, the populace still refers to the concert halls where calypsoes are sung as tents.

e. The first businessman to sponsor a competition was the

---

[o] Research shows that Kitchener left for London via Jamaica in 1947.
[p] A lighted torch made from kerosene in a bottle with a cloth wick.

father of deceased Ronald Williams, ex-chairman of the Carnival Development Committee.[q] The topic, according to Iere, was a chocolate drink called "Toddy" and Attila won the competition. This revelation by Iere doesn't seem to be true, for Unknown, Beginner, Lion and Pretender all speak of competitions way back in the 1920s sponsored by wealthy persons.

f. The Victory Calypso Tent was formed under Attila, Growler, Tiger, and Invader in 1941. Formerly, it was named by patrons the "Big Six" tent. In 1936, just before the War, it was called the "Marginot Line."

g. Lord Invader was the fastest "thief" he ever knew. According to Iere, "He would thief a song from out yuh brain and all. Once you sing a calypso for Invader, he would re-arrange it and sing it the very night."

h. Kitchener's first calypso was entitled: "Mary, Ah tired and disgust;" it was sung in 1944.

i. Attila the Hun was the first person to dramatize the calypso. "He would place more than one person on stage and he would sing different parts. He took minutes of the City Council's meetings and dramatized them in the tent." Indeed, calypsonian Attila entered politics and won a seat on the Port-of-Spain City Council, later becoming Deputy Mayor of Port-of-Spain. Winning the seat was an easy matter for Attila, for over the years, through the medium of his calypsoes, Attila gained the reputation of being a fighter for human rights and a champion of the poor and the down-trodden. His fight with the Colonial Government, his campaign against the censorship of the poor man's writings, his championing of the Marxists and the writings of George Padmore, his leaning with the anti-imperialist stance of Tubal Uriah Butler all caused him to win his seat. By 1950 too, as a member of the Trinidad Labour Party, he won a

---

[q] A Committee under the chairmanship of Mr. H.O.B. Wooding, appointed by the Government in 1957 to oversee Carnival.

Dr. Hollis "Chalkdust" Liverpool

seat in the National elections thereby serving as a member of the Legislative Council.[12]

j. According to Iere, the first Dimanche Gras was run by one Harold Khan at the Mucurapo Stadium. Years later, the Trinidad Guardian produced the show on the Queen's Park Savannah.

k. The idea of a calypso king, according to Iere, came from Attila who used to crown the king in his tent on the Saturday or Sunday preceding Carnival.

l. The Growling Tiger won the first official National Calypso King Competition. It was held at the Princess Building near the Savannah. Tiger sang on "The Labour Situation." The year was 1939. Iere's fertile brain also recalled a number of unofficial kings of calypso, since there were no carnival celebrations during the War. "Nevertheless, tent kings were crowned by the calypsonians themselves at the end of the season." For example, in 1941, Destroyer won with "A Mother's Love;" in 1943 Invader with "Rum and Coca Cola" and Pretender with "God Made us All" were the kings. In 1944, Caresser ruled the roost with his "Rule Brittania," while Attila the Hun was crowned king in 1947 with " Million Dollar Jail." Killer was the king in 1950 with "In a Calabash" before the C.D.C.[r] took over the competition in 1953 when Spoiler won, this time officially with his "Bed Bug." Continuing, Iere recalled that:

m. Sparrow was the person who first compelled singers to write the musical scores of their compositions.

n. The Roaring Lion was responsible for the innovation of the two (2) line or four (4) line chorus, which today is part of the structure of calypso.

o. King Fanto was the first calypsonian to die while performing.

Iere proved beyond the shadow of a doubt that because of his experiences, the many years spent on stage, his fantastic memory,

---

[r] Carnival Development Committee.

Dr. Hollis "Chalkdust" Liverpool

and because of his interest in the art-form, he was one of the most knowledgeable persons in the field of calypso. From 1948 to 1966, Iere stayed in the background, for as he himself said: "my composing was not one of note," whilst he wanted to "give younger singers a chance." After singing at the Calypso Theatre from 1966 to 1969, Iere who "always had an itch to go on stage," and who served his country as a masquerader, stickfighter, chantuelle, calypsonian, entertainer and comedian passed to his eternal reward in 1974.

ENDNOTES

[1] Hill, Errol. The Trinidad Carnival: Mandate for A National Theatre. (Austin, Texas: University of Texas Press, 1972), p.144.

[2] Simon Pete. Art and Man. (February 1969): p. 34.

[3] Liverpool, Hollis. Rituals of Power and Rebellion: The Carnival Tradition in Trinidad and Tobago; 1763 - 1962. (Chicago: FrontlineBooks, 2001), See pp. 257 - 292.

[4] Francisco, Slinger (Sparrow). "The Outcast" in The Outcast. National: NLP 4199. 1963.

[5] DeLeon, Rafael (Roaring Lion). Calypso from France to Trinidad: 800 Years of History. (POS: the Author, 1978), p. 187.

[6] Roberts, Aldwyn (Kitch). Personal Communication. Diego Martin. 1977.

[7] Benjamin, Sydney (Gibraltar). Snow Cone. 1968. The author's personal collection of calypso lyrics.

[8] Alexander Fitzroy (Melody). Ice Man. 1960. The author's personal collection of calypso lyrics.

[9] Mcfarlane, Mervyn. Personal Communication. Nelson St. Boys'R. C. School. 1966.

[10] The Author's personal collection of calypso lyrics.

[11] Gumbs, Carlton (Spitfire). Personal Communication. P.O.S. August 1970.

[12] Liverpool, Hollis. Calypsonians to Remember. (P.O.S.: Juba Publications, 1987), pp. 46 - 48.

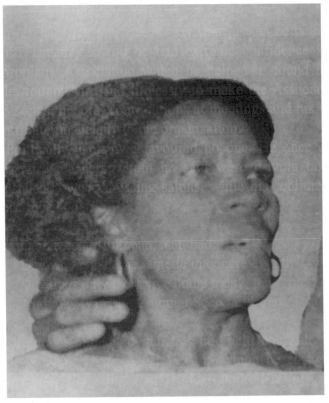

Lady Iere

Chapter 5

Aldric Adrian Farrell - Lord Pretender

For God made us all and in
him we trust;
So nobody in the world aint
better than us.

("God made us all"- Preedie-1943;
From the author's private collection).

Lord Pretender was born Aldric Adrian Farrell in Tobago on September 8th 1917; his Trinidadian father had gone there to work, he having been transferred from Trinidad where he was employed with the Ministry of Works for many years. Little of Tobago's unique way of life rubbed off on him however, for when he was one year old, his family returned to Trinidad and lived at Sackville street in Port-of-Spain.

Preedie, as he was fondly called by his adoring fans, was a short man with rather slim features and whenever I spoke to him, I always told him that he owed his long life on earth(he died in the year 2002 at the age of 84)to his size and physical build. An ardent horse race fan, it never took me long to find him whenever I needed him for a show or for a calypso-related activity; I simply went to the few racing clubs in and around Queen street in Port-of-Spain, and there he would be with a serious face in a corner studying the horses; it was his daily routine before he spent a few hours liming on Prince street with his non-alcoholic friends. When you spoke to him, you couldn't help agree with his many responses since he spoke honestly from his heart; he would react angrily when certain names of other singers came up or if someone should pass by and tell him anything that in his estimation was debased or undignified, but you couldn't help liking Preedie. "Ah too good too long," he would say to his detractors, "so all yuh hate me." In truth and in fact, no one I knew hated Pretender. If, however, you disagreed with his truisms when he pronounced on calypso, then you were sure to feel the wrath of his tongue, especially if you were not a calypsonian.

It must be emphasized that Pretender loved and adored calypsonians. He loved them because he saw them as men who had followed the African griot tradition of praise-singing, story telling, and documenting the history of his people. Pretender was strong in his belief that calypsonians were griots in Trinidad carrying out the same functions as have been done for centuries in Africa, for as validators, artisans, advisors, masqueraders, poets, singers and historians, griots held a special place and continue to do so in West Africa.[1]

Griots in 19th century West Africa had many functions: they were mediators in disputes; took part in the decision making process; challenged the decisions of kings; validated claims for power based on their knowledge of family histories; ridiculed lawbreakers, and, as embodiments of the ancestors, masqueraded on Carnival days.[2] They were also musical composers, composing songs on topical, philosophical and religious themes. M.G. Smith, who researched Hausa court singing in West Africa, found it to be "an informal regulative institution" through which social control was maintained. The Hausa griot was less concerned with the individual qualities than with the social and cultural ties which a person was supposed to embody. Thus, the griot gave praises where praises were due and derided those who opposed the values that the society or his patron held dear. Weddings, naming ceremonies, concerts, initiation ceremonies and masquerades found the griot singing, dancing, reciting poetry and informing the audience of their family history, the history of others, or tales of their heritage.[3]

From the research of Fr.Anthony DeVerteuil[4] and the writings of Mitto Sampson,[5] it has been established that Frenchman Pierre Begorrat and his son St. Hilaire held court in Diego Martin in the 19th century and employed native African griots to sing their praises to the other planters and enslaved men and women. This they did so as to drive fear into the hearts and minds of the enslaved and to appear as mighty, feared men in the area. Begorrat believed that the songs of his griots would make the enslaved less rebellious for, at the time, it was customary for the enslaved to rebel by poisoning masters and animals.[6]

Pretender thus felt that calypsonians were carrying out a treasured and noble function as griots in their own right and he got extremely angry when they didn't understand their role. When he got angry, he would rant and rave, curse and swear, and wish evil on the faulty singers. To him, when calypsonians sang "foolishness and things that don't make sense" they were in fact degrading the work of the griot. To Pretender then, calypsonians must first understand, before embarking on calypso as a profession, that they were first and foremost griots, and therefore had a responsibility to "sing the truth" at all times.

Pretender loved especially to see little children singing and would always be present at shows involving children, he himself having started his singing career as a "little boy." "I rhyming and singing extempo since I is a little fella five years old," he once remarked to me. His first calypso he sang at the age of eight (8); it was an ode to a little girl from the area of Corbeau Town where he lived in the 1920s. Corbeau Town in the 1920s was a poor, fisherman's village. It encompassed the area surrounding Sackville street with the sea water washing the beach that is today the reclaimed land called Wrightson road. The girl Pretender liked, but she having died, he told her in song:

I had a little girl by the name of Jane
Who died recently in Irving Lane.
She was so neat; she dressed very sweet.

Dr. Hollis "Chalkdust" Liverpool

Falling the young boys when they meet on Frederick street.
But this is what she say before she passed away:
Preedie we'll meet Resurrection day.

At age twelve in 1929, at the Red Head Sailor tent in Corbeau Town, he made his first professional appearance. There he sang:

I'm living fine this 1929
No woman at all to disturb mi mind (repeat).
What dem woman want is just what I need,
Therefore with me they cannot succeed.
And when you can't come up with the dough,
They take out dey bundle and walk out the door.

Pretender recalled that Railway Douglas opened the first commercial tent but the masquerade bands like the Red Sailor band used to also hold tents. Pretender noted that in the 1920s, "a singer could have gone into any tent and sing and collect your twelve cents or your six cents accordingly. If you aint good, they haul you down. They had crook stick, all kinda thing." Truly, there was the crook stick that hovered over the heads of singers from the 1920s to the early 1950s. Kitchener brought it back in 1967. It was reserved especially for singers of smut that didn't go down well with the audience or that, in the public's eye, was too obscene. Lord Pretender in his career never suffered the indignity of being pulled off stage with the crook stick. "I was always a master. That's why Chalkie does call me the master of them all," he would tell those who wish to underrate his ability to compose or sing good calypso. Attila reported that although Pretender appeared annually at the tents and started from an early age,

"it was not until 1936 that he was acclaimed when he sang a kaiso ridiculing an unpopular policeman…. The kaiso was extremely popular…from this time Pretender's stocks went up. His audience asked for him and if he attempted to remain in the background they would actually command his presence on stage. Pretender had arrived.[7]

For Preedie, a calypso wasn't a calypso unless it had "a message and more than a message; it must have an introduction and an ending." Too many of the modern day singers, according to him, didn't sing calypso for there was no message in their offering. "All my kaisos have message, a story, whether it is humour, smut, anything." As proof that all his calypsoes contained a story, he singled out one of his smut calypsoes entitled "Move yuh foot" to show that even in the smutty songs there must be an organization of ideas. In the calypso which he sang in 1969, Pretender is telling his fans that because of his age he can no longer get a sex partner. As such he has to resort to prostitutes. He tries therefore to show that though labeled a smut, his calypso yet contains a story. The first verse goes thus:

> Verse: Ah know it aint nice
> But fellas Ah bound to give this advice (repeat).
> Just face facts and know yourself;
> You aint have to hide on top a shelf.
> Ah say to live like sensible men,
> And you bound to move round the girls and dem.
>
> Chorus: Dem girls nowadays they aint business with me;
> Ah must respect mi age.
> I know I'm old and I think you'll agree
> That I must keep quiet at this stage.
> Ah done old mih old, me aint rude me aint fast;
> And mi flag flying at half mast.
> So, is doo doo darling hold on to this;[a]
> Move yuh foot leh (let) me pass.

Besides composing calypsoes with a story, Pretender was strong in his condemnation of calypsoes that didn't make sense. "A story aint all; sense make before book," he would often tell me. I recalled one day in 1989 when two of us were listening to singer David Rudder who was having one of his first concerts at Spektakula Forum in Port-of-Spain. Rudder was singing a calypso

---

[a] Creole for 'accept this money.'

entitled "Bacchanal woman," and was repeating lyric-wise the words, "a bacchanal" over and over. Pretender, though possessing a black face, turned red with anger. Sensing that he was raging mad, I asked him what was wrong. He promptly answered: "But what he singing? Dat don't make no sense! Dat is a calypso? Rudder lucky that I stop drinking rum." Two calypsoes from Rudder later, he was back to his normal self; his colour returned and his contorted face relaxed once more. "Now dat make sense! dat is a true true calypso!" he shouted loudly in reference to the song being sung by Rudder entitled "The Hammer." On another occasion, we both were at a concert featuring, among others, Natasha the child wonder. She was on stage performing her hit song entitled "One day." Preedie felt strongly that children ought not to sing calypsoes that were expressive of adult values and thinking. As such, throughout Natasha's performance he kept telling me how much he hated the song, since it was "too big for she." Suddenly, he showed me his hands with the follicles of hair standing straight and remarked: "Ah hate the song, but when she reach the high part and belch out 'one day' Ah does get goose pimples." In all things for Preedie, truth and honesty stood out, and he wasn't afraid to criticize adversely and creditably.

Pretender however believed that even though your song made sense, to be a calypsonian, you first had to compose your own work. For him, a calypso singer sang other people's work; a calypsonian composed his own. He recalled that calypsonians in singing their own compositions were telling people of their experiences and forcing their values on others. To Preedie, a singer cannot express another man's values since values come from within, the results of one's upbringing, socialization and community environment. "When you sing, you sing yuhself," he would say over and over again. "You can't be me and I can't be you. You must stay you and let me be me." Accordingly, he felt that there ought to be a distinction between the calypsonian and the calypso singer to the extent that those who do not compose their own songs ought not to be in competition with those whom he called "true true kaisonians."

> I don't understand dem kaisonians like Sandra and Prowler and Baron and dem. (They) can't write a line of calypso but you beating man who composing. I can't see with that. I aint vex with dem singing. They should have a competition for the calypso singers. You can't make a line and you beating people who composing? And the judges does do that for spite.

For Preedie, Relator, Duke, Black Stalin, Valentino, Kitchener, Luta, Rio, Penguin, and Chalkdust are great calypsonians because "dem doesn't sing other people's songs." For the same reason, he named as great calypsonians deceased singers Attila, Radio, Douglas, Executor, Mentor, and Growler. When asked in the year 2000 if he preferred Sparrow to Kitchener, he replied: "Sparrow is the greatest man in calypso (but) Sparrow is not the best kaisonian. He singing a million people kaiso. I don't understand that one at all. The whole world know that the greatest man in calypso was Kitchener." When asked how he ranked himself with Kitch, he replied: "I give him the edge with the melody; he can't compose high lyrics like me; his compositions are simple, but he have melody like peas grain."

In the world of calypso, Preedie had many complaints. He complained long and often. One of his pet peeves was the fact that although he won the National Monarch competition in 1957, he was never given the acclaim that he so richly deserved. He strongly felt that in terms of lyrics and the extempo-type song, there was none to compete with him. Worse yet, few producers invited him to shows and when they did they paid him less than others whom he saw as his "juniors." Moreover, although he had produced gems in calypso such as "Woman, the Masterpiece of Creation" in 1939, "Ode to the Negro Race" (God made us all) in 1943, "The virtues of a woman" in 1948, "Que SeraSera"in 1957, and "Move yuh foot" in 1969, he yet was not given the recognition by the media and the NCC as being one of the greatest lyricist and calypsonian. Whenever then we stopped to talk, he would complain and pull me in a corner to hear "this great song that the judges refuse." One rather rainy day in 1972, accompanying himself music-wise with a box of matches, he sang for me on Prince street this calypso entitled: "History in We Own Backyard."

Verse:
Trinidadians and Tobagonians
Like we aint have no sense at all;
We couldn't care less bout we native land,
But we is the first people that does bawl.
We know a lot of history bout Russia,
France, America, England and Rome.
And all this time
So much history knocking bout right here in we native home.

Chorus:
It was Irvin McWilliams, is he who put some
sense in we brain;
Listen masqueraders, don't bother with no
foreign history again.
Just last year Carnival, McWilliams make
plenty people know
With his Buccoo reef portrayal, that we have
plenty history in Tobago.

One of the reasons given by critics for Pretender not enjoying a higher place among the hierarchy of great singers is the fact that he continued to sing calypso throughout his life in the "double tone" styling of 16 bar verses and choruses, with greater emphasis on the lyrics than on the melodies. Pretender's style was a take off, as it were, from the "sans humanite" or oratorical minor key calypso and took the form of a ballad sung in the major key.

His style dated back to the 1920s and 1930s when the promotion of Jazz and Latin American music by big bands such as Lionel Belasco, Sam Manning, Walter Merrick and Gerald Clarke's orchestras impacted upon the calypso. In fact, Preedie told me that the melodies of the verses in his songs were really "Spanish music" and that they were first sung by "Douglas and dem." How did Spanish music come into the calypso? I asked him. He informed me that the calypso pulled from the African, the French, the Spanish, the English, and "Lion and dem even thief a set of Jazz from the Americans when they went there and had people down here going crazy when they came back." It is a fact that Lion used the melodies of the Four Mills Brothers in singing and recording a tribute to them in 1936 in New York.[8] Thus, from Pretender's reckoning, the calypso can be likened to a lake that caught the running waters of American, English, French, Spanish and African rivers.

Another reason why Pretender did not enjoy the status he claimed was the fact that he made few recordings. He would say that he recorded "God made us all" with Mr. SaGomes[b] and recorded it again in England with the BBC but received no royalties from either of them. Of his recording career, he noted:

> I had one or two records but is only one LP I have. Is Resistance[c] and dem who make it in 1989, I think. ... I sing kaiso in this country...but I didn't use to record nutten because you didn't used to get nutten. Sometimes, they want to buy yuh kaiso for forty-eight dollars and all this thing, and you aint getting no royalties or nutten. I used to work. I was stupid smart. I used to work on the docks. I was a dockworker.

Yet another complaint of Pretender was the fact that after winning the National Monarch competition in 1957, he won no more from then to his death in 2002. After every competition in

---

[b] Eduardo SaGomes, proprietor and record producer, he sent away Lion. Tiger, Attila, Beginner and Caresser to record their works in the mid-1930s.

[c] He is referring to calypsonian and Rapso artist Brother Resistance.

which he participated, he would always complain to me that the judges had place him low on purpose. "Dey hate me; dey don't want me around,"he would croon. In fact, in 1957, because of the fact that he was never crowned a champion, one of his calypsoes was entitled "Why Pretender Suffering So."

> "I sing some-a all kinda kaiso, but they wouldn't give me win. Why they wouldn't give me win? I was always there. They mus' pick me. They bound to pick me, Pretender. They bound to have me but they wouldn't give me win at all. Ah too good too long."

Conscious of the fact that he couldn't win anything in addition to his many other complaints, Preedie dropped out of the Calypso Monarch competitions after the 1986 contest. He added then:

> You know what a judge tell me? 'A judge tell me: if you win is a retrograde.' You aint see he want me to blind him! If I win, it carrying kaiso back! And he so dam stupid to tell me. A next one tell me one time: 'you know the competition always thirty points in front of you all the time.' A judge tell me so.

Perhaps because of the fact that Preedie was not as successful as he wished in competitions, he kept the names of all his adversaries and was therefore able to inform me and history of some of the details. For example in the first ever National Calypso Monarch competition held in 1939, the contestants were the Growling Tiger, Attila the Hun, Lord Caresser, Growler, the Mighty Ziegfield and himself.

> When Tiger reach to sing-he was number three-he was in Tunapuna singing. He lost already, cause he was to sing third, and the calypsonians say: 'nah nah, leh him sing.' And the man drop a boom (bomb) and beat everybody yes. Tiger, Attila, Pretender; is so it run.

The reader should note that in competitions in the past, many singers absented themselves on purpose especially when they feared to sing behind a strong singer or a hit calypso. Hence the rule was that should a singer not appear in the position he drew, then he or she would be disqualified. In the 1970s, it was felt that that rule was too harsh and so it was amended to state that should any singer not sing in his place as determined by the draw, then that singer would have to appear last on the programme. Pretender complained to me often too, of many "lies" that have been expressed in the writing of the history of calypso. Firstly, he was vehement in stating that Lion "never win nutten" and yet he has been hailed as one of the greatest of singers. Lion was "never even a good composer. Is lawyer Alston Huggins, the P.N.M. lawyer composed for him." Secondly, according to Pretender, Lion never had any calypso tent and was not responsible for Kitchener's success, as stated by many social historians.

> I is the man who bring Kitchener to Port-of-Spain! A day I coming down from Arima...is a whore place in dem days and dey call me: Preedie come and hear the Arima champion.... And he leh go 'Green fig' and some ...Ah say boy why you aint come in town? Dat is kaiso fadder! ... Is so he come in town. He used to stay by me.

It is indeed a truism that Kitch and Pretender were the closest of friends. The two of them could be seen walking through the streets of the city of Port-of-Spain well dressed in coat and tie busily chatting. They could be seen too at horse racing throughout the many racing venues in Trinidad. They were so close that at one time in the 1970s, Pretender refused to sing at the Revue Calypso tent which was run by Kitch. When I asked him the reason for singing elsewhere, Preedie informed me that he didn't want to get angry with Kitch; he felt they were too close and the conditions under which he had to perform at Kitchy's tent would surely have caused him to break up the fine relationship which they both enjoyed. Although Kitchener was his friend, never one to be dishonest, he stated:

> And Kitchener lie too. He say that when he came in town he used to stay by Lacou Harpe. Is me he used to stay by in Henry street dey...First tent he sing in was Victory tent, Khan

104

tent …1943…he mash up the place, mash up me and all.
Another misconception according to Preedie was that perpetuated by
many with regard to Kitchener's debut to Port-of-Spain and the start
of the Young Brigade Calypso tent. Many academics including
Professor Gordon Rohlehr, according to Preedie, had written that
Kitch was the driving force behind the start of the Young Brigade in
1947.

> 1943, Kitch was at Victory. 1944 was Victory. In '45, smart
> man Invader, just like Melody, come and snatch we and open
> a tent for Gaston Johnson's son named The House of Lords.
> '46, we went back by Attila, and Chalkie the singing was
> Pretender, Attila, Kitchener; Pretender, somebody Kitchener;
> Pretender, somebody, Kitchener. And Elias Moses whey
> (who) had the store, he used to come in; he see dat, so he
> telling we: leh we open a tent.' Kitch fraid. In dem days the
> crowd did like Attila and Lion. Ah say man Kitch, we could
> mash dem up, and Ah really believe it. Ah convince Kitch.
> …dem things Rohlehr have in he book, Ah never feel Ah
> could blind a man so. All way ah telling him! (He say) Killer
> and Kitch whey open tent! It is I whey squeeze in Kitchener
> cause I know calypso and I say dah is a great boy. We call the
> tent The Young Brigade. I even make this calypso: 'Young
> Brigade again! We young and we have the brain. Tell them
> we aint fraid; we go mash up The Old Brigade.'

Thus in Preedie's estimation, the Original Young Brigade was their
tent of 1947and not the tent of 1955 onwards that featured Sparrow
and Melody.

> The Singers at the Young Brigade in 1947 were Pretender,
> Killer, Sir Galba, Young Ziegfield, Kitchener and Small
> Island Pride. Spoiler came in as a helper. In Attila and dem
> days when you come in as a helper is a dollar or two a night
> you getting. It had no week in dem days; is every night they
> sharing money. And the manager get(s) the same share as the
> contracted men.

"According to many writers too," remarked Preedie, "Spoiler
was part of Victory Calypso Tent of 1943." Pretender corrected this

Dr. Hollis "Chalkdust" Liverpool

"dat is a next lie" in calypso history.

> It was 1947 dat Spoiler come in. Not 1946? 1947! He
> come... dey ha(ve) to come to me. I was the M.C. All dem
> talk whey you hearing is I invent them you know. Dem aint
> know dem language: sobriquet and appellation ...Is I is the
> first man whey bring dem talk in calypso... Good! Spoiler
> come with a 'Rum Bacchanal' and the only smut he sing in
> hi life-put dat in yuh book too-the 'Female Pork Vendor.'...
> Spoiler was something else you know! ...He could-a make
> any kind -a kaiso....good kaiso, but this humour thing!

The reader should note that terms like "sobriquet" and "appellation"
that are currently used for introducing singers by M.C.'s, may have
indeed come from Pretender, since these words form part of
extempo singing today, and Pretender was one of, if not the greatest
extempo singer to ever grace the calypso stage. According to
Preedie, to be a good extempo singer one had to "think quickly and
practice." Whenever he was encored on stage, Preedie would return
with an extempo verse, and this aspect of his singing the crowd
grew to expect and love. The secret of his extempo, he once told
me, "is God." "Is God whey singing, not Preedie." He would then
give me an example of God at work:

> Ladies and Gents Ah really must
> Sing about mi good friend Chalkdust (repeat).
> How the words come to me I do not know;
> That's why I am the genius of extempo.
> The words does come so constructively
> Couched, and so grammatically.

For many, however, calypsonian Gypsy is the best of the extempo
singers, he having won the championship of extempo singing on
more occasions than any other calypsonian. Pretender in his
lifetime, however, refused to enter the extempo competition to
compete with the likes of Gypsy. He felt that it was infra-dig so to
do, not only because he was elder than Gypsy, but more so,
because, according to Preedie:

Dr. Hollis "Chalkdust" Liverpool

"the man does sing nonsense and people does clap. Is dat whey does vex me. … Hear Gypsy 'Oh, Ah don't want to fudge; Ah go sing bout the judge.' Ah tell him dat is nonsense. You must say: Ah don't want to sing bout the judge immediately, cause you could get a million words to rhyme with immediately. No sense! And people clap! And it annoys me.

The reader would note the difference between a helper at the Young Brigade and the contracted singers. It would seem that young singers who were yet unknown and who did not as yet make a name for themselves in the field of calypso were hired as helpers. According to Gordon Rohlehr, who noted that Lord Melody worked as a helper with the Victory Tent in 1945, "a 'helper' was a singer without contract, who existed on the sufferance of the tent management, taking what was given him whenever he was lucky to get anything at all."[9] According to Preedie, after the contracted men were paid, helpers were given a "substantial" sum of money, "according to how you sing." He pointed out also, that money for the contracted singers varied; most top singers were paid according to the generosity of the tent manager or leading tent singer. In an angry tone, he told me:

I see I sing with Lion and Attila in Royal Theatre. Place sell out-no lie ah telling you-Attila gie me three dollars. This Lion, he vex till he want to dead; he find ah get too much. And Lion and Radio carry me in a restaurant that was opposite the market-first time I go there in mi life-and buy curry shrimps. Attila and Radio gie me a dollar more....A night a sing for Douglas in London and Olympic.[d] He say: 'you go be one of the great ones.' Six cents! Three penny! ...Ah went Tamana with Executor for five weeks, cause in dem days was chantuelle so they carry we up dey...licks down the line; dey gie we food and thing, and the Sunday we coming down, the Carnival Sunday. Two sixty cent piece and a bag-a orange! He (Executor) say: take care-a dem orange eh! Is Nabel orange.

---

[d] London and Olympic were cinema houses in Port-of-Spain where kaiso shows were very often held.

Dr. Hollis "Chalkdust" Liverpool

Preedie, in narrating to me how very often many singers were robbed by the big boys, is on good ground, for calypsonian Mighty Power informed me that his first salary as a calypsonian in the early 1950s was a piece of a roti. In fact, he noted that whenever it was salary time, Melody would send him to buy the roti so as not to pay him any cash. Power noted too, that in the 1950s when Sir Galba was paying the singers, he would pay them with one hand while holding a cutlass in the other. If the singer seemed not to be in agreement with his salary, Galba would raise the cutlass, lean forward and say: "You don't like yuh money? " At that moment, most of the recipients would smile quickly and nod to Galba assuring him that the pay was most adequate.[10] A most important consideration for the reader to understand was that the young singers, despite the fact that they might have been robbed were glad to sing under the tutelage of the senior men. According to Preedie, despite the poor wage, "I proud to be with Executor."

The *Trinidad Chronicle* reported that a calypso quarrel flared up at the Young Brigade tent on Park street, Port-of-Spain on the night of Thursday 12th February, 1959, when the manager Mr. Henry 'Spike' Clarke refused to pay the **calypsonians even though he was** given a grant of $1,000 by the C.D.C. Mr. Clarke was accused by singers Caresser, Pretender, Brynner, Director, and Spider of threatening them with a cutlass when they demanded their pay. Clarke informed the media that the money granted him by the C.D.C was meant to defray expenses he had incurred in running the tent, and "not to pay the 14 calypsonians."[11]

In this regard, calypsonian Observer, who served in the late 1960s as President of the Calypsonians' Association used to painstakingly inform me of the term used by singers in the 1940s to the 1960s called "pulling jacket." Young singers like him in the 50s simply had to physically pull the jacket of the M.C. or a leading singer, an action that signified a humble plea to be allowed to perform on stage.

Moreover, he would say, "the big boys loved it; they loved to see the younger singers scrubbing the bench and begging them. And many a time if you didn't pull jacket, the M.C. would take it that you not interested in singing."[12] I personally recall Mr. Syl Taylor at the O.Y.B. tent in 1963 and afterward, putting a bench for calypsonians to sit on and requesting that they be seated there throughout the show so that the Master of Ceremonies wouldn't have to search for them when they were needed to perform. The irony of it all was that the singers could be seen on the bench pleading with Cristo, the M.C., and literally "pulling his jacket" in an effort to show off their wares on stage. Moreover, if you were not on the bench when Cristo passed with his finger dangling in the air, you would forfeit your chance to be on stage for the night. I have personally seen the Young Creole pulling jacket at the O.Y.B. and the Mighty Dougla shamefacedly defending his ego by pretending to be suffering with toothache, when his friends, whom he had invited to the tent one night, wanted to know why he didn't sing.

Not all calypsonians, however, started as helpers. Preedie noted that singers like himself, Lion and Kitchener were never helpers but made a name for themselves from their very debut to the calypso world. And although Preedie spoke well of Lion, there were times in our interview when he spoke so ill of the man that it made me wonder if Lion was himself a great calypsonian. "The man is a thief," Preedie would say. "He thief mi kaiso 'Nettie, Nettie.' And when he sing it, I feel like Ah win a sweepstake, to hear the great Lion singing mi kaiso." Preedie is the second singer to claim to be the composer of the famous song: Nettie, Nettie. This shows the extent to which in the 1930s singers sang one another's song in public. Preedie's claim to the song, however, had some merit. He remarked that:

> Lion is a human gramophone you know! Is people song he use to sing. To sing in the tent a year, Ah had to give him mi best kaiso: 'Criminals in Trinidad, the Government say you

too blooming bad. If you know you can't stick the grind, make (up) yuh mind to taste the cat-o-nine.' Dat is why he hate we... me and Kitch... he hate we cause we from he time and we still singing.

Continuing Preedie observed:

In dem days he had a friend name Aines Perry.... Say he had some gyul but she belly big months, months, months, months. And dat is why Ah start to give him fatigue and ah sing: 'Nettie! Nettie! Gie mi de thing that yuh got in yuh belly.' Is so dat kaiso make. Ah aint tell you what he do in England?

It would appear that Lion and Preedie had a heated on-going battle over the song Nettie, Nettie, for in London, England, in 1999, after Preedie "mash up the place," Lion informed the large audience that Pretender "was never a calypsonian." Pretender therefore felt that Lion had done this through jealousy. Worse yet, one year, Lion in an interview referred to Kitchener as "a B class calypsonian." This caused Pretender to dislike Lion more.

Another misconception that caused Preedie to harbour "dislike" in his heart was the fact that critics had associated the famous line, "Ah want to fall" to Spoiler. Although he and Spoiler were good friends, Preedie, ever one for truth, noted that that was a cliché of Growler. "Dah is Growler thing....This is the Growler; Ah want to fall," he Growler would sing. "Growler was the most beloved kaisonian; He used to argue for all the money after a night's show. 'Gie me the pudding,' he would growl."

Because of his experiences, Preedie was able to clear up many misconceptions and give me clearer insights about calypsonians of the 1940 era, such as Spoiler, Terror, Radio, Kitchener and Douglas. He loved Spoiler. Both of them had toured Barbados in 1950 and so he was anxious to tell me about the character of Spoiler. For example, according to Preedie, Spoiler didn't stay too long at The Young Brigade. In fact, in 1948, he sang at Doug Hatton's tent on Richmond street.

Doug Hatton worked with the radio station in Port-of-Spain and was, as a result, anxious to work with calypsonians. At the tent Spoiler sang a calypso entitled: "A Guest at The Queen Wedding. It was never recorded." When Sparrow won in 1956, Spoiler was the king, he having won the Crown in 1955. Spoiler, however, did not contest, not through any fear of Sparrow, but, because he felt that the Crown should go to a younger person. "Spoiler was a genius; he and I were good friends and we never went anywhere without one another...Spoiler was a nice human being; everybody did love Spoiler, but the liquor." It is a known fact that Spoiler was a great singer but was an alcoholic. It is even said that he died because of the bottle. The reader would note that in the 1940s, most masqueraders, pannists and calypsonians spent their leisure moments consuming alcohol. It perhaps was the only thing to do during the day in a society that didn't give them due status and acclaim. Spoiler drank so much, according to Preedie , that he used to get convulsions. When Spoiler, in the course of his singing, uttered the words: "This is the Spoiler; Ah want to fall. He was actually feeling to fall down from the rum." "Ah want to fall" became the war cry of Spoiler, and, very often, he was announced on stage not by his name but by "Ladies and gents, Ah want to fall." The crowd knew instantly that the singer who was about to perform would be Spoiler. 1948, according to Preedie, was the year that Terror made his debut in calypso.

Many persons used to criticize Preedie about the fact that most of his melodies were the same. He informed me that this characteristic of him is part of the tradition whereby "in my days-dat wrong ah still in mi days-we had to sing six tunes every night. No tune! yuh singing anybody tune!" Preedie then was right on target for singers in the 1920s and 1930s usually went to other tents, after performing in their established tent, and sang with a view to collecting some more money for the night's work. "Nobody didn't care bout no tune." Radio, however, was different. "Radio was a tunemaster; he born too early." Preedie is definitely correct in his assessment of King Radio, for not only did Radio introduce more "swing" into calypso, but he gave the kaiso world tunes such as "Mathilda," "Brown Skin Gal," and "We Want Ramadhin on the Ball." These melodious, single-tone tunes helped to make the calypso not only "more singable," but caused the artform to become popular in the United States. Most Americans in the 1940s heard calypso for the first time and Radio's tunes formed the basis of their first impression.

Continuing his bid to provide me with a greater insight into the character of calypsonians, Preedie hinted that "the man who bring kaiso as it is now is Douglas; he move from the minor (key) to the major." According to Preedie, this change occurred in the song: "Why mi Neighbour vex with me."

"The man who gie kaiso bounce is Growler. He swing calypso." His first song with swing was "Ah want to rent a Bungalow." This characteristic of Growler was confirmed by Kitchener who often told me that his rhythm, melody and bounce came from his observance of Growler.[13]

Another singer who Pretender admired was Beginner. "Beginner was the only person who could-a play a guitar. In dem days we couldn't afford a guitar, so me and Spoiler use to use a box -a matches....Melody and Kitch was famous for the mouth bass." The ability to play a guitar must have helped Beginner immensely, for he was known for his sweet melodies. In fact, Preedie concluded that "he was a next tunesmith."

One of the outstanding aspects in the development of calypso noted by Preedie, was the fact that the emergence of the calypso tent forced the calypsonian into becoming an entertainer. Before, he was merely a folklorist singing the traditional tunes of his forefathers. In the calypso tent, with the world made smaller on account of the World Wars, the calypsonian was forced to become a professional performer of world class. According to Preedie, Spoiler was the man who led the change. "Spoiler had no voice like Baron and dem, but he had timing and expression. He's the man who bring expression in Kaiso."

Expression for Pretender meant acting out the concepts that were formulated in the mind. Thus the calypsonian became not only a singer but an actor on stage as well. His hands, his face, his clothing, his movements altogether told his story.

Moreover, before Spoiler came on the scene, calypsonians used to sing standard English in keeping with the values of the society that applauded persons for good grammar and literary expressions. According to Preedie, Spoiler brought into calypso the use of the vernacular, enriching the lyrics with pointed Trinidadian phrases and sayings and the kind of humour that can, only with the use of the Creole tongue, cause uncontrollable laughter in the audience. "Long time you couldn't say whey the great Chalkdust does say now; Ah went and look for she, instead of her. Spoiler whey bring dem rhyme in calypso….and the way he use to put he face…kaiso come sweeter through that." Spoiler was indeed an actor and a humourist, besides being a singer.

Another innovation in calypso, according to Pretender, was the initiation of dance as part of the repertoire of the calypsonian. The man who started dancing on stage was Commander. Commander who started singing around the year 1952 earned his plaudits in 1955 with a song entitled: "the Stuttering Witness." It was a case of a witness whose stuttering enraged the magistrate who felt that the witness was being obscene; the utterances of the witness caused the audiences to break out into laughter. Pretender may be quite correct in terms of Commander's ability to dance, for Commander himself was a tap dancer of some sort and used to dance on street corners for money when mere singing did not provide him with enough money to eke out a living.[14]

Always one for truth, Pretender remarked that he had sung "all kinda song in the Savannah and yet they never crown me." In the same way as it took foreigners to accept the musicality of the steelband, so too, according to Pretender, it took "singing a foreign song to win the crown." He had, he said, observed Lord Melody in 1954 successfully mixing his calypso with American songs and thus tried the same recipe in 1957. Melody in 1954 sang the melody of a song entitled "Second Spring;" in1957, he therefore used the melody of Doris Day's hit song "Que Sera Sera."

Another truth that came out of our conversations was the fact that Preedie admitted that he could have given me more information about the development of the calypso if he wasn't so drunk in the 1940s and 1950s. It was a known fact that Pretender was a drunk. People in Port-of-Spain knew him more for his drunkenness than for his singing. He would go from club to club whole day drinking out the few pennies he made from singing. When he awoke on the pavement, he would be so angry with himself that he would return to the rumshop and drown his sorrows in rum again, stopping only when his frail body could take it no longer. Then he would fall into a deep stupor whence some good Samaritan would pick him up and nurse him back slowly to health. Needless to say his drinking cycle would restart in a day or two. When he was unable to answer my questions, he would smartly retort: "Don't ask me nothing bout dem thing; ah was drunk all dem time; ah forget." So drunk was Pretender that one day on the Evening News, he was photographed having sex on a boxcart with another well-known drunk named "Drunking Joyce" while the shock of such an immoral moment was clearly expressed on the faces of the onlookers, some straining their necks to get a ring side view. I personally remember him in 1959 being put out of the tent on Duke street where I had gone to hear calypso. After being put out because of his drunken behaviour, he held court on the pavement singing to us who couldn't afford to pay to hear the saner bards inside. "Yuh know," he said, "dat is the only night I could remember bout mi drinking days? I use to get black out.[e] I remember sitting down on the window of Good Samaritan Hall on Duke street and Sparrow saying: 'Look at the king! The Lord!' And I proud." On the wall of his apartment on Nelson street, there hung a picture of Preedie "drunk as a fish. " He would tell me that he couldn't recall the moment, the place or the time of day that the

---

[e] To fall into a state of temporary unconsciousness.

Dr. Hollis "Chalkdust" Liverpool

picture was taken.Worse yet, in the photograph he was dressed with a beret on his head which, in his saner moments, he never wore, and with clothes that he couldn't recall being his own.

Fortunately, Pretender, after listening to a lecture in which the lecturer called alcoholism a disease, decided to seek help at the St. Ann's Mental hospital in 1964. "I never thought I could-a stop drinking…I never wanted to stop drinking…I felt that drinking was a part-a life. Is better you drink and dead than aint drink." How Pretender was cured of his habit makes good reading in my opinion for any would be alcoholics. His story too, provides, for psychologists and other interested social science thinkers, information on how the mind of an alcoholic works. He attributed his recovery to Dr. Beaubrun[f] and calypsonian Unknown who both spoke to him about his health. Noting that he saw many persons who went for treatment were coming back "more drunk," he refused all treatment at first. However, the persons who went for treatment were coming back "more fat and rosy." Being a very thin man he made a resolution.

> …Ah say ah go go up dey, rejuvenate the body and (still) beat the liquor. So ah went up weighing about 86 pounds…But God send me a day to hear whey dem people AAA saying…cause I so vex ah want to blind all-a dem…The chairman was saying that the alcoholic is not a bad man or worthless man, he is a sick man…and ah start to bawl: 'not guilty.' I thought it was me, so ah say: 'arrest him. I'm going to sentence alcohol to death, not no six months, not even lifetime, to death.' And I came out dey the 3rd of May, and from since that day, ah never even eat fruit cake, Ferrol, nutten. Man put dat in a kaiso nah man! I is de happiest man to know ah sick. I was happy to know ah sick; it aint me. I use to wonder what it is get in me. Dr William have he big party down Charlotte street. I go in and take up hi big chicken leg and start eating oui! And the more dey tell me….Chalkie you never wrong you know! You never wrong!

---

[f] Dr. Michael Beaubrun, well-known psychiatrist in Trinidad and Tobago and the Caribbean.

Dr. Hollis "Chalkdust" Liverpool

Preedie's talk confirmed what Andrew Carr once told me. Carr felt very much ashamed for calypsonians following the behaviour of Preedie who walked into Kimling restaurant and told Eric Williams, then campaigning for national elections, that if he wanted to run Trinidad and Tobago he must first "learn to share." "With that," said Carr, "Preedie picked up the chicken leg from Eric's plate and start to bite and eat it." Carr felt that were it not for Preedie, the police would have been summoned. Moreover, Eric Williams, according to Carr, "must have had a soft spot for calypso," for he dismissed the whole affair with a smile.[15] Years after in the comforts of the Regal Calypso tent, Eric confided to me about the importance of the artform and of the great contribution that guys like Pretender had made to the development of the people of Trinidad and Tobago. Though silent on many cultural issues involving calypso, Eric understood it all along. In fact, were it not for his pronouncement on my case when I was charged for singing calypso, I would have been found guilty and that might have been the end of my teaching career.

After surrendering himself to the various medicines and prescriptions, Preedie never again up to his death in 2002, touched alcohol. "Ah don't eat fruit cake and ah don't even take cough syrup, since those things have in alcohol." Pretender, it can be said, like Spoiler, Caruso, Jaguar and Unknown, were well-known street alcoholics who were characteristic of many mid twentieth-century artistes who faulted the society for neither recognizing nor understanding the talent they possessed, while adoring foreigners and lesser able European knights; these calypsonians demonstrated their hatred of the elite and those in authority by becoming what upper-class society perceived them to be, drunkards.

Another aspect of calypso that Preedie pointed out was the contribution of Sparrow to the art form. For Preedie, Sparrow brought status to the art form.

> Sparrow is the greatest man in kaiso...he aint no kaisonian like me and Kitch and you Chalkdust-composer, singer-but he do for kaiso plenty. Is he whey have kaisonian singing in club and thing...long time in hotel and all had 'no calypsonian and dog allowed'... dey aint want you, you can't go up dey. And as you open yuh mouth, "Oh ... yuh hungry calypsonian! Sparrow kill that...then Kitchener come, he strengthen it. And all kaisonians come and imbibe in it.

Another misconception cleared up by Preedie was the number of schoolteachers who sang calypso before Chalkdust. He would always inform me and others that I was the best of all the teachers who sang calypso, but that Mentor was the first schoolteacher to do so. "He sang one of the best Road March here, then we had one from Charlotteville, King Alpa, but dey aint in Chalkdust class." I would remind him that Pete Simon, a schoolmaster, also sang oft and on, and that schoolteacher Carlton Scott, to whom I owe a great musical debt, sang at the Calypso Theatre in 1968. Then came Shortpants and Penguin in the 1970s to display to all and sundry that teachers were possessive of great talent.

Preedie, of course, would boast that he had defended me "in battle," he having sung on the Chalkdust issue in 1969."

> Chalkdust give a fillip to kaiso...and is through me he singing you know...one-a the best kaiso, the Chalkdust Issue, is so he singing...I is the man defend him like Sir Stafford Cripps...Kitchener say is one-a mi best...man ah bring some points in dey ass...ah even mention how Guyana praise Canary...teachers singing reggae and a teacher cant sing we own kaiso....kaiso fadder man.

The reader would recall that in 1968, the government of the day felt that calypso was part of the lower class persons of the society, and that the nation's teachers were of the upper and middle class. Above all, schools were expected to underscore middle class values of which the calypso was not a part. Accordingly, I was asked by the

Ministry of Education to explain why I had decided to participate in calypso singing while being a teacher in a public institution and drawing an extra salary from the government for so doing, since I sang in a tent run by a government agency. The Ministry felt that it was immoral to draw two salaries, but at the base of their inquiries was the known fact that teachers were not to degrade the teaching profession through calypso singing.

The world will remember Pretender if not for his melodies, at least for his lyrics. Always stressing that it was the lyrics that made for good calypso, he sang some beautiful lines in calypso. In "Woman the Masterpiece of Creation," sung in 1939, he called on men to

> "Always remember that their presence on earth,
> Was due to the women who gave them birth....
> Don't prove yourself to be unworthy,
> Of your maternal rich legacy...
> And we should recognize another woman
> As the masterpiece of creation's plan"

Another lyrical masterpiece of Pretender was one sung in the 1940s when the society tended to degrade children who were illegitimate. Marriage then was looked upon as noble and moral, while society frowned on common-law unions and the so-called "bastards" the name given to the offspring of such relationships. There were cases where "bastards" could not get into the public schools of the country and unmarried women, by law, were not entitled to the wealth or material assets of their common-law husbands. Up to his death in 2002, he felt that the concept of illegitimacy was wrong. On illegitimacy, Pretender commented beautifully thus:

> Verse 1
>
> Day after day as time marches on
> Some children must regret the day they were born (repeat)
> They are always treated contemptibly
> And subjected to a life of pure misery.
> But why should a child suffer a bitter fate?
> Simply because he was born illegitimate.

Dr. Hollis "Chalkdust" Liverpool

Verse 2

Friends I must explain that I personally
Don't agree with those who say a man must marry.
My mother and father made me out of matrimony,
Yet I cannot say that I was a better man you see.
Thousands of your children who were born in bastardy;
Carry their picky heads straight to university.
That is the point I am trying to elucidate;
You can't condemn a child who is illegitimate.

One of the finest pieces of creative writing that has ever been sung was a calypso by Preedie called "Lock and key." In it he likened the female vagina-without using the term-to a man's property, and wished that somebody could invent a lock and secure it to the extent that on the property "water can't go in; water can't come out." Several critics have hailed it as a masterpiece simply because of it bordering on smut, and yet the lyrics are creative, imaginative and crafty, without being obscene. The lyrics of the first verse which made audiences shout in the tent "kaiso! Kaiso!" went thus:

Every day Ah reading the Guardian,
Ah always hearing bout a new invention (repeat).
They inventing things to destroy mankind;
Things they invent could put we out-a work all the time.
But to me they not so intelligent,
I wll gie them the right thing to invent.

Chorus: If somebody could invent a lock and key
          Whey a man could lock up hi own property;
          Go where he like, brag and boast as much as he can,
          That not a soul could trespass upon hi land.

Chorus (2): But if on hi property he had a lock
          Anybody coming, he sure to hear dem knock.
          And as a trespasser, he had to peep and hide,
          Cause try as he want, he can't get inside.

Yes siree! Preedie was one who ate, drank and slept calypso. There were those who disliked him because he felt so strongly about his art; there were others like me who loved him because he was honest in everything he said and did. He would oft remind me of the need to use the palm of the hand as a spade when singing. The spade was the instrument that reflected the inner thoughts of the kaisonian. The hand as a spade, must twist and turn, dip and rise, in keeping with the lyrics of the kaiso. Those who didn't use the spade could not be good kaisonians in Preedie's opinion. All such comments brought on enemies, but Preedie never wavered from his informed stance.

Although he would tell me that his best song was "The Gomes Commission Report," all his critics favoured "God made us all." The lyrics summed up his life. He felt that there was no art form better than calypso, no place on earth better than Trinidad and Tobago, no people better than Africans and no singer/composer better than himself. He lived a most down-to-earth life, rising above the clouds at times when he sang, but quickly returning to the earth and the humble abode of his poor friends afterward. And to his poor friends, he extended his mighty hand of sympathy, love, caring and understanding, advising them in song:

> Never ever worry; don't mind how things looking sad.
> Never ever worry; don't care if you suffering bad.
> Never ever worry; what I'm saying is true.
> Always consider; somebody suffering more than you.

Pretender therefore rode with kings but never forgot the common touch since he knew the virtues of humility and caring in his heart, and based every action and every aspect of his being on the philosophy which he gave the world, namely, that: "God made us all and in him we trust, so no body in the world aint better than us."

Dr. Hollis "Chalkdust" Liverpool

120

ENDNOTES

1 Liverpool, Hollis. Rituals of Power and Rebellion: The Carnival Tradition in
   Trinidad and Tobago, 1763 - 1962. (Chicago: Frontline Books, 2001), p.190.
2 Liverpool, op. cit., pp. 189-190.
3 Smith, M.G. "The Social Function and Meaning of Hausa Praise-Singing," in
   Africa, Vol.27, No.1, pp. 26 - 43.
4 DeVerteuil, Anthony. A History of Diego Martin. (Trinidad: Paria Publishing Co.,
   1989).
5 Pearse, A. ed. "Mitto Sampson on Calypso Legends of the Nineteenth Century,"
   Carribean Quarterly 4, Nos. 3&4 (March - June 1956): 250 -56.
6 Liverpool, op.cit., pp. 190 - 196.
7 Quevedo, Raymond (Attila). Attila's Kaiso. (Trinidad: UWI, St. Augustine, 1983),
   P. 111.
8 Spottswood, Richard. "A Discography of West Indian Recordings." Appendix 2,
   Unpublished T.S.
9 Rohlehr, Gordon. Calypso and Society in Pre-Independence Trinidad. (P.O.S.: The
   author, 1990), p. 458.
10 Francois, Sonny (Power). Personal Communication. Regal Calypso Tent, P.O.S.,
   January 1973.
11 Trinidad Chronicle. "Calypso Row in the Young Brigade." February 13th 1959, p. 1.
12 Lord Observer. Personal Communication. Calypso Theatre, P.O.S., January 1969.
13 Roberts, Aldwyn (Kitchener). Personal Communication. P.O.S. March, 1973.
14 Lord Observer. Ibid.
15 Carr, Andrew. Personal Communication. P.O.S., July 27, 1966.

Kitch and Sparrow in their Heyday-Courtesy Irving Rauceo

Chapter 6

Gaston Nunes - Lord Smiley

Ah want somebody
to understand
Nowadays my friend a man
is a man.
Never mind what's your rank
Today my friend each
man important.
So men like Chalkie
Can't cry down you or me.
Because we never went UWI
and we have no degree
That don't mean we aint nobody.

(A Man is A Man - Smiley - From the
author's private collection).

In 1969, I was hospitalized at the General Hospital in Port-of-Spain to remove a polyp from my larynx; the doctor had correctly diagnosed that I had overtaxed my voice organ and had thus caused the cells there to multiply to the extent that I was getting hoarse nightly. In fact I was even thinking that my singing career was coming to an end having to teach in the day and sing in the night. While on my bed thinking of my fate, up came this singing hospital attendant to cheer me and give me hope; he was Gaston Nunes and was known in the calypso world as Lord Smiley. Working at the hospital, where he eventually laboured for 34 years, was his first love; calypso, he informed me, was his second. "I am Nunes," he would say, while stressing on the letter s; "it is Portuguese." I looked forward every day at the hospital to his singing and took a special interest in his personality for to all the attendants and nurses, he was "Cous," the abbreviated pleasantry of cousin. Over the years our friendship grew by leaps and bounds and in many circles people expected to find Chalkie with Smiley in all our escapades and endeavours.

Smiley is indeed a cousin to all, calypsonians as well as the people, and he is a fitting example of the love that the public in the 1940 to the 1970 era had for the singing bards. During that era, whenever persons from the general public saw the calypsonian, they would approach him with respect for the singer was looked upon as the voice of the people, especially the oppressed. As such, they were always ready to give him advice and to offer him tunes and topics upon which calypsoes could be composed.

Born on January 15th 1930 in the same district where I came into existence-Chaguaramas, Trinidad-Smiley grew up in Carenage, but at the age of ten, moved for a short while to the fishing town of Cedros, and the two fishing environs allowed him to be exposed to the calypso art form as a child. Today in Carenage, he is a living example of that love that could be found in all communities in the 1940s, for everywhere Smiley goes in Carenage, he is greeted with "Cous" to which he would reply "right cousin." Everybody in Carenage is Smiley's cousin. In fact, he prides himself by saying that he is the unofficial "Mayor of Carenage." Sometimes he would cause me to break out in laughter when in reply to a fan who has just hailed him, he would retort: "that is mi third cousin," meaning that the person was a bit far in the line of kinship. Of course the reader would realize that I became his first cousin, and as such, I had access on countless occasions to interview and communicate with him.

Smiley grew up in Cedros but started his career in Diego Martin in the early 1950s and won the St. George West Calypso crown in 1958. Having done so, he passed the audition the following year to join the Original Young Brigade on Wrightson Road, and although he said his song " went down well with the audience," he left because of an altercation with another singer who had threatened him with violence. At the tent, he observed that many singers were never accepted as part of the cast and in fact "scrubbed the bench" for the greater part of the season.

"Scrubbing the bench" is a term used in the calypso world for singers who are not given the opportunity to sing although they are selected by the tent management as a performer and advertised as such. Young singers, in particular, suffered that fate in the 1930 to 1980 era, for the management would often times select a singer only to see him booed by the audience. Besides, there was no guarantee that a song that went down well in an audition would be a hit with the tent. Accordingly, the management on most occasions did not guarantee a singer's spot on the programme until the tent audience had given him or her the right to sing, and that was usually done by a resounding round of applause at the end of the singer's debut. Moreover, some songs would be well received by a Saturday night crowd when the audience overflowed, and poorly received by a sparse Monday night crowd. As such, the management kept a bench to house all such singers handing them the microphone only when an outstanding calypsonian was absent or late and, as a consequence, they were needed to fill the breach. More importantly, the singers had to sit on the bench if they wanted to sing or be a part of the tent. The master of ceremonies would never search in the crowd or the bar or the confines of the tent to locate a young or inexperienced singer; the debutant had to make sure that the master of ceremonies found him seated on the bench.

It was indeed a ritual to see Christo, the master of ceremonies at the Original Young Brigade, approach the bench. As Christo approached, dozens of young singers who had left the bench or who might be chatting with friends at the sides of the calypso tent would suddenly scamper back to the bench with the hope that they would be fancied by Christo. Christo had a way of whistling and pointing his fingers around and up in the air before descending on a singer. When Christo's finger rested on a singer, it meant that that singer would be next. All young singers prayed that Christo's finger

124

would rest upon them. When that happened, the selected singer would rise, put on or borrow a jacket, fix his shirt, straighten his tie, clear his throat, sometimes drink a rum and practice his lines to face the uncompromising audience which most times had no mercy on the young.

Smiley thus felt pity for those who scrubbed bench at the O.Y.B. for the entire season and who were never put on the programme. One singer, Young Creole, informed me that he scrubbed bench from 1964 to 1966 at the O.Y.B. and that the manager of the tent, Mr. Syl Taylor, bought a special bench to house the singers backstage. Syl Taylor and his benching policy became so much a part of the tradition that even his son, Nap Hepburn, also had to "scrub the bench." Nap, the reader would realize, became an outstanding calypsonian and chorus singer, but his chorus singing took root only because he feared sitting on the bench. In other words, to get away from the bench, Nap embarked on chorus singing as another option. In 1973, for instance, calypsonians Dougla, Rajah and Clipper could be found "scrubbing the bench" at O.Y.B. Dougla, the reader should know, won the Calypso Monarch title in 1961 with two beautiful renditions namely: "Lazy man" and "Split me in two." But 1973 was not 1961, in Syl Taylor's eyes, and so poor Dougla had to "scrub the bench." It was a poor year for him; his songs were not particularly liked by the audience and one night a number of white foreigners came to hear him. To their dismay, Dougla was not allowed to sing by the management that night. At the end of the show, Dougla's friends inquired as to why he did not perform and approached Dougla for the reason. Poor Dougla, ashamed to say that he was put on the bench retorted by holding his mouth and whispering through his teeth: "Ah have a tooth here giving me beans; it paining me for so."[1] It must be emphasized that the calypso tent always had singers who were not sure to sing. In the 1920 to the 1940 era, they were called helpers. Most calypsonians started off as such, so that "scrubbing the bench" was considered a part of the calypso tent tradition.

There were even a few outstanding singers who "scrubbed the bench" but who were paid salaries for their services.

Fearing the bench to some extent, Smiley joined the Calypso Theatre in 1969 at the corner of Abercromby and Hart streets where he was a hit with his song entitled "Mi Indian Wife." That year the Calypso Theatre was headed by the Roaring Lion who received the princely sum of $250 weekly.[2] The theatre began in 1966, when the Calypsonian's Association, founded by George Goddard, decided to open a tent so as to allow calypsonians who couldn't find a place in the more popular commercial tents to be able to air their calypsoes. The then Carnival Development Committee with Mr. Ronald Williams as chairman, assisted by way of the provision of galvanize and lumber and the tent was situated at 100 St. Vincent street in keeping with the calypso tent tradition.[a] In 1966, although in the Calypso Monarch competition the theatre produced four semi-finalists in Gibraltar, Funny, Leveller and Unknown, and one finalist in Leveller, it was, to say the least, a financial flop for the public did not patronize the venture. The little cash that was made was spent on soft drinks on a Friday night, whilst at times, the singers used to encourage people to come in freely so as to get an audience.[3] In 1968, I joined the Theatre and was paid sums ranging from $2.00 to $18.00 weekly. It is indeed ironic to note that while being paid such small sums of money, I was dismissed by the Teaching Service Commission for singing for "emoluments under the Crown"[4] while being employed in the teaching profession. The truth is that my dismissal from the teaching service was not so much based on singing for gain as much as it was due to the fact that a teacher in those days was not expected to engage in an "undignified art"[b] as calypso. It was not until Duke, Chalkdust, Psycho, Young Creole, Bopee and Lord Smiley joined the Calypso Theatre that people began to patronize the gates and the singers began to get a respectable fee for their performances.

[a] Some of the early tents were located at !00 St. Vincent street.
[b] In reference to the issue at the time, the term was used by Rudolph Allen well known educator at the University of Woodford Square.

Dr. Hollis "Chalkdust" Liverpool

126

Smiley came up the calypso ranks the hard way; he procured an average of fifty dollars a week in 1969 while the tent leaders, Duke and Chalkdust, were paid $200 and $150 respectively. Smiley remembers that in 1969 and 1970, the elder singers such as Lion, Tiny Terror and Gibraltar claimed that they were foundation members of the Theatre and the Association and thereby drew sums in excess of what the two leading stars, Duke and Chalkdust, received.

Another interesting aspect of the Calypso Theatre that Smiley remembered was that with Chalkdust as Secretary of the Association in 1970, the calypsonians were graded A, B, and C, based on their popularity, their ability to perform, and the crowd response to their songs; they were therefore paid accordingly. In addition, small sums of money were given to singers weekly for being (a) the best dressed calypsonian, (b) the most disciplined and (c) the cleanest shoe. In the category of best dressed, Lion and Spitfire, two of the most senior bards, always topped the cast.[5]

Smiley, whose songs then were more or less based on the domestic scene and targeted the lower-lower, still favours the melodies of the double and single tone singers of the 1920 to 1940 era, and has, he claims, acquired "a lot of knowledge of the history of the calypso from my wife's grandmother."

> "Grandma says that calypso began as the slaves used to extempo in the field when the hot sun burn them. She remembers a circus company coming to Trinidad in the early 1930's and she took me to see it. She says that I was asking for the circus to come home and perform, where-upon a calypsonian heard my cry and sang:

> > Mama buy that camel for me.
> > Mama buy that camel for me.
> > No my child, that's not for we
> > It belongs to the circus company."

The reader can thus see how quick-witted calypsonians of the past were, but although Smiley loves to hear the extempo of the past, he says bluntly:

> "I am not that type of singer; when I sing I wish to tell a story. I want people to understand that amidst their poverty, their misery and squalor, culture pervades. They must be proud of their culture patterns for it is their very own, and they ought to learn to unite for a better life, a better nation and a better world."

Smiley who grew up a poor lad in the squalor of Cedros and Carenage was nurtured and socialized by his environment and thus understood only too well the nature of poverty. Amidst the poverty, however, he was taught, like many others of his day, values of honesty and love for his fellow man. As such, in 1970, he castigated his fellow men for not living up to their responsibilities while yet aping other ways of living. He thus sang:

> It worries me whenever
> I think of my Negro brother.
> 'A Negro don't help a Negro!'
> Ah hearing that anywhere I go.
> And yes Ah roam about plenty
> And everywhere Ah go is the same old story.
> But last year February, Ah prove it for myself up in the country.
> Chorus: You know Ah open a grocery up in D'Abadie [c] -
> (Oh Lard) [d]
> The people trusting [e] from me and
> buying cash from the Chinee. [f]
> Why my people so? Tell me Ah want to know.
> Good Lord ah can't understand!
> What is wrong with the Negro man!

---

[c] A district in North-east Trinidad.

[d] Smiley's favourite cry. A localized way of saying "Oh Lord."

[e] In local Creole it means that they were "crediting."

[f] Creole term for the Chinese.

Dr. Hollis "Chalkdust" Liverpool

Only a brave man can tell it like it is and Lord Smiley is fearless when he sings calypso. In 1969, in his song "Indian wife," he displayed anger at those who felt that he shouldn't be attached to an Indian woman, he being an African, but he gave listeners his reasons for leaving Doris his first African wife. In the calypso, he captures, as few can, the essential differences in culture between the African and the East Indian in the 1960s. He sang:

> Mi Indian wife don't like to pose, or wear no saga clothes
> She even selling mangoes.
> No pound, guineas or pence, but she have common sense
> And she's a boss in dollars and cents.
> Is to see she in the bank when she banking
> And I with a big cigar smoking!
> But Doris with she big mouth
> Use to run down a fete East, West, North and South.

> Chorus: But since Ah marry Ramdaye
> The Indian from Debe
> Up to now Ah living okay.
> Ah eating Bhaji and roti
> For breakfast, lunch and tea
> But now Ah have big gram[g] and T.V.

The song not only paints a picture of the love and assistance that East Indian women give to their husbands, but is indeed, in Smiley's opinion, a comparison between the ways of living between the two ethnic groups; these differences he captures so well. When today we hear lecturers from the University of the West Indies saying that calypsonians are one-sided and racists and sing only to demonstrate the qualities of the African race,[6] they should revert to the calypsoes of Smiley, Power, Hindu Prince and Shah, all of whom extolled the virtues of East Indians in the calypso tent.

---

[g] Short for "Gramophone."

Dr. Hollis "Chalkdust" Liverpool

To loud applause, the Mighty Power in 1969-1970 showed the cultural differences of the two major ethnic groups in his calypso entitled "Different ways of Living." While East Indians, according to Power, stress good family life values, Africans on the other hand are only showing hate for their fellowmen and women. Listen to Power:

> But dem Negroes would a (of) talk bout obeah and light,
> And when Jane see Joan face first in the morning, whole day she blight.
> And keeping things in utensils till they smell evermore,
> Wake up next morning and dash it in front your neighbour door.[7]

Continuing his attack on those who did not live up to their civic responsibilities, Smiley in 1973/1974 turned the heat on the Chinese. We both went to the Oval in Port-of-Spain to see a football match involving Pele the Brazilian wizard. Smiley pointed out to me that in the crowd of approximately thirty thousand all he could see was one Chinese man. He boasted that if there were more than two to be found, he would pay me a huge lump sum of money. Try as we did, we only found two persons of Chinese descent. Smiley thus composed "The Chinese Man." Although the calypso was unfavourably received by the University students at St. Augustine, patrons, nevertheless, applauded it vociferously all over the country. A stanza from it goes thus:

> The Chinese man
> Is a man Ah can't understand.
> Here in Trinidad
> Ah say friends they selfish too bad.
> Yes Ah talking facts
> So they can't vex for that.
> I am a calysonian you see
> Ah singing on anybody.

---

[h] Creole for the word "nothing."

Dr. Hollis "Chalkdust" Liverpool

Chorus: Dem Chinese don't spend
        They don't take part in nutten.[h]
        Ah wonder what's their reason?
        According to Mr. Guy,
        They sucking the country dry.
        Ah want the Government to pass a law
        And tax them twenty-five times more.

I always pointed out to Smiley that he was a bit hard on the Chinese for they do take part in society's functions and many of them have been outstanding in their contributions. Because they are in the minority, many do not note their participation. There have been Chinese such as Carlisle Chang and Edwin Hingwan who contributed immensely to the field of visual arts; carnival bandleaders such as Max Awon, Neville Aming and Edwin and Elsie Lee Heung who have made a name for themselves in the production of masquerades and carnival bands; Sir Solomon Hochoy, the nation's first Governor General, and Patrick Jones who sang calypsoes in the 1920s to the 1940s under the sobriquet of Chinese Patrick. Smiley however feels that the Chinese need to do much more and put the energy that they usually display for business into other cultural concerns. Again one sees the fearlessness of the calypsonian and the method by which he gets themes for calypso. He is there to tell the nation his story as he sees it, regardless of the outcome. In this regard, Smiley longs for a more united fraternity of men, regardless of their ethnicity, race, belief or religion. One cannot disagree with him, especially when we realize that there still exist many men who, as individuals in the nation, pursue different goals using, at times, subversive routes.

Not every calypso touches Smiley or makes him yearn to listen to it; songs that are smutty are valueless in his thinking.

Songs, whereby no morals are gained, "float through one ear and pass out the other. A good calypso must make me feel something and carry a message whenever I hear it, even if it is fifty years old. It must not only make me feel to dance; it must set my brain dancing." This is exactly what famed folklorist and artist Professor Errol Hill meant in his article on the development of calypso, a section of which centers around the outstanding calypsoes and their characteristics.

> "A good calypso should be timely and timeless. It should have wit and humour. It should be couched in colourful language (similes and metaphors) with images that seem original yet ring true. Its verbal and musical form should be dictated by its content, not merely the story element, but the composer's interpretation of his material, his own point of view of the life experience. The melody and rhythm should strengthen the impact, and although it is a form of entertainment, there ought to be morals to be gained.[8]

Several calypso lovers, including many journalists, over the years have attempted to establish a list of the best fifty calypsoes ever sung. In doing so, they have used several yardsticks for measurement, but I am of the opinion that Professor Errol Hill's criteria remain the best. For Smiley, indeed for Errol Hill, one of the great songs of yesteryear was Destroyer's "A Mother's Love" of 1941 which goes in part:

> A Mother's love we cannot forget
> Wrong things we do we bound to regret ...
> You can have diamonds, rubies and pearls
> A mother's love is the master key of this world.[9]

Perhaps because Smiley loved this song so much, and perhaps because his mother didn't give him the love that was rightfully his, or perhaps because he knows that there are so many unfit mothers today, Smiley castigated his own mother in a calypso sung in 1970.

His mother left him, he said in the calypso, to go to the U.S.A. to work as a domestic, a custom that was very prevalent in the 1960s and 70s. A verse of it goes thus:

> Mother I can't live with you,
> Cause I will be dead in a year or two.
> You never brought me no joy,
> For Christmas you never gave me a little toy.
> Sumintra (his foster mother) gave me tricycle
> And when I get bigger she gave me bicycle.
> Now you want me to leave her to come to you.
> You want a lash with a big boutou (baton).

> Chorus: Mother, mother darling!
> You are my mother, yes that is true,
> But I cannot leave Sumintra, mother
> To come back to you.

It is to be noted that in the 1930s and 40s especially, several singers extolled the virtues of motherhood at a time when the role of women in everyday life was emphasized in hundreds of calypso songs. With women as their theme, singers sang about the good, the bad, the ugly and the prostitute, but they were extremely careful in singling out mothers for particular mention as if to be a mother then erased all the sins that women committed or could commit. Pretender and Caresser in 1937, Radio and Lion in 1939, Terror and Beginner in the 1940s and Sparrow in the 1960s, to name a few, all paid glowing tribute to their mothers. Radio noted that:

> Children the time is growing hard,
> Don't treat your dear old mama bad.
> There is a debt we all have got to pay
> For treating mothers in a naughty way.
> For you never miss the water till the well run dry,
> Like a mother when she close her eyes.[10]

Pretender, waxing rhetorically, noted that women were "the masterpiece in creation's plan." In one verse he explained the role of woman thus:

> The zenith of a woman's ambition in life
> Should be to be a loving and a pleasing wife.
> For thus they are by nature intended,
> Not as overlords or slaves, but to man subjected
> To join with him in love and connubial unity
> In generating humanity.[11]

Speaking about calypsoes of old particularly those of the 1920 -1930 era, Smiley believes that much of the rhetoric used then never made sense; "it was just big words hastily put together." Some songs, he believes, were excellent, while most of them were aimed at "creating an impression on the audience, and bearing no topic." Smiley may be correct for many singers, in trying to paint images, did use words that made no sense whatsoever. However, the reader must understand that the rhetoric was indeed the style of the era, with most singers seeking to paint images using figures of speech. It was this skill in the use of words that singled them out as calypsonians and educated ones at that. Some may have used words wrongly or even waxed warmly with malapropism, but the idea was always oratory in keeping with the ideals of British liberal education and values.

In the history of calypso, it is a well known fact that elder singers have always criticized the younger ones in terms of the changes that debutants bring to the art. A well-known commentator in the daily newspapers of 1946, Mr. J.R. Best, at the time pointed out that "some of our calypsonians seem to have begun to experiment on their art. There is a tendency among them to dazzle and amuse - not to create and develop."[12] When in the late 1940s and 1950s, however, calypsonians such as Terror, Christo and Spoiler began to create new themes for calypso by exploring the world of fantasy and make-believe, they were soundly thrashed by Executor who declared in 1950 that "in my time, 30 or 40 years ago,

134

calypsoes were more factual; we sang mostly on local topics. Now the songs are mostly things of imagination." [13] The Roaring Lion in the 1970s was extremely critical of the singers then claiming that they were no longer singing calypso. Perhaps because of his secondary education, or perhaps because of jealousy of the younger singers, or perhaps because of his preference for the double tone over the single tone calypso, calypsonian Attila always felt that the young bards of the 1950s "were spoiling calypso." [14] Even Professor Errol Hill, writing on the oratorical calypsoes that characterize the 1930s, 40s and 50s noted:

> "A peculiarity that resulted from the calypso ode was the use of polysyllabic words and the attempt to cram as many words as possible into the melodic line. The display of eloquence, especially in the hands of second rate singers, tended to sink the calypso into a morass of elaborate verbosity rattled off with unintelligible speed. It seemed as if the calypsonian was parodying himself." [15]

Here , Professor Errol Hill seems to be agreeing with Smiley, but the reader must note that Hill was referring to the "second rate singers." Calypsonian Pretender had the same trouble with second raters most of whom he disliked. He referred to them as "calypso singers" and "calypso mongers" and not calypsonians. [16] Lord Short Shirt of Antigua in the 1980s informed me that the singers who were bent on singing the fast soca tunes should not be called calypsonians, for everytime they were so called, he was being insulted. Lord Kitchener had a standing comment for all the young singers who in the 1980s and 1990s were trying to infuse new rhythms into their calypsoes. He would smilingly say: "Ah hope all who cross over could cross back when the time come." [18] Kitch therefore felt that the basic calypso rhythm would win in the end.

It must be understood that there will always be differences of opinion as regards old and new calypsoes, but those differences serve to show the interest that calypsoes generate. Moreover, each generation tends to fall in love with the fads, crazes, dances, musical art forms and patterns of its day. The calypso itself has always shown change; it moved from the call and response pattern to the single tone, to the double tone and then to the strophic eight line verse and chorus. Nowadays singers show very little respect for rhyming or for any special length of line, meter or verse. In fact many of those who break the so-called laws of calypso tend to have the bigger hits in the calypso world and are lauded by the majority of calypso fans.

The point that younger singers are not singing calypso has been argued as far back as 1914; the Port-of-Spain Gazette carried an article then in which the writer complained that: "none of the carnival bands sang any properly composed songs, most of them being merely a jingle of words uttered with lightning-like rapidity and ending with the monotonous 'sans humanite'."[19] I shudder to think what that writer would have said if he heard today's singers like Tallpree and Ajala, who according to calypsonian Sparrow are fast approaching 200 meters per minute on the metronome.[20] The reader would note that the writer of 1914 perhaps did not appreciate the talent of the calypsonians or perhaps did not understand their background. If he did, he would never term the beautiful and meaningful phrase "sans humanite" as being "monotonous." Today, the phrase has been retained even though it may have lost its original force. The writer didn't understand that the emphasis on the phrase showed the self-aggrandizement, the power and strength of the singer who aimed at the oratorical defeat of his enemy. The writer did not understand too, that to sing so many words so quickly was a feather in the cap of the calypsonian, a tribute to his genius and skill for matching and rhyming words and a mark of true greatness in terms of composing lines within a measured musical space.

The reader must note that although Smiley is against the "sheer big words" of past singers, their music finds favour with him, for most of his songs tend to flow along the chord structure of the 1940s,[i] whilst he himself is a lover of the minor key. Patrons at the Regal Calypso Tent looked forward annually to hear Smiley sing his war cry "oh lard" in the minor key. Smiley is so much in love with the minor key that at the Regal Calypso Tent which opened its doors to the public in 1973, Smiley was dubbed and advertised as "the minor key calypso king." Smiley was told by the elders in Carenage that the enslaved people brought the minor key to Trindad and used it in their stick fight songs. "It is from stick fight minor key singing come from," said Smiley. The reader may know that many of the old Kalenda songs were sung in the minor key. "When I'm singing minor," according to Smiley, "I sing from here (he places his hands on his stomach). I feel the minor key in mi big toe. It's an African thing." Smiley may be right for J.D. Elder has postulated the theory that the calypso descended from the kalenda and that the chantuelle of the stickfight band was the first calypsonian.[21]

That the Africans brought the minor key to Trinidad and used it in their kalenda songs is a truism for as early as 1820, planter Mrs. A.C. Carmichael showed that the enslaved in Trinidad were deliberately setting fires to the canes and were celebrating the cane burning sessions with songs which were set "in a minor key."[22]
Professor Errol Hill has shown that the Belair,[j] which he said had the greatest impact on the calypso, was a creolized "song of praise or dance" and was "plaintive and melancholy" in terms of its melody.[23] All musicologists know that such descriptive words aptly describe the minor key which when played provides a saddened atmosphere for the listener. J.D. Moreton who wrote in 1790, was also struck by the "deep melancholy" with which the enslaved Africans in the Caribbean sang their worksongs.

---

[i] Minor Key :Am/Am/B7/Am//: /Am/Dm/G7/C//Am/Dm/B7/Am//
  Major Key :C/C/G7/C//: C/F/G7/C// C/F/G7/C//
[j] Belair - sometimes spelt Bele or Belay.

Another 18th century writer, William Beckford, noted that all the songs of the women working at the mill at nights were "of a plaintive cast." Elder calypsonian, the Growling Tiger, was particularly influenced by the early 19th century stickfighters in Siparia, South Trinidad. As a result, Tiger was able to sing some of the early stickfight minor key songs, while the minor key heavily influenced his own singing style and compositions. One of the songs that Tiger sang was termed "Iya to bi mi." Tiger claimed that it was handed down to him by the elders of his day. He claimed too, that "it was sung on the slave ship." Linguist Maureen Warner Lewis showed from her doctoral research that not only was the song sung in the minor key, but that the words and melody can be traced to the Yoruba people of West Africa.[24]

In 1993, Smiley sang an up tempo calypso in which he tried to show the audience that the young people today do not take dancing seriously. Several persons applauded him for it and some even exhorted him to try a Road March. But road marches are not for Smiley. In fact, he says, "I leave that for Kitch and Superblue; Kitch is the boss of the Road March." Smiley may be quite correct for Kitch himself informed me that he was the first person to use the term. "I invented that," Kitch told me. It was 1946, according to Kitch, and he had just made the tune called "The Birth of the Steelband." Seeing all the revellers in town rhythmically chipping away to the same musical piece in all the bands, he noted that it was the Road March and from the very next year he kept using the term. Soon, the Carnival Development Committee picked it up and the concept of the Road March was born.[25] In fact in 1963, he sang "The Road Make to Walk on Carnival Day."

The Carnival has always been blessed with road marches. They represent the tunes that find favour with the revelers. The newspapers of 1888 record that the revelers were singing "an obscene distich of the most indecent character of the crudest words."[26] Thus the singers were rhyming as they sang along.

Dr. Hollis "Chalkdust" Liverpool

At the turn of the century, the songs of the revelers were called the "leggos" and sometimes the "lavways." A "leggo" means a "breakaway;" it is the tune that allows people to let themselves go or to break away in dance to the music. A "lavway" is a sing-along song. In other words, as people tramped, danced or chipped to the music, they would sing along, and would often add their own lyrics to the tune. One such song sung in 1946 after the war went thus:

> The Governor say no mas
> The Governor too dam fast.

The revelers however changed it to:

> The Governor say no mas
> The Governor haul hi ass. [27]

At the end of World War 1, when Trinidadians celebrated Victory Carnival, the leggo of the day was:

> (Refrain):"Hold yuh cup for yuh ginger tea, hold yuh cup.
> (Chant) : The matron behind you"

While before 1919, several leggos were sung, this calypso was sung by all and sundry and could be aptly described as the official leggo. of the day. The calypso demonstrates that the carnival revelers were responding to the conditions of the prison when ginger tea was served. In the 1900 to 1930 era, in the absence of any official leggos, several tunes, year after year, were sung and sung over. Among these were "Prisonniers Levez" a leggo dating back to the 1840s; "Fire Brigade Water the Road," a tune that dates back to the days of dirt roads in the city when the water was needed to keep down the dust; and stick fight songs such as the following:

> 1.Refrain: Jour ouvert bas wayo, pas levez la main asuyo
> (Jour ouvert morning block them, don't let them raise their hands on you;

2. Refrain: Sergeant Brown moi vlai gormay (Sergeant
   Brown ah want to fight)

   Chant: Sergeant Brown bas moi battonier (Sergeant
   Brown pass mi stick).

3. Refrain: Millington wayo, Millington bas moi battonier
   (Millington Oh! Pass me mi stick).

   Chant: Bas moi battonier, mama moi kay pleway pour
   moi (pass me mi stick, mi mother go cry for me).

One can easily tabulate the road marches of Trinidad and Tobago
beginning with the year 1900. The table would read as follows:

1900 -1918	Stickfight chants.	
1919	Hold yuh cup for yuh ginger tea.	
1920 -1927	Stickfight chants	
1928	One cent a Honeycomb	Roaring Lion
1929 - 1931	Stickfight songs	
1932	Tiger Tom Play Tiger Cat	King Radio
1933	Wash Pan Wash	King Radio
	After Johny Drink Mi Rum	Douglas
1934	After Johny Drink Mi Rum	Douglas
1935	Dingolay Oh!	Roaring Lion
	Advantage Could Never Done	Roaring Lion
1936	Ask No Question	Roaring Lion
1937	Netty Netty	Roaring Lion
1938	Ah Nora Darling	Roaring Lion
1939	Mathilda	King Radio
1940	Run Yuh Run	Beginner
1941	Whoopsin Whoopsin	Roaring Lion
1942 - 1945	(No carnival - World War 11)	
1946	Mary Ann	Radio
	Lai Fook Lee	Kitchener

Dr. Hollis "Chalkdust" Liverpool

1947	Voosh Kay Voosh Kay Voosh	Pharaoh
1948	Canaan Barrow Went To Town	Melody
1949	Ramgoat Baptism	Wonder
1950	In A Calabash	Killer
1951	Tiny Tiny Davis	Terror
1952	Post Post	Spitfire
1953	Bow Wow Wow	Spitfire
	Madeline Oye	Vivian Comma
1954	Mama Look a Band Passing	Kitchener
	Steelband Clash	Blakie
1955	Happy Wanderer	(ForeignTune)
1956	Jean and Dinah	Sparrow
1957	PNM	Spitfire
	Drink Tisane De Dourbon	Nelson Caton
1958	Pay As You Earn	Sparrow
1959	Run the Gunslingers	Caruso
1960	Mae Mae	Sparrow
1961	Royal Jail	Sparrow
1962	Maria	Blakie
1963	The Road Make To Walk	Kitchener
1964	Mama Dis Is Mas	Kitchener
1965	My Pussin	Kitchener
1966	Obeah Wedding	Sparrow
1967	Sixty-Seven	Kitchener
1968	Miss Tourist	Kitchener
1969	Sa Sa Yay	Sparrow
1970	Margie	Kitchener
1971	Mas In Madison Square Garden	Kitchener
1972	Drunk and Disorderly	Sparrow
1973	Rainorama	Kitchener
1974	The Bassman	Shadow
1975	Tribute To Spree Simon	Kitchener
1976	Flag Woman	Kitchener
1977	Tempo	Calypso Rose
1978	Soca Jam	Calypso Rose
1979	Ah Tell She	Poser
1980	Soca Baptist	Blue Boy
1981	Ethel	Blue Boy
1982	A Deputy Essential	Penguin
1983	Rebecca	Blue Boy
1984	Don' t Back Back	Sparrow

Dr . Hollis "Chalkdust" Liverpool

1985	Soucouyant	Crazy
1986	Bahia Girl	David Rudder
1987	Thunder	Duke
1988	Dis Party Is It	Tambu
1989	Free Up	Tambu
1990	We Aint Going Home	Tambu
1991	Get Something and Wave	SuperBlue
1992	Jab Jab	SuperBlue
1993	Bacchanal	SuperBlue
1994	Jump and Wave	Preacher
1995	Signal To Lara	SuperBlue
1996	Movin'	Nigel Lewis
1997	Big Truck	Machel Montano
1998	Footsteps	Wayne Rodriguez
1999	River	Sanell Dempster
2000	Pump Up	SuperBlue
	Carnival Come Back Again	Iwer George
2001	Stranger	Shadow
2002	Trinidad	Naya George.
2003	Display	Faye-Ann Lyons

Patrons at Spektakula Forum on Henry Street from 1981 to 1996 looked forward annually to hear Lord Smiley and his minor key calypsoes in his own inimitable style. It was a joy to see patrons singing along with him as he crouched low, his left thumb and forefinger joined as he bellowed his famous war cry: "oye, oye, oye." Smiley, unlike a number of calypsonians, aims at pleasing the audience. "I is a fellow once I please the audience, I happy. I don't look at judges."

Two of his songs were considered good enough to find favour with Pat Nurse's selection of the "calypso classics" of all time.[28] Regardless of the selector, to be considered among the best calypsoes of the century is a feat for any composer. It means that Lord Smiley is indeed one of the giants in the calypso arena. The two songs were the "Negro Man" and "The Snake." In the Snake Smiley mused:

The housewife some men must know
Need some recreation also.
But some men have dey wife pen up
They can't even go to the shop.
Take neighbour Elsa - poor thing
She never go to the cinema
That stupid man, she husband, his name is Buchanan
One day nearly break she hand.

Chorus: Because she went with some friends to the cinema -
Oh mi Lard,
You know Buchanan nearly dropped down with heart failure.
Like he fraid if she go to town a snake will bite she - Oh mi
Lard;
Ah can't understand why some men so stupidy.
Even though she home
Snake is a creature that like to roam.
She can't go no way
But she still getting bite every day.

Smiley, the reader may observe, loves to sing on the different races and ethnic groups in Trinidad and Tobago. Not one to treat any group with special favours, in 1994, Smiley castigated his own race with "The African's Worst Enemy is the African." As if to destroy the myth that the African in Trinidad and Tobago is incapable of running a commercial enterprise or having a sense of commerce, he sang in 1995 "African Millionaires." Smiley used calypsonian Trini as the scapegoat, possibly because Trini is of Syrian/Lebanese descent. In the calypso, he explained to the audience that he and Trini had a conversation and Trini was boasting about the amount of money that Syrians had made from investing in business ventures in Trinidad. One of the choruses that I particularly liked went thus:

Dr. Quamina, Dr. Ince and Butler
Dem is millionaire.
Dr. Bartholomew and Dr. Henry from the avenue

Dem is millionaire too.
Dr. Jeff Davidson and others from Tobago
They are millionaires also.
Ah now start the song as you can see
So much millionaires called already!
So Trini only fast, or he blasted bias,
Or he talking up in hi - #$*.

In 1997, Smiley left Spektakula Forum and vowed never to sing there again in his life, on the grounds that the management had ill treated him. Had I known that he was made "to scrub the bench" by the management, I might have been able to change the picture and bring the two sides together. I usually sing in the second half of the programme, so that when ever I arrived, I was of the opinion that Smiley had already sung. One can then imagine how shocked I was to learn the he was "on the bench" and that after two weeks of that treatment, he had walked out. What management did not know is that Smiley hated the bench. He hated and despised it so much that he disliked what he saw at Sparrow's O.Y.B. and, as a result, joined the Calypso Theatre in 1969. He therefore sang with the Calypso Theatre in 1997 and has been doing so up to Year 2003. I never interfere with tent managers and their decisions, but I was forced then to explain to them that Lord Smiley had contributed immensely to Spektakula's success, and if even his calypso was not up to mark that year, his past contribution ought to have negated any thought of putting him on the bench.

The patrons of the Calypso Theatre were therefore thrilled when in 1998 he dished out another "ethnic" song; he was then on the legal luminaries of the nation. The first verse went thus:

Some people in Trinidad and Tobago, Ah can't understand
Why when they want a lawyer they sending quite to England.
I do not know what they playing!
They showing off or something!
England have top lawyers that is true
But Trinidad and Tobago have top lawyers too.

Chorus: Guerra, Desmond Allum and Shastri Persad
They know law too bad!
Allan Alexander and Prakash Ramadar
Dem men is thunder!
With Douglas Mendez and young Carlton George,
Ivor Archie, Sebastian Ventour,
They know plenty law
Of that I am sure,
Like dem English lawyers or more.
More top lawyers to call but ah just getting set,
Clinton Bernard Ah aint mention yet.

Perhaps because he spent the greater part of 1998 in the U.S.A., he sang in 1999 "God bless the U.S.A." The first verse goes thus:

God bless the U.S.A.!
Ah don't care what nobody say.
I'll shout it out night and day
God bless the U.S.A.
If we disagree well then it is shameful
Or if not, we dam ungrateful.
Once you have a conscience man you must agree
The U.S.A. does help people from every country.

Chorus: People from Europe and Africa,
Asia, Australia, South America,
The people from the Caribbean
For that matter is the whole world Ah mean;
As a man ketch hi tail and he can't see hi way,
He heading straight for the U.S.A.
And as things start going nice with he
He sending for hi family.
The U.S. have millions on their feet today!
Ah tell you - God bless the U.S.A.

One aspect of the calypso that Smiley misses very much is the audition. When calypsonians of the1940s, 1950s and 1960s speak of the audition, they were referring to that annual event put on by tent managers to select calypsonians for the ensuing season. It was a most delightful event, for not only would the singers and fans get a taste of what was to come, but it was also a time to judge which singer was strong and which ones were weak. Many a time too, some calypsonians or debutants were so weak that the audience would be in fits of laughter especially when the judges say "next singer" in the middle of a calypsonian's performance. Lord Kitchener, for example, would stop a singer sometimes at the end of the singer's second line; one could imagine the peals of laughter that would ensue. Kitch used to say that "you don't have to sing a whole calypso to know if it good or not; from the way the song break, after the first two lines, you could tell." And so Kitch used to stop them because time was important in an audition (there were at least about eighty to a hundred singers lining up to sing for the judges). Kitch used to hold his audition at his home in Diego Martin; Sparrow held his at his tent and sometimes at his "hideaway;"[k] others were held at the Regal calypso tent, at Balisier house[l] and at the office of the Carnival Development Committee which eventually changed to the National Carnival Commission. There were other auditions to select singers for tents in Arima and San Fernando and so calypsonians used to have many a meeting place to enjoy the company of one another.

Judges for auditions would normally be persons who were known to have knowledge of the development and history of the art form. They were men such as George Goddard who was associated with both calypso and steelband; one Mr. Alston Huggins, who was a lawyer and a calypso composer; Mr. Andrew Carr, the well-known folklorist; calypsonians Growling Tiger, Kitch, Sparrow and Lion; Mr. Lance Heath who contributed so much to the development of the art among children; Mr. Jonah Regis who was

[k] Sparrow's Hideaway - a night club and calypso tent adjacent to Sparrow's home in Diego Martin.
[l] The headquarters of the political party known as the PNM.

respected for his knowledge of the art and Mr. Tony Mitchell a respected journalist who worked with the Trinidad Guardian newspaper. It was important to have good judges for many a calypso that was not well received by the audience did not mean that it was not a good composition; the same calypso would "mash up the calypso tent," to use Lord Pretender's words, later on. Similarly, many a calypso that was well received by the fans at an audition, fell flat in the tent later on. It took judges of the caliber of Lance Heath, Rocky McCollin and Tony Mitchell, who had an understanding of what will go down well with a tent audience, to judge singers at the audition.

Auditions in the 1950 to 1990 era called for good guitarists to accompany the singers. While some guitarists accompanied the singers before the judges, other guitarists and singers could be heard at some distance away practicing and getting their keys and chord patterns right. So important were the guitarists that a singer could have failed the audition if the style of strumming didn't fit the song or the chords were not right. Most singers wanted the "Coleman rapaap-pa-pap" strum made popular by the great guitarist and musician Fitzroy Coleman. Of all the guitarists in the audition business, most singers of 1960 to 1980 era still speak of calypsonian Caresser who was not only a master guitarist, but was one of the best hustlers in the calypso industry. At any audition, Caresser was always in demand, for he knew the calypso chord pattern well and had the ability to accompany a singer regardless of how unusual the chord pattern in the calypso flowed. Besides Caresser, there was Andrew Hudlin with whom most singers were comfortable. Other good guitarists were calypsonians Panther, Robin, Superior, Relator, and Viking. Auditions attracted not only calypsonians and calypso fans but legislators, business men and union leaders. Many of them came others came to hear if their names were included in a calypso, for it is well known that a calypsonian, to use the words of Lord Kitchener, had the power to "make and break" someone.[29] In fact, to the calypso tent nightly, many politicians and businessmen flocked. At the audition to select singers for the 1968 season, I was introduced to Dr. Eric Williams, the prime minister for the very first time. The prime minister was brought to the audition by Mr. George Goddard, who at that time headed the steelband movement. In September of that year, the prime minister appointed George "adviser on the improvement of steelband music" which post George reluctantly accepted, since he felt that that post was meant to silence him, he having had a reputation for speaking out on matters cultural. So important were auditions that on several occasions, the prime minister accompanied by the minister with responsibility for culture continued to come to those to select the cast of the Calypso Theatre, during the period 1968 to 1980.

In the 1940 to 1980 era also, the majority of calypsonians had to face judges, who on most occasions were the tent owners and managers, at an audition annually. The singers auditioned, not so much to satisfy judges, but to enable the master of ceremonies and the tent manager to hear their offerings for the season. As such, most of the top singers had a private audition with the master of ceremonies and the tent manager. It was important that the master of ceremonies and the tent manager hear the songs, for singers wanted to impress the tent manager and perhaps to demand more money for their services, while the master of ceremonies had to understand the merits of a calypso in order to place the singer in the most favourable singing position on the programme. It is a well known fact that the master of ceremonies had the ability to heighten or lower a singer's performance, by the position on the programme where the singer sang.

148

There were some singers who had the ability to wake up an audition in the sense that things would be going rather cold, but when they came to sing, the whole place would come alive. They would, by their personality (which calypsonians call their gam), the loud guitar strumming and large chorus group that accompanied their performances, and the resonance of their voices change the atmosphere of the audition. Such strong singers included Viking, Viper, Spitfire, Tiny Terror, Young Creole, Gibraltar, Lord Funny, Penman, Popo, Scaramouche, Jaguar, Supreme Happiness, Durango and, of course, Lord Smiley. Some singers at auditions, like King Wellington and Power were known to be tunesmiths (they composed beautiful melodies); some, like Pretender and Short Pants were called lyricists; they were famous for strong lyrics. Others like Terror, Brigo, Relator, Composer, Gypsy, Penguin, Superior, and Drake were noted for always having good tunes and strong lyrics.

In Smiley's opinion, Spoiler was the greatest calypsonian who ever lived. Spoiler, to him, was imaginative; Spoiler had foresight. Spoiler was never smutty, but witty and humourous. In Smiley's opinion, "for a man to think of topics such as 'Talking Backward,' 'Pick Sense out of Nonsense,' 'Mi Twin Brother,' 'The Magistrate Trying Hi Own Case,' and 'Rum Bacchanal,' he has to be a superman." Little wonder that Professor Gordon Rohlehr once referred to Spoiler as "a genius of the absurd."[30] Calypsonian Bill Trotman, who was a close friend of Spoiler and who toured Barbados with him, informed me that although Spoiler never sang smut in a tent or on a show, yet on that tour, Spoiler sang "some of the dirtiest, nastiest, stinkest songs he ever heard. Spoiler," according to Bill, "would sing some unbelievable dirty songs to private audiences that included firemen and policemen." In fact, Bill sang for me one such ditty which he said was composed and sung by Spoiler. I would have loved to give readers a taste of it but the words are unprintable.[31]

For Smiley, Chalkdust and Pretender remain the "greatest composers in the calypso business." Says Smiley:

Dr. Hollis "Chalkdust" Liverpool

"Pretender could compose a calypso on anything, from the jawbone of Samson's ass to Mary had a little lamb. Chalkdust is great. I once saw Chalkdust recording a calypso and while they were taping the music, Chalkdust was in a corner writing the lyrics. By the time the band was ready, say ten minutes, Chalkdust was ready with the calypso, and to crown it all, he recorded it with one take and without a mistake. Chalkdust has, over the years too, provided us with calypso classics that would make Douglas and Houdini look like little boys."

Enough of me Smiley, I had to tell him. Perhaps our friendship has distorted your perception. Smiley believes too, that Christo and Bomber are the two most unlucky singers, for both of them have always composed good songs yet their performances have never brought them the laurels they deserve.

Without a doubt, Lord Smiley, termed the minor key calypso king, has not only showed that he has gained considerable knowledge of the development of the calypso both from his grandmother and from his personal experiences, but he has added much to mine.

Kitch, Supie and Melo—Musicians all—Courtesy 'Calypso Dreams'

Dr. Hollis "Chalkdust" Liverpool

150

ENDNOTES

[1] Ali, Clayton (Dougla). Personal Communication, P.O.S., August 1974.
[2] From Calypso Theatre records kept by the author.
[3] Goddard, George. Personal Conversation, Diego Martin. August 10th 1980.
[4] Teaching Service Commission, correspondence from Commission to Liverpool, April 1968.
[5] From Calypso Theatre records kept by the author.
[6] See Keith Smith's columns on the Express, December 2nd - 6th, 2002.
[7] Francois, Sonny (Power). "Different Ways of Living." Calypso Theatre, 1970.
[8] Hill, Errol. The Trinidad Carnival. Texas: University of Texas Press, 1972.
[9] Morris, Clifford (Destroyer). "A Mother's love." The Author's Collection of Calypso Lyrics.
[10] Spann, Norman (King Radio). "Tribute to Mother." The Author's Collection of Calypso Lyrics.
[11] Farrell, Alric (Pretender). Personal Communication, P.O.S., August 1972.
[12] Best, J.R. Trinidad Guardian. February 24th 1946.
[13] Naipaul, S. "Almost Blind, Lord Executor Hums Calypsoes to Himself," Trinidad Guardian. February 16th 1950.
[14] De Leon, Raphael (Lion). Personal Communication, Mt. Lambert, Trinidad. January 1973.
[15] Liverpool, Hollis. "From the Horse's Mouth," Undergrad Thesis, UWI 1973, p.48.
[16] Farrell, Alric. Personal Communication, P.O.S., August 1967.
[17] Emmanuel, Maclean (Short Shirt). Personal Communication, St. John, Antigua. August 1981.
[18] Roberts Aldwyn (Kitchener). Personal Communication, St. Thomas, USVI. April 1981.
[19] Port-of-Spain Gazette, February 25th 1914.
[20] Francisco, Slinger (Sparrow). Personal Conversation, Brooklyn, New York. December 12th 2002.
[21] Elder, J.D. "Evolution of the Traditional Calypso of Trinidad and Tobago: A Socio-Historical Analysis of Song Change," Ph.D. diss., Univ. of Pennsylvania, 1996. pp. 91 - 98.
[22] Carmichael, A.C. Domestic Manners and Social Customs of the White, Coloured and Negro Population of the West Indies, Vol. 2 (London: Treacher & Co., 1833), pp. 301 - 302.
[23] Hill, Errol. Quoted in Liverpool's Rituals of Power and Rebellion. (Chicago: Frontline, 2001), 197.
[24] See Rituals of Power and Rebellion, p.197.
[25] Roberts, Aldwyn (Kitchener). Personal Conversation, St. Thomas, USVI, April 1981.

151

26 Port-of-Spain Gazette, February 15th 1888, 3.
27 The Author's Collection of Calypso Lyrics.
28 Nurse, Pat. Carnival Woman. (New York: the Author, 2002), 217.
29 Roberts, Aldwyn (Kitch). Personal Conversation, St. Thomas, USVI., April 1981.
30 Rohlehr, Gordon. Seminar on the Calypso. Univ. of the West Indies, St. Augustine. March 6-10, 1986.
31 Trotman, Bill. Personal Conversation. National Museum, P.O.S., October 2002.

Sparrow–Courtesy 'Calypso Dreams'

Dr. Hollis "Chalkdust" Liverpool

Andrew Ma
(Lord Sup
You must disco⸱er
disⲟv ⲣo
Mohammedans di ⸱er
Buddhist ⲛd Christians
discover Jew.
Whites mu over Blacks
to avoid lation. - Yes,
If we wan find peace on
earth man first must
discover man.

(Superior - Man In Space- From
the author's collection of lyrics).

Lord Superior, who has since renamed himself Brother Superior, was born Andrew Marcano in the rural district of Rio Claro, Trinidad in 1937. I first met him at a barber shop on George street, Port-of-Spain, in the early 1960s. At the time, I was passing by when I heard the sweet strums of a guitar and entered the shop ostensibly to get my hair cut in a style that, I remembered, the barber didn't like. The barber said to me then that the haircut reminded him of a goat or a monkey or some such animal. I cared for neither him nor his hair-cutting remarks; I was interested in Supie (the more pleasant name used for Superior), and his guitar playing and singing. I again met Supie as a singer at a Buy Local audition in 1966 and by 1973, we were such good friends that he asked me to join with him in providing Trinidad with a new calypso nt. As a result, he, Calypsonian Duke and I formed an organization which we called Dusuchalk[a] in 1973, and, using its resources, instituted the Regal Calypso tent.

George Street, where I first met Supie, served as the headquarters of the calypsonians then. Few calypsonians, if any, had telephones, and, as a result, when a promoter or anyone interested in a show wanted to find a calypsonian, he simply had to leave a message with either Dougla who was a calypsonian and barber, Zachary a barber of note, calypsonian Coffee who lived and limed in the area, or with any of the other barbers and tailors whose shops were located in the vicinity. In the absence of an office or a building to house the Calypsonians' Association, most calypsonians frequented the area up to the 1970s and even in the 80s. They met at the corner of George and Queen streets to do a number of things. Some like the Mighty Piper could be seen playing a game of draughts on Queen Street between George and Nelson streets; some like the Lord Black Hat, Mighty Caresser and Mighty Viper met there to decide where they would hustle that evening; some like the Mighty Coffee, Explorer and Jaguar(another good hustler)drank their morning tea at the Chinese parlour situated at the corner of Queen and Nelson streets; some like Viking, Rainbow and Viper came there daily to play the horses at the racing outlet on George street; some like the Lords Melody, Christo and Blakie limed continuously in the barber shops; some like Unknown, Brigo, Lester and Zebra simply had to pass there daily to say hello to the rum shop crowd; others like Spoiler, Gibraltar, Lion, Pretender, Iere and Spitfire simply entertained themselves with a flask of rum in the rum shop at the corner of George and Queen streets. Singers met there also, not only to visit the barbers and tailors who made them look special for shows or for the upcoming season, but very often the very barbers and tailors would provide them with materials for their songs.

---

[a] Dusuchalk stood for Duke, Superior and Chalkdust.

Dr. Hollis "Chalkdust" Liverpool

Barber shops, rum shops and tailor shops served as social sites[b] for the population; there the people would discuss the happenings of the day and such happenings would be passed on to the calypsonian. There too, the unspoken riposte, stifled anger, and bitten tongues created by relations of domination found a vehement, full-throated expression. Like in Europe where the alehouse, the pub, the tavern, the inn, the cabaret, the beer cellar and the gin mill were seen by secular authorities and by the church as places of subversion, the barber shops, tailor shops and rum shops in Trinidad served as unmonitored areas where people gathered to discuss social issues and from where themes for calypsoes took root. In such shops all privilege was suspended, and yet amid the noisy atmosphere, there prevailed forms of discourse excluded from the world of hierarchy and etiquette: parody, ridicule, blasphemy, the grotesque, scatology, revelry, and obscene language. In the rum shop especially, the piety, humility, servility, seriousness, respect and physical deportment of official onstage conduct were replaced by patterns of speech and conduct that were otherwise disapproved. Yet serious discourse took place there and several strands of friendship were knotted and many ties cemented. As a young singer, I got my first taste of the rum shop culture from Lion, Gibraltar, Coffee and Jaguar who amid the drinks and the loud noise would make me change a line in my compositions and would censor my songs, in return for several flasks of rum which I had to purchase if I wanted to retain their friendship, composing skills and camaraderie.

Lord Superior, who often times strummed his guitar to accompany singers in these social sites, was always a guy who would utter some anecdote from which a young singer could improve in the art of calypso singing; Supie always had a story to tell that would illustrate the error made by the young or even the experienced singer and, by so doing, the development of the

---

[b] Special liming spots for a vast number of the lower class especially artists, pimps, whores, drunks and badjohns.

Dr. Hollis "Chalkdust" Liverpool

calypso became much clearer and simpler to me. If, for example, a singer forgot his lines, Supie would tell you a dozen stories of singers who in the past forgot their lines. If a singer mispronounced a word, Supie would fill you in on a true story of a singer who ten years ago pronounced a word badly, as well as some juicy details of the way the singer fared with the audience then. Besides being a prolific guitar player, Supie is one of the most serious singers in the calypso world. A friend of mine, deceased Mr. Ulric Smith, once described Superior as a person who is in love with Trinidad in general, and with calypso in particular. [1] In this regard, Mr. Smith is so correct, for Supie is one of the bards that a person is sure to find wherever calypso is being sung.

Although Supie began to sing professionally in 1954, like most artistes, his interest in the art started six years previously, he having witnessed the "Madame Olindi" show that originated from Guyana, with performing stars such as Lord Coffee and the Mighty Dictator. Like most calypsonians, an elder singer motivated him, and in his case it was Lord Dictator. It is sad to note that like Lord Coffee, so many of the singing bards ended up as vagrants on the streets of Port-of-Spain. Lord Brynner, who thrilled listeners in the late 1960s and 1970s ended up as a vagrant in the late 1980s before he died. Lord Creator, who in the early 1960s was hailed by the best cultural circles as being the best entertainer in Jamaica, ended up as a vagrant on the streets of Port-of-Spain in the 1980s. Lord Coffee lost his home on Nelson Street and lived on Tamarind Square, Port-of-Spain before he was found dead in the 1990s. The Mighty Commander lived in the squalor of the streets of San Juan, rummaging in the garbage bins there before he died. So fed up with life was the Growler, that he threw himself over the wall of the Dry River in the 1950s and consequently died. The Mighty Penman who thrilled calypso fans with his witty and well-composed lyrics in the 1960s, and who was the original composer of "Portrait of Trinidad" sung by Sniper and "Professor Broom" sung by Bomber, is, at the time of writing, still living on the city's streets. Lord Dictator, who Superior admired fortunately migrated to the U.S.A. and helped to promote the calypso art form there before he passed away. Of him, Supie exclaimed: "I was moved by Dictator's song "The Shortest Way to Prosperity," for it pointed out a new way, an innovation for one to succeed. I said there and then: I want to become a singer like him." Superior has indeed proven to be a singer like Dictator, for the majority of his songs has that message of urging people to live better, or inspiring them with new hopes for a better country. For example, in the "Republic" he wrote:

> When Ah get the news
> That we going republic,
> Ah jump out mi shoes
> And Ah say: that is terrific.
> For if we are to be a nation,
> We must cut all ties from Britain.
> It's stupidity
> To have ties with your enemy.

Of the Space programme he wrote:

> Why all this haste
> Spending money to enter space? (repeat)
> It looks as though very soon
> Man will be making plans for the moon.
> But why fool with the universe?
> We have things on earth to discover first.
> Chorus: For instance, you must discover me;
>   I discover you.
>   Mohammedans must discover Buddhists
>   And Christians discover Jew.
>   Whites must discover Blacks
>   To avoid tribulation.
>   If we want to find peace on earth
>   Man first must discover man.

Dr. Hollis "Chalkdust" Liverpool

The year was 1954 when Superior made his debut as a singer in a tent situated at 100 St. Vincent Street, where stars such as Lord Melody, Sir Galba, Pretender, Cypher, Lady Pearl-White, Striker and Wrangler sang. It was nicknamed "Victory" tent and was looked upon as the tent whereby, according to Superior, singers would achieve financial victory over the poverty that characterized calypsonians then. On looking back at the year 1954, Lord Superior recalled the systems of management that were instituted in the running of the tent and feels strongly that modern day tents ought to be organized along similar lines. For example, he stressed the point that the revenue gained from the Victory Tent was distributed among the singers in a more equitable manner than in the 1960s and early 1970s. In 1954, shares were allocated to tent personnel based on the contributions they made to its organization. The financier or manager received one (1) share of the revenue. Speaking of the 1970s,[c] Supie observed: "Nowadays, managers get too much for doing next to nothing." The reader should therefore understand that when Duke, Supie and I organized the Regal Calypso Tent, as managers, many a week we received no pay, since the revenue was used to pay the singers, the band, the workers and the many other expenses of running the institution.

In 1956, Sparrow won the Calypso Monarch title; his vivacity, bounce, melodious voice and deportment caused thousands to flock to the calypso tent and ushered in a new dimension in calypso, in that Trinidadians began to esteem the art more highly. Sparrow's tuneful chorus lines as well as his jovial energetic personality influenced not only a great many persons into taking a second look at the art, but it made the calypso more famous overseas. Superior, however, is no ordinary calypso fan or fanatic, for while to him the years 1956 and 1957 represented the "zenith in the calypso's acceptance," and were to him "the years of craze," he certainly does not attribute the rise in the popularity of the calypso then to the advent or influence of Sparrow. Superior should certainly know for Sparrow noted that the two of them were considered the two youngest and fastest-rising singers at the Original Young Brigade tent on Wrightson Road in 1956.[2] To Superior, that fame, that

---

[c] I interviewed him then in 1972.

Dr. Hollis "Chalkdust" Liverpool

foreign acceptance, that craze, that shot in the arm for calypso music came from Lord Melody's "Boo-Boo Man," Harry Belafonte with his "Jamaican Farewell," and the other folk songs[d] of the Caribbean which Belafonte at that time recorded and sang to large audiences in the United States.

An interesting aspect in the development of calypso that was mentioned by Superior was the art of "hustling." "Hustling" was so called because of the art, guts, expertise and energy it took to jostle the tourists in order to make a living out of calypso singing. "Hustling" which still goes on today, has always been the part-time occupation of most singers from as early as 1920. It means understanding the world news and events of the day, arming oneself with a guitar or cuatro, learning a few outstanding calypso compositions and rhythmic oratorical lines, and then entertaining guests and patrons by singing notable calypsoes and composing ditties extemporaneously on events taking place. Such hustlers could be seen at night clubs, street corners and tourist spots. In the 1940s and 1950s, the red light district on Wrightson Road was the famous place for "hustling;" in the 1960s and 1970s, the Botanic Gardens around the Savannah as well as the look out on Lady Young Road, found favour with the hustlers. Today, one only has to visit Maracas Bay, the lookouts on Lady Young Road and the Saddle Road, and one would get a fair picture of the art of "hustling."

In Superior's heyday, 1954 - 1960, all calypsonians hustled during the off season,[e] but Superior was quick to point out that there were A grade hustlers like the Growling Tiger, Skipper, Panther, Dictator, Sir Galba and Lord Melody who hustled in night clubs and posh entertainment centers; B grade hustlers like Sparrow, Striker, Intruder, Caresser, Spitfire and himself who hustled at street corners, barber saloons or wherever a crowd might gather; and C grade hustlers who aped the songs of the graded

---

[d] Belafonte also recorded tunes composed by Lord Melody such as "Boo Boo Man" and "Shame and Scandal in Mi Family."

[e] The off season was the period when the calypso tents were closed. This usually took place on the Saturday before Carnival until January (New Year's day) of the next year.

Dr. Hollis "Chalkdust" Liverpool

159

singers and tried their learnt-by-rote art in rum shops. Some of the
C grade fellows even pretended to be graded singers by assuming
the nom-de-plumes of their more famous fraternity before an
unsuspecting or otherwise ignorant audience. In the 1970s, Viper,
Scaramouche, Lester, Jaguar, Young Killer and Caresser were
famous singers who hustled all the year round, both during the
official calypso season and the off season. So good were Caresser
and Viper at hustling that in the 1980s, they were brought to Hilton
Hotel by the hotel's management to sell their wares there. Other
good hustlers in the 1980s included Robin, Organizer, Inventor and
Baker. Caresser in 1972 brought out the reason for hustling when
he sang:

> Government! tell me what is wrong?
> Everything Ah do, Ah doing it wrong.
> No money, no work, Ah bad luck for so,
> So it look like Ah go dead singing calypso.[3]

Not all social sites welcomed the hustlers. In fact, many
hustlers, according to Supie, were hustled outside, for some night
club owners felt that the hustlers were encouraging the wrong
crowd to gather on their premises. In this regard, I remembered
seeing in 1968 a huge sign at a Chinese eatery at the corner of
Frederick and Park streets that read: "No Calypsonians and Dogs
Allowed." Such a development ought to make the reader aware of
the struggle with which singers, up to the 1960s, had to put up in
order to gain recognition. Little wonder that Sparrow in his calypso
of 1963 entitled "The Outcast" mentioned the problems that singers
faced when they indulged in the art of calypso.[4]

Knowing that most fans, especially the American soldiers,
favoured the smutty songs, most hustlers sang same, or else
composed lines on the audience. A favourite trick in hustling is to
know the lines by rote, but change a few words to make the listener
feel that it is being done extemporaneously.[5] For example, a
favourite of hustlers goes thus:

Welcome my friend! Welcome good man!
Ah glad you come to this sunny land.
Here you'll find the natives nice,
Beautiful, sensitive, this is paradise.
I do hope you really enjoy your stay,
Drink plenty rum and bathe in Maracas Bay.
Since yuh come here, yuh already looking fat,
So put a five dollar in mi old black hat.

If a tourist (A) gives them a dollar, and another one (B) refuses or is in a doubt, they would add two more lines to (B) and say:

Your friend over there (B) gave me ten dollars,
please understand;
Don't make him shame, for all of you come from
the same land.

As the reader can see, the emphasis was on extolling the beauty of Trinidad and Tobago in particular, and the Caribbean in general, to tourists, or telling them how beautiful they looked; to the natives, on the other hand, local tent compositions, the smuttier the better, were sung. A favourite hustling composition of the B grade hustlers, according to Superior, went thus:

Ah can't play mi instrument,
Since Ah marry Millicent (repeat).
In the night she won't leave me alone;
She only want to play the saxophone.
She say she like to play the tune,
It reminds her of the honeymoon.
Chorus: Saxophone - leave the saxophone.
            Saxophone - girl, you blowing without a tone.
            Saxophone - baby, you can't make the note.
            Saxophone - darling, take care you hang your throat.

Last night's behaviour was the worse;
Millicent determined to rehearse.
Ah lay down trying to relax,
Inside she mouth she put the sax.
Ahoula-houla-hou she start to blow;
All how Ah try to tell she: no.
The reeds went soft and out of tone
You know she leave me with a broken saxophone.

Chorus: Saxophone - leave the saxophone.
Saxophone - girl, you blowing without a tone ...[f]

Most persons are quick to condemn the hustlers as being no-good drunks, pimps, touts and women runners. Yet it must be realized that to qualify as a hustler demands a good memory, quickness of thought, and knowledge of the audience, for different audiences demand a different variety of songs. It is not uncommon for tourists to ask for old compositions such as "Brown Skin Gal," "Rum and Coca-Cola," "Day-Oh" or their favourite "Yellow Bird." Besides, the hustler most times had to learn to play an instrument, usually the guitar, and although seemingly happy (he tells foreigners how beautiful they are or how shapely they look with their blond hair and straight nose), he is in fact, to use a local term, "mamaguying" them, aiming to rape them of a few coins, in return for a few choice, well-rehearsed lines. For some hustlers, the tourist represents the slave master, the unrepentant capitalist, the forces of oppression that have kept him down, the trading stabs that have bled his country and the colonial exploitation that has placed him in his miserable condition. For these, hustling is, as it were, a form of passive resistance.[6]

It was the thinking of the society's middle and upper classes in the late 1940s and early 1950s especially, that calypsonians were obscene, degrading, opponents of the political system, and, as such, many prominent persons called for a ban on them. In addition,

---

[f] The calypso itself was composed by the Lord Kitchener and was a favourite in the calypso tent.

many felt that calypsonians were carrying Trinidad and Tobago into a morass of dirt, smut and muck and openly poured shame on them as scandal mongers and trouble makers. Lord Superior not only testifies to this but has been a victim of the society's values then. To underscore the point for the reader, in 1943, the police regarded as irreverent Pharaoh's song "The Governor Tall, Tall, Tall" and demanded a copy of the words from Atilla, then manager of the Victory Tent.[7] In 1950, the Growling Tiger's two songs "Leggo the Dog" and "Daniel Must Go" caused an upheaval in upper class society and many articles were written in the press calling for a ban on the songs, and describing them as "vile, cowardly, scurrilous."[8] All that these songs were doing was commenting on the unfairness of the society in terms of the poor treatment meted out to the lower class, as opposed to the high esteem in which the upper class members were held.. The Trinidad Guardian editorials of February 8th, 9th and 10th and letters to the press on the same dates all denounced the singers and their songs.[9] Tiger's song "Daniel Must Go" landed him in court, and although the case was dismissed, one can see how clearly out of touch the upper class was with the lower class; one can see how the Trinidad Guardian championed the cause of the upper uppers; one can see how the real political and social issues of the period were misunderstood; one can see how the calypsonians suffered. A typical suggestion was:

> Let's cleanse the calypso of its dirt and muck and let us insist on its staying cleansed; for, after all, if we allow the songsters to continue with their more offensive and abominable productions, it means that we are adopting a complacent attitude in allowing them to think that our morals are so low as not to be offended by egregious insults to our intelligence and ethics.[10]

163

Superior then, was caught up in this network of stupidity; he was trapped in the campaign by the privileged classes who sought through the Police Force, the courts and the white-owned Trinidad Guardian, to restrain the growing criticism of the poor down-trodden masses whose rights they had oppressed for more than a century. In 1955, while hustling with Sparrow, Intruder and Striker on the Gaza strip,[g] the quartet was raided by the police. Quick-footed Sparrow, then in the prime of his youth got away, but Intruder, Striker and himself were arrested and charged with "molesting the passers-by" (white personnel), and "obstructing the free passage way." After spending two days in prison, they were fined five dollars ($5.00) or seven days in prison. From the cash gained from hustling, they promptly paid.

Superior has always regarded his fellow calypsonians as nothing short of genius. He loves them best when they attack the privileged class. He is ready to die for them, especially when they understand their role, that of "mirroring the evils under which the poor people live." Indeed, he sprang into the limelight championing the cause of his fellow calypsonians. It was 1957 that the country at large took notice of this guitar-strumming lad from Rio Claro; he had left his job as an apprentice carpenter to join the singing gang of underprivileged men at the youthful age of sixteen, and at age twenty he was attacking in song those who sought to esteem the white carnival queen and denigrate the calypso king. In a calypso entitled "Brass Crown" he told the affluent upper uppers:

> A calypsonian
> Needs more consideration (repeat).
> Take the Carnival Queen competition
> And the King Calypsonian;
> The Queen getting everything,
> And nothing goes to the Calypso King.

---

[g] An area on Wrightson Road, Port-of-Spain that was heavily patronized by American soldiers,Whites and upperclass society who frequented the area in search of "high-cultured" prostitutes.

Dr. Hollis "Chalkdust" Liverpool

Chorus: She gets refrigerators,
Machines, radios and even motor cars;
Sometimes a Simmons bed;
And all the king gets is a Brass Crown on his head.

Supie sang that calypso because while the entire nation was praising Sparrow for his calypso "Jean and Dinah" and dancing to the sweet refrain of the melody, he having won the Calypso King and Road March competitions with it in 1956, the authorities only awarded Sparrow with fifty ($50) and a brass crown.

During the Lenten season, it was customary for radio stations to stop playing calypso. Those who controlled the stations felt that Lent was a time of penance to make up for the sins committed against God, especially the sins of the flesh that occurred during the carnival. This non-playing of calypso lasted up to the late 1970s when singers like Kitch, in song, began to call upon the authorities to lift the ban. As early as 1970, Kitch sang a calypso entitled "Kitch have No Season," in which he explained that he was planning to dance and sing during Lent. But Superior may have been the first to do so, he having sung in 1959 a calypso in which he begged the news media and the religious prudes to "Play Calypso in Lent."

In 1973, he condemned steelbandsmen for only playing tunes composed by Sparrow and Kitchener on Carnival days, whilst so many beautiful compositions of other singers "waste their sweetness in the desert air." Sparrow and Kitch had in fact shared the road march prize between them since 1963, and this caused Superior to sing:

I'm begging all dem steelbands,
Combos and musicians,
Remedy the Road March competition.
Yes, for all calypsonians
Not just this two man domination.

Chorus: If Supie tune sweet - play it.
   If it got the beat - play it.
   If the melody strange - play it.
   With good chord change.
   I'm begging steelbands to stop and take my tip:
   It's time to stop this Road March dictatorship.
   Ah say fellas stop this Road March dictatorship.

Again in 1973, he denounced the judges for being biased in their adjudication and for their lack of objectivity. Supie felt then that the calypso should be judged thus:

   Give forty points if a song have good lyrics.
   Give thirty points if the tune is properly fit.
   Give twenty points for rendition;
   Ten for the crowd appreciation.
   Tell every judge in the land,
   That's how to judge a competition.

Up to 1972, the calypso was judged thus: Lyrics - 40 points; melody - 30 points; originality - 10 points; presentation - 10; and rendition 10 points for a total of 100 points. The Original Young Brigade (OYB) represented by Sparrow and his tent manager, in a meeting with the Carnival Development Committee chaired then by Mr. Ivan Williams, raised the point that melody and lyrics should be equally weighted, and that it was important that the CDC seek to "make Carnival more musical."[h] In keeping with the wishes of the OYB, the criteria for judging the Calypso King competition was changed in 1972 to read thus: Lyrics - 30 points; melody - 30 points; rendition - 15 points; originality - 15 points; and presentation - 10 points.[11] In 1976, with the participation of so many female singers in the National Calypso Competition, the name Calypso King was changed to Calypso Monarch. Chalkdust was therefore the first person to win that award in Trinidad and Tobago.

---

[h] As Secretary of the Calypsonians' Assoc. then, I represented the Association at the meeting.

Dr. Hollis "Chalkdust" Liverpool

In order to uplift the art, to which Supie is dedicated, he has on many occasions called upon his fellow singers to "pull up their socks," and, like King Short Shirt of Antigua, he has denounced the "calypso singers," a term he uses to denote those singers who do not compose, as being men and women who are unworthy of the name calypsonian. It is truthful to say that in keeping with the tradition of calypso, the singers of calypso tunes are expected to compose them. Supie's song composed in the 1950s goes thus:

> Too many mock calypsonians
> Making fame in this island.
> It have some mock calypsonians
> Going around in this island.
> Always bad talking Sparrow,
> Sometimes Superior, sometimes Melo,
> But they will not try to compose.
> What is wrong with dey brain, well the devil knows.

> Chorus: They always know who can sing; who cannot sing;
> And who is the calypso king.
> But take it from me!
> Carnival Committee
> Encouraging them in this thing.
> By putting them in competition
> To sing people compositions,
> Leaving out real calypsonians.
> But the day that Nelson Caton and Rocky
> McCollin dead
> These imposters go beg their bread.

In the history of calypso, there have always been many composers, too numerous to mention, who, perhaps unable to sing, prefer to compose for others; there are others who can sing but they prefer to sell their compositions for a fair price. It is a well-known fact that sociologist Pete Simon helped many, including Sniper, with their tunes; Reginald "Piggy" Joseph composed many tunes including "No Money no Love" for Sparrow; Winston "Joker" DeVignes composed many tunes for Baron, Sparrow, King Austin, Crazy and Trini; the Mighty Bomber has turned out a large number of singers, including Singing Francine, with his songs; Calypsonian Merchant made a living out of his compositions for Designer, Explainer et al; Rocky McCollin composed most of the hits sung by Nap Hepburn; Nelson Caton composed for Prince Valiant; Christophe Grant and the Mighty Crusoe composed a fair majority of the songs sung by Singing Sandra; calypsonian G.B. has composed for many including David Rudder and Prowler; calypsonian DeLamo has composed for Baron et al; calypsonian Kurt Allen has assisted Denyse Plummer; Duke assisted Lord Nelson with a few of his compositions and the Mighty Penguin has composed for many including Explainer.

An outstanding event in Superior's life, he claims, was in Madison Square Garden in 1960, when thousands of patrons flocked to hear Sparrow. He was overjoyed almost to the point of tears, to see how the calypso from its humble beginning had spread overseas. Supie sees the calypso and the calypsonian as the initiator of many policies, for after singing the "Brass Crown" in 1957, the Government set up the Carnival Development Committee replacing the Guardian which was responsible for staging carnival competitions. Even as early as 1957, the very year his song was recorded, the first calypso king, Lord Pretender, received one thousand dollars ($1,000.00) when the previous year Sparrow got fifty. It is interesting to note, however, that up to 1976 when I won the Calypso Monarch competition, the prize was still one thousand dollars.

Dr. Hollis "Chalkdust" Liverpool

In terms of calypsonians being the initiator of policies, Superior is right for Attila, Tiger, Destroyer and Spoiler mirrored many of the feelings of the lower classes and certainly were initiators of change, both political and social. Attila himself mentioned that:

> As time rolled on, we find with the riot of 1903 that calypso was not only a form of amusement but a decided and potent factor in shaping public opinion, one song actually causing a public outburst at the alleged brutality of a member of the Constabulary which, eventually in its repercussion, caused investigations to be instituted and the alleged murderer brought to trial. He was subsequently found not guilty and was discharged. The song went like this:

> Lawyers of the Bar we must form a deputation.
> Jurors of the land, not to acquit Holder;
> We must try him for murder.
> If he escapes the rope, he must die in Carrera.[i]
> Perry waiting with the rope
> To break his manima.[12]

Spoiler in the early 1950s, it must be remembered, whether he was being imaginative or not, called upon the authorities to establish a woman police unit. Today, beginning from about 1959, women police carry out duties all over the country. Around 1988, police calypsonian, "The Supreme Happiness," called on the Police Commissioner to stop the eurocentric practice of having policemen in short pants. Soon after singing his song, the reformation was made.

Contrary to many beliefs, Superior was quick to point out that in looking at changes in the art form, Sparrow was not responsible for singing the eight line modern chorus, for he himself had heard Terror and King Radio singing same in the early 1950s.

---

[i] An off-shore prison in North Trinidad.

Dr. Hollis "Chalkdust" Liverpool

One of Sparrow's great contributions that few may know, however, is that he was partly responsible for calypsonians having their melodies musically dictated so that a band can accompany them. In 1955 or thereabout, musician Roderick Borde informed me that at the request of Sparrow especially, he began the task of writing music for the singers at the OYB calypso tent.[13]   Roderick, now deceased, for his feat was instituted into the Sunshine Awards Calypso Hall of Fame in 1993.

In comparing the calypso before 1956-the year of the calypso craze-and after, Superior sees a decline in lyrics, with the emphasis today on leudness.

> A calypso stage was a dignified thing and even if smutty songs were sung, there was beauty in it. It was a common thing to hear calypsonians in the early 1950s say: I have composed four songs for the year, two tent songs and two Theatre songs. Smut was for the Theatre, whilst philosophy was for the tent.

The point needs no further explanation, for Superior puts it so well.

Supie spoke often of the calypsonian's form of dress, always pointing out that, before a singer went on stage, he had to be nattily attired. "Sometimes we kept a special jacket for those who had no clothes." The point was re-echoed to me many times by singers Kitch, Spitfire and Cypher. They pointed out to me that one of the reasons why a wooden barrier was built across the stage, was that if a jacket did not fit the singer, the crowd nevertheless hardly ever noticed. The use of a jacket, the reader would realize, was all part of the calypsonian's striving to attain a higher class in society. Jacket men, whether black or white in the era up to the 1960s, demonstrated to society that they were an educated breed, and the African jacket men strove too, by the language they demonstrated, to prove to the lower class that they were a rung above them on the ladder of social stratification and esteem.

Superior's view of the calypsonian's dress is traditional and goes back to the chantuelle days of 1900 - 1920 when singers attired themselves so well. A 1903 description of Norman Le Blanc, chantuelle of the White Rose band, carried this commentary in the Trinidad Gazette of February 26th:

> The cutaway jacket - short, tight-fitting knicker bockers made of white flowered silk elaborately and profusely trimmed with imitation ermine and gimp... Breast of Jacket - sparkled from sequins sewn in an artistic ground of gold and silver braids studded down the center with a double row of silver buttons...cloak of Japan silk bordered with imitation ermine flowed from his shoulders to the ground.[14]

In the early 1950s, according to Brother Superior, "the tent was still a place for Whites. It was poor entertaining the rich." Even the manager and financiers were from the rich upper class. "I remember that there used to be one black woman in the audience - Miss Audrey Jeffers." Audrey Jeffers was a nominated member of the Legislative Council of Trinidad and Tobago from 1946 to 1955, and as a notable African woman in the community she was even appointed honorary consul for the state of Liberia in Trinidad. In 1931, she founded the Coterie of Social Workers organization which aimed at uplifting working-class women in the society in terms of gaining for them employment, better conditions of labour, and establishing breakfast sheds to feed their underprivileged and generally poor offspring. Her organization, however, was neither very strong nor vocal on the political rights of women especially at a time when a fairly large percentage of women were not eligible to vote. But Audrey Jeffers' home was situated in St. Clair, a district that is still regarded as being the site of the upper class, and for all intents and purposes, Audrey mixed with the upper uppers. So close was she to the Governor and his friends, that she was nominated by him to serve on the highest constitutional assembly of the land, and thus visited the tent many a time as part of the Governor's entourage. As such, she may not have been a lover of the calypso, but having identified with the privileged minority, it was fashionable for the Governor and his party to visit the tents. Professor Gordon Rohlehr understood this when he wrote:

> Albert Gomes understood the real nature of politics in Trinidad, better than a person like Audrey Jeffers, who was against Universal Adult Suffrage. Ironically, in outlook she was much nearer to the White ruling classes than he, though in complexion and wealth, he was nearer to the Whites than she.[15]

It is a well-known fact too, that many Governors and government officials and, later, Prime Ministers and Ministers of Government visited the calypso tents to link with the people socially and politically, or otherwise to get a feel of how the electorate was thinking. Since calypsonians to a fair degree of accuracy, record the feelings of the general populace, it is only fair that the Government can tap into this rich arena of the people's social site and come away either nourished or bitter, but at least educated. Every Prime Minister that I have known, from Williams in 1962 to Manning in 2003 have ensured that they and their party visit the tents, especially when they are of the opinion that the calypsoes being sung are in their favour. In year 2002, especially, Prime Minister Manning who regularly attends the semi-finals of the Calypso Monarch Competition in San Fernando, made it his business to ascend the main stage and join the singer Sugar Aloes to sing the calypso entitled "Jubilation Time" that underscored the victory of the party in the elections of that year. Aloes, needless to say, went on to win the competition.

In terms of privileged, upper-class visitors to the calypso tent, Superior remembers Sir H.O.B. Wooding, the noted lawyer who became Chief Justice and Chancellor of the University of the West Indies, "as being snobbish to calypsonians when he (Wooding) was among his White friends, whilst Eric Williams in 1955 and 1956 used to encourage them to sing."

Eric used to say: "Let me hear the people's mouthpiece," and, Superior continues, "You sure to get a twenty dollars from him." H.O.B.Wooding, although he defended the Growling Tiger in 1950, was perhaps of the same mettle as Audrey Jeffers, black outside and white inside, whereas Eric Williams, then aspiring to oust Albert Gomes from the legislature, knew that calypsonians could bring him the feelings of the electorate. I had the privilege, as Secretary of the Calypsonians' Association of hosting Eric Williams at the Calypso Theatre in 1969 and 1970, and he would seek my attention to explain him every line in the calypsoes that he didn't understand or was made unintelligible by the sound system, so interested in calypso was he.

Superior bears testimony too to the fact that in the early 1950s, calypsonians in the calypso tent were classified as contracted men, percentage men and helpers. The contracted men were the big boys like Sir Galba, Lord Melody and Pretender. Percentage men like Striker, Nap Hepburn and Intruder received sixty percent (60%) of the contracted men's pay, whilst the helpers were paid as the contracted men saw fit. In the early 1950s, the prices of admission for three different areas of seating were one dollar, one dollar and seventy-five cents, and fifty cents respectively. Singers were paid nightly and Superior believes that, "were this system in operation today,[j] calypsonians would have been better off financially." One tends to agree with Superior for in 1973, the Original Young Brigade raked in an average of fifteen thousand ($15,000) weekly in revenue and yet Supie's highest pay as a Grade B singer was seventy-five ($75.00) dollars, whilst he received as little as fifty ($50.00) dollars. In the year 2002, top singers at Kitchy's Revue, Klassic Rouso and the Calypso Theatre raked in, on an average, six thousand dollars ($6,000.00) weekly.

Superior sees as impediments in the march of progress, the fact that Trinidadians themselves, do not give the singer his due, whilst "nothing is being done at governmental level, that is the C.D.C. and the Tourist Board to help the damned thing."

---

[j] I interviewed him in the 1970s.

The Governmental bodies do give assistance to the calypsonians. In fact, under the Prime ministership of Basdeo Panday, the then Minister of Culture, Dr. Daphne Phillips, initiated a system whereby TUCO, the calypsonians' body, was given the princely sum of two million dollars in 1997 to run its affairs. Formerly, the C.D.C. and later the N.C.C. was given the grant to run the business of carnival. What Superior therefore means is that although Trinidadians support the calypso more than any other art form, yet the calypsonian as a man or a woman is not treated with the dignity and respect that ought to go hand in hand with his or her contribution. For example, he says, "there are persons who still want calypsonians to perform voluntarily or for little financial reward." One of the songs most favoured by calypso fans in the late 1980s was one by calypsonian Rio; it was entitled "The Free Show Calypso King." In the calypso, Rio complained that patrons were seeking him out all the time to sing for them in concerts and shows for no pay, but when money was involved, they, the same patrons, sought other well-known and famous singers.

Superior himself castigated his fellow Trinidadians for wanting calypsonians to always sing free of charge at parties. According to Supie, "dentists, doctors, nurses and other professional men never work for charity, yet calypsonians are expected to sing for rum." He is of the opinion too, that calypso can literally "take over" the whole Western English-Speaking world in a few years, but calypsonians have got to be prepared first to sing on more world issues, so that foreigners "could appreciate our cultural traits." He himself told me in 1973: "if I get the break, in five years I can shake up calypso by starting a radio station, a calypso magazine, a record producing company; employing expert public relations personnel; and making a film." Thus far in 2003, Supie has started a radio station, produced some of his own records and has, in conjunction with a film company from the U.S. co-produced a film on calypso.

Indeed, Superior's whole life(his thinking, his love for the art form, his past experiences and his sufferings as a calypsonian)is beautifully summed up in his calypso entitled "Play Calypso in **Lent.**"

Chorus: I think they should play calypso in Lent
For its lovers' entertainment.
If a song is immoral
Then don't play it no time at all.
In Lent they will play
Rock n'Roll, Meringue and Mambo;
And some of these songs more vulgar than calypso.

Verse: Close your eyes ten minutes or so
And tune in your radio.
You wouldn't know if you in Cuba
Puerto Rico or Venezuela,
Because they only playing Spanish
When most of the people here speak English.
What bothers me is that I don't know
If them Spaniards cussing on the radio.

ENDNOTES

[1] Smith, Ulric. Personal Conversation, Diego Martin, December 1986.
[2] Francisco, Slinger. Personal Conversation at Calypso Rehearsal. Brooklyn, N.Y. December 12th 2002.
[3] Joseph, Randolph (Caresser). Personal Conversation. P.O.S., August 1972.
[4] Francisco, Slinger. The Outcast. National: NLP 4199. 1963.
[5] Farrell, Alric (Pretender). Personal Communication. P.O.S., August, 1967.
[6] McFarlane, Mervyn. Personal Communication. P.O.S., August, 1970.
[7] Trinidad Guardian. January 10th 1948.
[8] Rohlehr, Gordon. "Political Calypsoes." Unpublished Typescript, November 1970, 9.
[9] Rohlehr, Gordon. Ibid.
[10] Trinidad Guardian. February 16th, 1950. 11.
[11] Minutes of Meeting of the Carnival Development Committee, February 1972.

Dr. Hollis "Chalkdust" Liverpool

[12] Quevedo, Raymond (Attila). <u>The Growth and Improvement of Calypso</u>. P.O.S.:   The Author, 1947), 13.

[13] Borde, Roderick. Personal Conversation. Tortola, B.V.I., August 1989.

[14] <u>Trinidad Gazette</u>. February 26th, 1903.

[15] Rohlehr, Gordon. Political Calypsos. Nov. 1970, 9.

Indian Prince–Pioneer East Indian in Calypso

Chapter 8

Daniel Emmanuel Jardine Gilchrist (Young Killer, 1933-2001).

It's not the world that confusing;
Is the people and the names that
they using......
And a black woman name
Miss White;
And a White woman
name Miss Black;
And a brown-skinned woman name Green
Is the funniest thing I've seen.
And a black-head woman name Redhead
Make me laugh till Ah nearly dead.
And a brown-skinned woman name Grey;
That is what have the whole world confuse today.
(The Author - Personal Collection of lyrics).

I remember with pride 1968 when the cast of the Calypso Theatre was discussing who would lead us for the calypso season and Lord Observer, who was the then President of the Calypsonians' Association nominated Daniel Emmanuel Jardine Gilchrist, known in the calypso world as the Young Killer. I didn't vote or comment for I knew little of him then. However, I had seen a clipping of him performing at Expo 67 in Montreal, Canada, and said to myself that with such charisma as that which he displayed on the screen, he ought to make a fit and proper leader of the tent. At the time, the Calypsonians' Association had taken the decision that all members performing at the Theatre had to pass the audition, yet here was the cast agreeing that Young Killer be allowed to sing and lead us without passing or participating in the audition of 1968. Such was the magnificence and pulling-power of the Young Killer, there being an elder Killer of the 1940-1950 era.

During that season of 1968, I would meet and chat often with Killer, for I was anxious to learn of calypso's art and history. As such, I fell in love with his confident personality on and off stage, especially when he announced to the world that I was his calypso horse for the Calypso King[a] title that year, and that he was the official jockey. That year, the tables of championship hopes kept turning and turning. Some were saying that Young Sniper was unbeatable with his "Productivity;" the next week the newspapers predicted that Duke with "What is calypso" would overturn the tables. "No, no," cried the senior calypsonians, "there is none to upstage the tried and trusted Cypher, the Clown Prince of Calypso." Cypher had won the title in 1967. All the while, however, the Young Killer was reminding them that whoever wins have to first defeat his horse, the Mighty Chalkdust.

As the Master of Ceremonies at the Calypso Theatre in 1968, Killer, backstage before the show started, called on several calypsonians to do the honour of opening the programme; all, including Viper, Gibraltar, Viking, Tiny Terror and Lord Coffee turned him down. No one wanted to be the opener; no one wanted to face the new ball. Killer turned to me therefore and said: "Chalkdust, let's pray." He held my hand and we both prayed asking God to bless our efforts to entertain. Then he said: "Get dress; you're the opener; we go teach dem big kaisonians a lesson." Killer knew that I had good songs, he having heard me at the audition at the CDC's headquarters on Sackville street in the presence of the Prime Minister, Dr. Eric Williams. He therefore knew that my songs would go down well and that not only would I be a good opener, but that the fellas coming behind me would be hard pressed to keep up with the standard that I would set.

---

[a] The title was changed to Calypso Monarch in 1976.

Dr. Hollis "Chalkdust" Liverpool

So say; so done. I went on stage and rendered the immortal "Brain Drain" to thunderous applause and lots of encores from the audience that included the members of the West Indies Cricket team, officials from the Prime Minister's office, permanent secretaries and members of the diplomatic corps. I can't recall who followed me, but I remember Killer having to give several jokes to make up time and allow the poor unprepared guy to get dressed to face the highly-charged audience. At half-time (intermission), the cast, including teacher Carlton Scott,[b] was introduced to the specially-invited (VIP's) guests. When asked by Lord Observer, the then President of the Calypsonians' Association, what they thought of the first half of the programme, all mentioned that they had liked my offering the best, and fast bowler Wes Hall hinted that I would become a great calypsonian in the future.

At the Calypso King competition that year, Duke (Kelvin Pope) eventually won the championship and did so for the next three years. He is therefore the only calypsonian to have won the crown for four consecutive years, 1968 to 1971. The 1968 competition was one whereby it was most difficult to separate the six finalists: Duke, Chalkdust, Rose, Baker, Cypher, Shorty and Sniper.

In those days, the Master of Ceremonies (MC) decided the order of appearance of the singers; he knew the calypsoes and the calypsonians and he had the unenviable task of so mixing the singers that the audience would at no time get bored. In addition, the singers had great confidence in the MC's who were looked upon as men filled with knowledge of the art form. Accordingly, Young Killer at the Calypso Theatre, Mighty Stalin (now Black Stalin) and Nap Hepburn at the Revue, Lord Melody at the OYB, Robin who conducted his show at the Hilton Hotel, and calypsonians Impressor and Alligator at the Southern Brigade in South Trinidad were held in great esteem by calypsonians. In 1974, when Regal was formed by Duke, Supie and me, the Mighty Composer, who

---

[b] Carlton Scott sang as the "Stylist" at the Calypso Theatre in 1968 and was a finalist in the Buy Local competition promoted by the PNM in 1967.

served as the Emcee (MC), was given a free hand to manage the programme. Composer decided where and when a singer appeared on the programme. He decided when Duke, Supie and I would sing. In addition, Composer assisted young singers with their offerings, changing a line here and there for better effect. The power of the Emcee (MC) can be gleaned from the comments of Stalin at Kitchener's Revue. Stalin noted:

> I put together the entire calypso program not only in Trinidad and Tobago but I went down the islands as emcee. From'72 I run all the auditions; I put who I want on the cast. I had a first-hand view and being able to be first-hand in the thing…I was emcee the first time Explainer sing in a tent; I was emcee the first time Maestro sing in a tent…Merchant, Mudada. I had the opportunity to see the men in auditions, to put them on stage. I was emcee when Shadow win Road March. Being able to put on the Road March year after year, I was able to look at every individual calypsonian whether Kitch or Sparrow…Kitchener leave it up to me to run the auditions, to run the show. Kitchener leave it to me to tell him when he going on and these things. In a management position at the Revue I was able to look at kaiso from over it instead of inside it.[1]

An emcee had so much power that he was almost a feared man. It is a fact that the calypso future of many a young singer lay in the sometime-shaky hands of emcees. Valentino and Power informed me that in their early days, Melody used to call upon the crowd to "bawl down" a singer. Of course, it was all in good fun, especially if the singer seemed more a comedian than a calypsonian. I personally witnessed Melody calling upon the crowd from the sidelines at the Naparima Bowl in the early 70s to "bawl down"[c] calypsonian Scraper. To add to the humour, Melody, as emcee, would call back Scraper, and then to the delight of the audience, ask them to boo him again. Poor Scraper, not knowing the

---

[c] Showing contempt for a singer on stage using catcalls, whistles and stamping of the feet. Crowds at Skinner Park in San Fernando by 1990 began to use toilet paper.

Dr. Hollis "Chalkdust" Liverpool

joke, went back on stage about four times, until calypsonian Harmony begged him to stop making a fool of himself. At one time at the Regal, singer Rex West refused to go on stage complaining to me that "Composer does incite the crowd to "bawl me down." Valentino confided to me that the way Melody used to put him on stage, if he wasn't good, the audience would have certainly booed him. Melo would say: "It have a fella who call hiself Valentino. If allyuh like him, gie him a clap. If allyuh aint like him? well!" And Melo would give the audience the thumb down sign.[2] I saw Kitch in St. Croix in the 70s refusing to talk to Stalin one morning because he didn't approve of the manner used by Stalin to bring him on stage the night before. Kitch intoned: "Chalkie, you aint hear how he put me on last night?" In a most subdued voice Kitch continued: "When it was time for me, he say ladies and gentlemen, the Lord Kitchener." Then Kitch raised his voice loudly and bellowed: "And when Sparrow come on, he bawling out Ladieees and Gentlemeeeen, the Mighteee, the Mighteeeee, Sparroooooooooow." Although Stalin was certainly innocent, Kitch reacted, for he knew the power that an emcee wielded over the audience. Today, most emcees are simply comedians who have nothing to do with management or control of the programme.

In the 1960s also, when a singer was given an encore, he was expected to go onstage and render a verse of his song; usually the audience looked forward to hearing the last verse. I was encored so much in 1968, that I changed the expectations of the audience and started giving them a new verse.[d] These new verses I composed backstage before the show and that practice of mine led to the breaking of the tradition where a singer was expected to sing the last verse. When singers after me didn't come up with a new verse and chorus such as I had done, the audience showed their disapproval by booing. Accordingly, new verses and choruses had

---

[d] Calypsonian Watchman at Spektakula in the 1990s was very prolific at composing new verses to songs every time he was encored.

to be sung when encores were obtained. Today, a new verse and chorus, after an encore, is accepted as the norm.

In terms of opening the calypso tent programme, today's singers have the same attitude as those in 1968; they do not like to be the first to be exposed to the audience. They fear that the microphone levels are not yet standardized or well set by the technicians and that they are therefore the guinea pigs in the audio experiment. Worse yet, the crowd at the beginning of any show is always small; calypsonians like to sing or sing best when the crowd is large and tuned up, the vociferous receptiveness of the large audience being a test to know if their songs are good or not. Moreover, it has become the cultural norm for the more experienced singers to sing late on the programme and the audience normally regards the lateness of a singer's appearance as an indication of his esteem on the card. The more established singers too, are allowed to sing more songs on a programme than the lesser established ones. All such appearances on the show's agenda have become over the years part of the cultural tradition with regard to calypso and its method of performance.

In 1968, Killer and I opened the tent with a prayer. Since then, I have always prayed before I go on a stage, offering up my performance to God to thank him for the gifts which he has bestowed on me and others, and to ensure that he stays beside me during my performance. I pray too, in reparation for my sins, the sins committed by calypsonians and the sins which calypsonians by their art have caused others to commit. At Spektakula Forum which began in 1980, stage manager Lennox Toussaint initiated a moment of prayer nightly. Before the show started, all singers, tent workers and musicians would bow heads, join hands and offer a word of prayer to the Almighty in the hope that their creative efforts would be truly blessed. It was a most beautiful scene to see the tent sweeper joining hands in prayer with the calypso monarch and the show producer, thereby underscoring the importance of each person to the tent's overall mission, that of performing the calypso to the best of one's ability and thereby fully entertaining the audience.

Young Killer was born in Port-of-Spain on November 20, 1933, the son of Agartha and Wilfred Emmanuel Gilchrist. He was educated at Success Village and Nelson Street Boys primary schools. At age 17 when he left school, like other young men of his community then, calypso was already in his blood. As a young man, besides calypso, scouting, boxing, painting and learning to play the guitar were his hobbies. He was so taken up with his guitar that "while other young men slept with women, I slept with my guitar." This is certainly true for the editor of the <u>Trinidad Chronicle</u> recorded that Killer "loved (calypso) more than food."[3] It was this guitar that allowed him to practise the musical fundamentals of calypso; it was this guitar that helped him to master the art of hustling in calypso and allowed him to earn a living; it was this guitar that served him up to his dying days in New York. In Young Killer's day, most calypsonians were accomplished guitarists; they learnt the art of guitar playing even before they made their debut on the stage. Killer recalled great guitarists like Viking, Wonder, Robin, Intruder, Panther, Superior, Jaguar, Caresser (the Younger), and Relator to name a few.

His nephew Gil Figaro recounts young Killer's debut:

> The first time Uncle Fats[e] sang on stage was in the company of two boys with whom, in later years, he would share a friendship which lasted up to the time he left this world. Those boys would later become known as the Mighty Sparrow and Lord Blakie. Uncle Fats himself was then a young boy scout who had been encouraged to enter a

---

[e] Killer in New York became very fat. At one stage he was a hefty 469 pounds, yet he possessed such a sense of humour that he made fun of his weight and told his nephews and nieces that he was Uncle Fats. He was thus so called.

Dr. Hollis "Chalkdust" Liverpool

singing competition. He placed third, with Sparrow winning first prize and the young Lord Blakie capturing second place. Interestingly enough, he did not initially pursue the stage as a performer. In his early years, he was more interested in writing than in singing calypsoes, and in fact he wrote many songs for a great number of well-known calypsonians.[4]

Killer, however, informed me that in 1955, one of his friends who hailed from Fyzabad informed him that one Dan, a calypsonian from the Southland had died, and that the calypso body in South was looking for a replacement. The newspaper at the time recorded his debut thus:

"The Young Killer's eyes sparkled as the idea revolved in his head. The 1956 calypso season was to open in a few months time, so without much ado, he dropped paint brushes, packed up and left for San Fernando. Sure enough the manager of the tent gave him an audition and, pleased with what he heard, he decided to let him fill the gap.[5]

Young Killer said that he started his career in South Trinidad in 1956 with the Southern Brigade tent, where he performed his "pedal pushers" calypso among stalwarts such as Impressor, Alligator, Syncopator, Ambassador, Clipper, Sad Sack and Power. The "pedal pushers" was a new pants craze in Trinidad then, and so Killer's song was particularly timely and welcomed by all. The chorus goes thus:

The girls in town nowadays they wearing these
tight, tight pants,
And if you catch dem at night time friends, bet your
life you have no chance.
So listen carefully to what the Young Killer will now say:
They should only wear these tight, tight pants on
Carnival day.

Management, according to Killer, paid him nine (9) dollars weekly and paid the other singers like Duke thirteen (13) dollars. When he asked the reason for being paid less, Duke informed him that as a newcomer he was put in class B. At the time Duke was in class A. Killer said that he informed Duke there and then that he was going in to Port-of-Spain. "If I have to be a B class singer, let it be under Pretender and Melody in the city of Port-of-Spain." He therefore came to Port-of-Spain in 1957 and joined the Young Brigade Calypso tent then held at the Good Samaritan Hall, on Duke Street, under the management of Mr. Sam Bodie. In Port-of-Spain, Melody, the MC, put him on stage and he was an instant hit. In fact, like calypsonian Syncopator in 1956, he was a finalist for the Calypso King competition in 1957. That Syncopator from the Southland could reach the finals of the competition, testifies to the high standard of calypso that emanated from the southern-based singers.

1957 was a most successful year for Killer seeing that he reached the finals of the Calypso King contest. His other calypso songs for that year were: "German Mopsies," "Thelma Haynes" and "Maintenance." His fertile brain therefore remembered that the other finalists were Pretender who won with "Que Sera Sera;" Fighter with "Why B.G. don't want to Federate" and "Animal Beauty Contest;" Spitfire, singing "Royal Romance" and "Corporal Leo;" Mighty Striker; and Lord Coffee with his "Unlucky Me." It was the year too, when Sparrow and a number of calypsonians boycotted the C.D.C competition on the grounds that the prize for the Calypso King was far too small in comparison with the blue - eyed Carnival Queen, Sparrow chiming "who want to go could go if they want, but me aint going no way."[f] As such, in another Calypso King contest held at the Globe cinema in Port-of-Spain, Sparrow placed first with his "Carnival Boycott;" Melody was second with "The Creature from the Black Lagoon;" and Spoiler was third with "Himself told Himself" a tune about a magistrate trying his own case. Killer recalled that in 1957 too, there were other great songs such as "Jacob from Panama" by Christo;

---

[f] Meaning "no where."

Dr. Hollis "Chalkdust" Liverpool

"Advantage" by Superior; "Shaver man" and "Election Bacchanal" by Cypher; "The Keskidee Bird" by Dictator; "The Lying Competition" by Eisenhower; and "The Naughty Boy" by Chang Kai Shiek.

In 1958, Young Killer again was in the limelight singing "Emelda's Nightmare" at the Senior Brigade located at 50 Park Street and managed by Mr. Henry Clarke. There, he shared the stage with Pretender, Small Island Pride, Viper, Striker, Wrangler, Director, Protector and Bomber. He recalled that the Young Brigade at Good Samaritan Hall on Duke Street was comprised of Melody, Sparrow, Spitfire, Cypher, Commander, and Viking, while Victory Tent on St. Vincent Street had singers such as Attila, Lord and Lady Iere, Skipper, Superior, Tiny Terror, Blakie, Destructor, Spider, Sir Gallagher and King Radio. He recalled then singing songs such as "Shango Experience," "Mutt and Jeff," "Women's Mistake," and "The Negro Downfall."

Asked to describe the 1959 and 1960 calypso seasons, Killer remembered that in 1959, Striker won the King contest followed by Blakie and Nap Hepburn. Striker sang: "Ban the Hula Hoop" and "West Indians versus Foreigners"; Blakie sang "Bring Back the Queen" and "Is the Mind that does Make the Man; and Nap's song was "We want back Chaguaramas." The Road March for that year was: "Gunslingers" by Caruso and Lord Smiley won the St. George Calypso Crown in Diego Martin with a calypso entitled: "The Jimmy Wilson Case." That year, 1959, according to Killer, a new tent, The Original Young Brigade, opened its doors to patrons at the Good Samaritan Hall, 106 Duke Street, Port-of-Spain. It featured Sparrow, Melody, Christo, Zebra, Fighter, Viking, Commander, Coffee, Power, Cobra, Chang Kai Shiek, Nap Hepburn and himself. The cast of the Young Brigade at the Waldorf Club on Park Street with Henry Clarke as manager comprised Spider, Distresser, Pretender, Brynner, Jaguar, Impressor, Destructor, Protector, Observer, Skylark, Surpriser and Caresser. The Senior Brigade then moved to St. Vincent Street and employed singers Cypher, Superior, Spoiler, Bomber, Wrangler, Striker, Tiger, Small Island Pride, Conqueror and Eisenhower. The Southern Brigade for that year was held at OWTU's Palm Club and there could be found singers Duke, Injector, Rock of Gibraltar, Sniper, Sad Sack, Clipper, and Indian Fighter, who Killer believes was the first East Indian to sing in a tent, and who paved the way for other East Indian singers over the years namely: Indian Prince, Hindu Prince, the Mighty Shah, the Mighty Rajah and Ricky Jai.

In 1960, because of the high standard of calypsoes, for the first time eight finalists were chosen to challenge the Mighty Striker for the Calypso King Contest. These were: Sparrow, Christo, Melody, Spoiler, Tiger, Blakie, Brynner and Small Island Pride. Sparrow eventually won with his "Ten to One is Murder" and "Mae Mae." Duke won the crown in the South from Lord Ambassador and Injector, and, like Impressor did in 1959, he proceeded to travel to the North to seek more wealth and fame. That year, Conqueror was crowned King in Princes Town and two new tents came into being: the Southern All Stars Tent in Fyzabad featuring Ambassador, Sad Sack, Scraper and Conqueror; and the Big Bamboo tent on 53 Park Street, Port-of-Spain, featuring Skipper, Inventor, Creator, Warrior, Eisenhower, Vocalist, Young Sparrow, Spitfire, Young Growler, Crooner and Chicky Chong.

Between 1957 and 1967, Killer was selected for the Calypso King contest on eight occasions, and though he never won the contest, most calypso lovers agree that Killer has been one of the foremost singers of the era. During his career which stretched into the 1970s, Killer gave to the calypso world hits such as "Is a Policeman," "Millie Small," "Report from Expo 67," "This is Carnival," "The Cry of the West Indies," "Doctor Say to Buy Local," "Old Time Calypsoes," "German Girls," "Leave Jackie Alone," "West Indians in New York," and "Air Pollution."

Because of his guitar-playing and extempo skills in particular, he was chosen to represent Trinidad and Tobago at the World's Fair in Montreal in 1967. All Trinidad and Tobago, indeed the Caribbean, hailed Young Killer for his high standard of performances at the Fair. All who saw him live or on video spoke about the excitement which he brought to the shows and of the fact that he put, by his exuberance, Trinidad and Tobago on the map of the world.

In 1965, Killer, a very charitable man both in things material as well as non-material, was instrumental in organizing the first calypso show for school children. It was held at Queen's Hall and was thoroughly enjoyed by the overflowing crowd of eager hearts. While Killer organized the first calypso show for children and continued to do so with my input in 1968 and afterwards, Wally Emmanuel, a teacher at Nelson Street Boys' R.C. School, organized, in the early 1960s, a calypso competition for schoolboys of that hallowed institute. As a teacher myself at Nelson Street Boys, I continued the great tradition of teaching the students the art of composing and at the same time holding calypso competitions from 1966 to 1973. In fact, so backward were the Ministry of Education officials, that I was summoned in 1968 to the office of the permanent secretary who promptly asked me boldly and loudly: "who gave you permission to organize calypso in the school?" My response was just as bold: "I need no permission to organize calypso in the school." To Nelson Street Boys' R.C. school would annually come superstars in the calypso world such as Black Stalin, Jaguar, Young Creole, Gibraltar, Smiley, Grabbler, Viking, Roaring Lion and Growling Tiger to pass on hints to the students on the art of calypso singing and to judge the school competition. Today's soca star "KC" who operates out of the United States and calypso giant Sugar Aloes-to name a few-were moulded from that Nelsonian cast. Similarly, when I was sent to teach at Mucurapo Senior Comprehensive Secondary in 1977, a Carnival Committee which came into being in 1978 annually invited all the top calypsonians to the school's calypso competition until I retired from the institution in 1993. Thus, students of Mucurapo were privileged to hear bards like Explainer, Duke, Sparrow, Tambu, Gypsy, Super Blue, Swallow, Short Shirt, Arrow and Lord Nelson. I recall having to hide Tambu in a special room on the compound from the band of roaring schoolgirls who wanted to tear him apart in order to get a piece of his clothing or any of his belongings as a souvenir. Such was the fever built up annually at Mucurapo, for before bringing the singers, the students were shown in their lesson plans the beauty and richness of calypso and calypsonians. In addition, Roy Cape and his orchestra not only accompanied the singers but demonstrated to them the skills of notation and the musical chord patterns that embellish the calypso. Out of this rich Mucurapo experience came singers like Eastlyn Orr in the late 1980s to soar to the top of the female calypso world in 1990 and 1995 when she was crowned Calypso Queen. The Queen competition which began in 1974 lasted only a few years; it was revived by the National Action Cultural Committee in 1985 and was won then by Twiggy. The following were the winners since then: Lady B in 1986; Singing Sandra in 1987; Denyse Plummer in 1988, 1989, 1990[g] and 1991; Singing Sonia in 1992; Bianca Hull in 1993; Queen Shaka in 1994; Eastlyn Orr in 1995; Lady Wonder in 1996 and 1997; Shirlaine Hendrickson in 1998, 1999, 2000 and 2001; Heather Mc'intosh in 2002 and Marva McKenzie in 2003.

Young Killer was especially pleased to see the rise of women in calypso. He noted that while Petit Belle Lily and Boadicea were outstanding female singers of the 19th century, Lady Trinidad sang in the 1930s and Lady Iere was the female stalwart of the 1950s. As a young man, he was privileged to see and hear Lady Iere who usually accompanied her husband Lord Iere in song. "Lady Iere was also the first calypsonian to bring music sheets to a calypso tent singing a song about "Love" in 1955," according to calypsonian Striker.[7] Striker may be correct because in the first place, he was there, and secondly, it is a known fact that musician Roderick Borde[h] introduced the skill of music notation at the Young Brigade calypso tent in 1955.[8] In the 1950s too, there was singer

---

[g] Denyse shared the championship in 1990 with Eastlyn Orr.

[h] Roderick Borde migrated to Tortola BVI where he got married to a Tortolan and taught music to many youngsters there before he died in the late 1990s. In 1993, he was inducted into the Calypso Hall of Fame by Sunshine Awards.

Dr. Hollis "Chalkdust" Liverpool

Pearl White who, according to Striker "had a sweet voice."[9] In the 1960s-Killer thinks it was 1964-Calypso Rose came on the scene. She was followed by Barbadian-born Singing Francine who made her debut in Trinidad with Lord Blakie's Victory Calypso Tent in 1970 at the Port Services Club then situated on Wrightson Road. Before that however, Francine sang as a chorister for many singers before being given the break as a solo performer by Blakie. In the mid 1970's Francine and Rose were joined by Singing Diana who possessed "a most beautiful fine voice," according to Killer. The three women ruled the roost until the 1980s when with the onset of the Calypso Queen contest, "women like lentil peas"-to use Killer's words-entered the calypso fray. It was because of the fact that Francine, Rose and Diana were regular semi-finalists in the Calypso King competitions of 1973, 1974 and 1975, and because of the fact too that Francine reached the Calypso King finals in 1973 and all three of them in 1975, the CDC, fearing that a woman might have won, changed the name of the contest to the Calypso Monarch. By 1974, there were so many female singers that a private entrepreneur in South Trinidad organized the first Calypso Queen contest. The contestants then were: Calypso Rose who eventually won, Singing Francine, Lady Lilly, Lady Judy, Calypso Princess (wife of Lord Blakie and sister of Lord Allrounder and Calypso Prince), Lady Bird, Lady Macbeth, Singing Diana, Lady Sugar and Lady Tiny. In 1975, Calypso Girlie, Lady Jane, Lady Makeba, Countess and Twiggy joined the group of singing women. The contest was won by Calypso Rose again followed by Singing Diana and Calypso Girlie. Rose won again in 1976 withPrincess B and Singing Diana as runner-ups, and in 1978 with Princess B and Calypso Darkie and Francine. With Rose dominating the scene so overwhelmingly, it would seem that the contest drifted into oblivion and was resurrected in 1985 by the National Action Cultural Committee, the cultural arm of the National Joint Action Committee. As years rolled by, hundreds of women joined the fray. These included Lady Wonder (daughter of Lord Allrounder), Lady Ruth, Lady Iere (the second), Singing Sandra, Lady B (now deceased), Lady Venus, Tigress, Denyse Plummer, Singing Sonia, Ella Andell, Lady Chaconia and Kizzy Ruiz, to name a few.

In the late 1960s, Ms. Anna Mahase at St. Augustine Girls' Secondary took up the baton of staging carnival and calypso competitions among her charges; hundreds of school principals have since followed in her footsteps. In 1974, following a petition which I made to the C.D.C., a committee, comprised of George Goddard, Lennox Straker, Canute Spencer and I, was appointed by the chairman Mr. Ivan Williams to initiate the first children's carnival for schools in Port-of-Spain and its suburbs. Goddard, Spencer and I chaired the sub-committees for pan, mas and calypso respectively. The shows were so successful and with the groundwork established, the contests were broadened to cater for schools in North Trinidad. Thus, a representative of the Ministry of Education was invited to become a member of the parent committee, since carnival itself is a tool for educating young minds. As such, Ms. Phyllis Mitchell, School Supervisor, joined the Committee and carried out yeoman service to the children of Trinidad and Tobago from the late 1970s until she retired in the late 1990s. In terms of grooming young children in the art of calypso singing, Mr. Lance Heath and Mr. Peter Pitts have done yeoman service, they helping through the auspices of the Junior Carnival Committee of the NCC to turn many an untrained rusty voice into a calypsonian of note. Mr. Heath in 1989 started the Roving Calypso Tent; it allowed children to sing in different school arenas throughout the nation. Top singers of today, such as Devon Seale, Kerwin Dubois, Roger George, Destra Garcia and Heather Mc'intosh, are all products of the Roving Tent.[10]

191

It was Killer in 1967 who organized a day of sports for calypsonians, and for many years afterwards, calypsonians would meet in friendly matches of soccer, cricket and All Fours.[i] In addition, a game of cricket between calypsonians and pannists used to be held annually with George Goddard, Mighty Composer and Young Killer as organizers. In the 1960s too, the sport-loving public of Trinidad looked forward to the annual soccer match played between calypsonians and barbers. In a famous calypso of the era, Lord Melody referred to the goalkeeper of the barbers thus: "hungry, long-legged, knock-knee Zachary."[11]

In 1968, Killer migrated to New York where he lived for the rest of his life. There he continued his merry self, yet performing in cities throughout the United States, especially on shows to help children and the elderly. From New York to Washington to Atlanta, California and Maryland, West Indians in the 1970s and 80s were treated to first class calypso by the Young Killer. Not only was he a fine singer, but a fine entertainer as well, for jokes would flow from his lips in such an impromptu manner that the audience would be left in stitches of laughter. His flair for entertaining the public was a skill that he developed after years of singing in night clubs and tourist centers. He loved to laugh and made the audience laugh with him, especially when he made fun of "the shortcomings and follies of society."[12]

In 1973, Young Killer was the featured Caribbean artist in a documentary film of the Caribbean islands produced by Eastman Kodak Company of Rochester, New York. In 1999, he was inducted into the Sunshine Awards Hall of Fame. The Hall of Fame was inaugurated by Mr. Gilman Figaro, the nephew of Young Killer, to award musicians and singers of the art form for their contributions toward human development. It is hosted annually by the author. The "Sunshine" awards are promoted by Calypso and Steelband Music Awards Inc. of Teaneck, New Jersey. The organization came

---

[i] A game of cards that is played by four persons; it is very popular in Trinidad and Tobago.

into being in 1989 and its first inductees were Lord Executor, Walter "Chieftain" Douglas, Attila the Hun, Lord Pretender and Lord Kitchener in the realm of calypso, while Neville Jules, Winston Spree Simon, Ellie Manette, Rudolph Charles, George Goddard and Taspo were inducted for their contribution to steelband. Since then, several notable calypsonians, including Sparrow, Beginner, Growling Tiger, Roaring Lion, Houdini, Chinee Patrick, Spoiler, King Radio, Lord and Lady Iere, Frankie Francis, Art DeCoteau, Cypher, Superior, Melody, Spitfire, Caresser, King Fighter, Brigo, Unknown, Dictator, Viper, Christo, Viking, Blakie, Striker, Short Shirt, Ras Shorty I and yours truly have all been inducted.

One Sunday morning in Tobago where we had gone to sing for Tobagonians as part of the CDC's annual show, Young Killer passed on to me an important and interesting piece of information; it concerned the start of the calypso tent in Tobago. In the 1960s, 1970s and 1980s, the CDC would organize calypso shows in various country distrticts carrying the cream of the calypso crop to Rio Claro, Siparia, Mayaro, Toco and Tobago. Those singers who were selected for Tobago were seen as the "crème de la crème," and were expected to be in the running for the Calypso King/Monarch title. In addition, the sum of money paid to singers for their one day sojourn in Tobago very often superseded their weekly pay in the tent. Two shows, one in Roxborough and the other in Scarborough brought out, "the whole of Tobago," to use Killer's dictum, and paved the way for the discovery of young Tobagonian talent such as Shadow, Tobago Crusoe, Axeback, Lady B and Danny Boy.

As the conversation underscored the rise of calypso stars in Tobago, especially one Lord Professor, Mr. Cecil Caruth, whom I had known as a boy, Killer informed me that the first Calypso tent was opened in Tobago by the Hon. Ulric Lee, the then Parliamentary Secretary for Tobago Affairs in January 1957. The tent was situated at Wilson Road in Scarborough and about one hundred persons attended the gala opening. In truth and in fact, the newspaper of the day described the performers that night as "comic brigadiers." [13]

The newspaper's account was partly correct since, according to Killer, "the audience howled in delight at Mighty Bougie's humorous "Shanty Town Housing Scheme." Killer performed that night as a guest artist and remembered that other calypsonians who performed on that opening night included the Mighty Zenith, Aggressor, The Arrow, Mighty Philco and the Mighty Poison.

The reader, I am sure, would have noted the rise of calypso and calypso tents in Tobago since then. In 1961, for example, Tobago crowned its first king; he was the Mighty Rainbow. Rainbow sang in a tent managed by one Leo Jones in Tobago. Other members of the cast were the Mighty Popo, Lord Impressor, Spitfire, King Solomon and Calypso Rose. In 1962, the tent, held at Club La Tropical, featured Chris Alexander and his Merry Makers music band with singers Rainbow, Calypso Rose, Avenger, Hollis, Bison, Johny Pancho, Caresser, Sunshine, Senator and Adventure. In 1963, Rose, though singing in Trinidad at the Independent Brigade Tent on Duke Street, won the Tobago King crown. Seeking greener pastures overseas, Rainbow, Tobago's first Calypso King, sang with the Calypso Theatre from 1967 to 1970. He died soon afterwards. Cobra won the Tobago King title in 1968; that year, the tent in Tobago really came into its own as crowds poured into the Bamboo Terrace in Scarborough to hear Sweet Georges, Young Astronaut, Mighty Jerry, Mighty Cut Cake, Lord Roscoe, Mighty Mouse and Young Saltfish accompanied by Ray Lyons New Sound Band. Since then, the Tobago tent and its singing artists have risen to great heights in the calypso world.

It is ironic that Young Killer and his best friend Lord Observer, who in their heydays were two very energetic men, would both end up in wheel chairs in a hospital in Brooklyn, New York. Mere weeks after Observer died, Young Killer succumbed to cancer on October 26, 2001. The world lost a man who understood that life was meant to be lived and who therefore lived it to the fullest in that he never lost an opportunity to laugh, to smile and even to deride his own self when the event of the day seemed too serious. Young Killer, like the elder Killer before him, was indeed one of the top calypsonians of the century.

Dr. Hollis "Chalkdust" Liverpool

ENDNOTES

1   Regis, Louis. Black Stalin; The Caribbean Man. Trinidad: The Author, 1986.
2   Phillip, Emrold (Valentino). Personal Conversation. Dominica 1975.
3   "No More Paint Brushes for the Young Killer." Trinidad Chronicle, January 31, 1957.
4   Figaro, Gil. Young Killer's Eulogy. New York. November 1, 2001.
5   "No More Paint Brushes For The Young Killer." Trinidad Chronicle, January 31, 1957
6   Ali, Sookram. Trinidad and Tobago Carnival Winners, 1932 - 2000. P.O.S.: Needss, 1999. 14.
7   Oblington, Percy. The True History of Calypso. Trinidad: the Author, 2000.
8   Borde, Roderick. Personal Conversation with the author. Tortola, BVI, 1993.
9   Oblington, Percy. op.cit.
10 Heath, Lance. Telephone Conversation. May 25th 2003.
11 Alexander, Fitzroy (Lord Melody). "Hungry Barbers." The Author's collection.
12 Figaro, Gil. Young Killer's Eulogy. New York. November 1, 2001.
13 Trinidad Guardian. January 29th 1957.

Viper, Striker and Young Killer Serenade movie-star Cary Grant at Piarco in the 1960s

194a

Killer and Observer in their heyday-Uniformingly Dressed

Killer visits Observer (Lennox Clarke) at Linden Nursing Home, Brooklyn, Sept. 19, 1998

Kitch visits Killer in hospital-August, 1997
Pictures courtesy Gil Figaro

Chapter 9

Garfield Blackman (Ras Shorty I)

(October 6, 1941 - July 12, 2000.)
Watch out my children!
Watch out my children!
It have a fella call Lucifer with a
bag o' white powder.
And he don't want to
powder yuh face,
But to bring shame and disgrace
to the human race.
(Ras Shorty I - from the author's collection of
calypso lyrics).

I first met Ras Shorty I in Port-of-Spain in 1968; Prince Cumberbatch, then the Secretary of the CDC, had picked up both of us on Independence Square in Port-of-Spain and was taking us to his office to discuss, among other things, formalities concerning the Calypso King competition. In the car when I was introduced to him, this tall well-dressed man smiling from ear to ear impressed me with his dignified posture and sense of self-esteem. He appeared calm and self-assured and thanked Mr. Cumberbatch on behalf of the CDC for selecting him. He assured me and Mr. Cumberbatch that he will give a good account of himself at the Finals for which he was selected, and proceeded to say that he ought to have obtained the judges' nod several years earlier, when, in his opinion, he was singing well enough to have been so selected. Shorty,[a] as he was called then because of his height on the

---

[a] He loved basketball and being about six feet in height, he was called Shorty. Later, he renounced all wordly items, gave his life to God, grew his hair long and called himself Ras Shorty I.

basketball court, had made it to the finals from the Southland and, in those days, that was indeed a feat for a southern singer. By 1968, the southern-based singers were a force to reckon with. Guys like Shorty, Duke, Amuser, Bitterbush, Sweet Georgie, Dynamite, Stalin and Spider had proven that they could beat the best in the North. Some like Duke, Power and Young Killer were by then singing with their northern counterparts and were making a big impact on audiences to the extent that Duke won the crown that year.

In 1957, following a dearth in calypso tents in the Southland, the Rock N Roll Calypso Brigade swung open its doors in Palo Seco. The brigade comprised singers such as Young Lion, Lord Successor, Mighty Beginner, Spider and Southern Pride. By 1959, Duke, Injector, the Rock of Gibraltar, Sniper, Sad Sack, Clipper and Indian Fighter were pulling in a fairly large number of patrons at the Southern Brigade Calypso Tent held at the Oilfield Workers' Palm Club in San Fernando. In 1960, Duke won the South Trinidad Calypso King contest with Ambassador and Lord Injector as runner-ups respectively. In 1962, Stalin was declared the winner and in 1963, Shorty, as a newcomer, beat the field which included Duke, Power, Maestro, Composer and Stalin. It is a truism that the 1963 finalists for the South Trinidad Calypso King title were such good singers that they all were accepted in tents in the North afterwards. Shorty had sung in 1963 two beautiful songs: "Sixteen Commandments" and "A Tribute to Rudrunath Capildeo." The songs were considered by many of us[1] to be original in terms of lyrics and melody, and thus Shorty felt that he ought to have been selected that year for the Calypso King contest.

Shorty, Stalin, Crepsole, Dynamite and Bitterbush continued to dominate the calypso world in South Trinidad in the mid and late 60s. By 1967, Stalin, Composer and Young killer-Southerners all-reached the "Big Yard."[b] Composer placed 2nd with "Talent in the

---

[b] The name Kaisonians use for the Queen's Park Savannah where the Finals of the King Competition is held. The elder calypsonians use to say "Ah touch grass," whenever they qualified.

Waist" and "Carnival Fever;" Young Killer placed third and Stalin with "Beat My Tune" and "Culture First" placed 4th; Melody and Baker were the other two finalists in the competition. In 1968, Stalin singing "Bring back the Ole-Time Carnival" and "How to Build a Nation" won the North Calypso King Crown, the first time it was ever held. There were however, other good shoots from the Southland during the 1960s; they included Maestro who won the Princes Town Calypso King competition in 1963, Young Tiger who was king of Siparia in the same year, Mighty Scraper and Lord Santa who after conquering Fyzabad became well known in Port-of -Spain in the 70s, Magic who became famous for his calypso entitled "Obey the Highway Code," Squibby whose antics were applauded in the North in the 1970 - 2000 era and Crepsole, a teacher, who won the Southern Crown in 1969.

I had the pleasure of speaking intimately with Shorty several times after 1968; we would chat for long hours at Scott's hotel in St. Thomas, USVI. The CDC in St Thomas as early as 1953 (their carnival was resuscitated in 1952) would invite Trinidad singers to participate in their calypso tent and their World Calypso King Contest, and Shorty, Duke, Kitch, Sparrow, Christo, Zebra, Composer, Rose, Melody, Power and Stalin from Trinidad and Tobago, as well as Fighter, Arrow, Short Shirt and Canary from the other Caribbean lands were regular invitees during the 1960s and 1970s.[2] The world contest stopped in the mid-1980s after I had won it on eight occasions, a feat that was not bettered by any other singer. Other winners of the title included Mighty Zebra (the first person to do so) in 1954; Beryl Hill in 1955; Lord Melody in 1956, 1958 and 1960; Lord Creator in 1961; Mighty Power in 1962;Calypso Rose in 1963; Sparrow in 1964; Duke in 1968 and 1969; Sparrow again in 1970; Kitchener in 1971 (the first international contest he ever won);[c] Sparrow in 1972; Chalkdust in 1973 and 1974; Singing Francine in 1975;[d] Chalkdust in 1976, 1977, and 1978; Lord Blakie of St. Thomas in 1979; Chalkdust in 1980, 1981 and 1982 and Allrounder in 1983. Shorty and I would chat too, at Skinner Park, South Trinidad at the annual semis for the Calypso King/Monarch title, and, of all places, at the home of Chester Rogers in St. Vincent, a teacher and carnival lover with whom we both shared a mutual friendship. Chester has since died.

Shorty was born Garfield Blackman on October 6th 1941. Though I never asked him where was the land of his birth since I presumed that he was a "Trini to the bone,"[e] I was informed by a few Southern based singers[3] that Shorty was actually born in Barbados, but grew up in Lengua, a village of predominantly East Indians in South Trinidad, and as such, he learnt and practiced many East Indian culture traits including the speaking of the Bhojpuri language which many East Indians in Trinidad still speak.Trevor Marshall, a historian, friend and citizen of Barbados informed me that "the majority of 'Blackmans' in the Caribbean are of Barbadian roots; the term is as Barbadian as Guinea corn coo coo."[4]

Of his youth, Shorty informed me that growing up in Lengua had not only taught him East Indian dances, but he learnt to respect their art forms and culture. As a young man too, he was fascinated by the mouth organ. His bigger brother George had one as a Christmas gift and would often give him "a blow" on it. From the mouth organ, he went on to play the tassa drum of his East Indian neighbours and then the guitar which, by 1968, he mastered. Like Young Killer, that guitar helped him immensely to play chords, to practice chord patterns and to build sweet melodies around them.

---

[c] Duke and Kitch actually tied. The judges called for a "sing off" in that they both had to sing a third song. Duke, showing his humility and respect for Kitch, surrendered. Thus Kitch was declared the winner.

[d] The author was not invited that year owing to the fact that I had sung on the Chairman in 1974. Shadow and Duke were the runner-ups respectively.

[e] The title of David Rudder's hit of 2003; it refers to traits that typify a true Trinidadian.

In the realm of guitar playing, there have always been outstanding calypsonian-guitarists: Superior, Panther, Wonder, Viking, Sparrow, Merchant, Robin, Caresser, and Relator, but Shorty had such a "sweet technique"[5] that I remember times in St. Thomas when all of us, including Duke, Brigo, Allrounder, Art DeCoteau,[f] Sparrow and Kitchener used to simply stop whatever we were doing during our leisure moments and listen to him strum tunefully-sweet chords on his instrument while crooning in his favourite minor key.

Music was not Shorty's only pastime; he loved sport and played cricket, volleyball, billiards, besides being a strong swimmer and a fairly good boxer. Music, however, filled his entire being in the end, especially when he heard and listened to the calypsoes of Blakie, Sparrow, Melody, Brynner and Kitchener. As a budding musician in his singing youth, he understood the importance of having good lyrics, but swamped with the East Indian melodies which he heard especially at East Indian weddings and social feast days, and the road marches of Sparrow and Kitch over the air waves, he was greatly attracted to the tuneful aspects of the calypso. Accordingly, his aim in calypso had always been, he said, to provide the listener with "good lyrics and sweet music."

Professor Kenneth Ramchand of the University of the West Indies noted:

> "Ras Shorty I grew up among Indians in Lengua in rural Trinidad and spent the last twenty years of his life in the countryside. From childhood he was exposed to cultural ferment on a daily basis. He would speak Hindi/Bhojpuri and he knew Indian songs and dances. It is no wonder that he introduced, and knew that he was introducing (into) calypso Indian rhythms and effects associated with Indian instruments. His unforgettable composition 'Om Shanti' and his retreat to the forest in later life suggest that he was

---

[f] Art DeCoteau was the band leader who notated the music and accompanied the singers on stage.

Dr. Hollis "Chalkdust" Liverpool

consciously or unconsciously influenced by Indian religion and philosophy:

> The song you hear
> Is an Indian prayer;
> From ancient times
> Created to soothe your mind.
> In danger, in anger, remember
> Sing this mantra, this golden mantra from the master.
> This song is doing a good, people,
> To struggle against the devil.
> Chorus: Sing Om! Shanti Om! Shanti Shanti Om!"[6]

It is true that Shorty was consciously influenced by East Indian music and culture and in his later days saw the devil as a forceful person who strove to corrupt and ruin the world, but he would tell me that he disliked Indian religion for its polytheistic concept. "Indian people believe in one set o' gods, but the plain truth is: there is only one God and Jesus Christ his son is one and the same God," he exclaimed. As such, he saw the Indian mantra as coming not from Shiva, Ram or Vishnu but "from the master." Hence he sang Om Shanti as "a form of praise to God." He sang Indian tunes too, to "pull the East Indians into the thing." That thing, for Shorty, was the fact that too many East Indians in his day felt that calypso was only for Africans. Accordingly, Shorty wanted to expose more East Indians to the beauty of calypso. And although "he had a feel for Indian melodic lines and Indian intonation, as is evident in 'Indrani' where there is no parody or patronage to be heard,"[7] Ras Shorty I, as he called himself then, was consciously basking in Indian melodies to woo East Indians to calypso, "to show the Africans the richness of East Indian music and culture... to unite the two races"... and not least of all his intentions "to sell more records nuh." In a similar vein, although Shorty respected the Rastafarian faith, adored some of their principles such as their vegetarian lifestyle, grew his hair in Rasta style, he did not believe in the smoking of marijuana or the use or abuse of any illegal drugs. In fact, he would tell me: "I am a Christian to mi toe...How could Selassie be God? God was in Selassie and Selassie displayed the power of God but he aint God...he can't be God... Jesus Christ is the only true God; he always was; he is and he ever shall be."

Shorty became known in the calypso world as the Father of Soca, he having first used the bass pattern that underscored the musical change that occurred around the year 1974. There are those who believe too, that Shorty coined the term "Soca" or "Sokha" because of his exposure to Indian music; some even feel that the "Soca is an Indian beat."[8] Some, like Professor Kenneth Ramchand, are of the opinion that Shorty brought

> "to the (so) of calypso the 'kah' of Indian influence. This Trinidadian person knew that 'kah' is the first letter of the Indian alphabet and the first syllable in 'kahalwah'...if Sundar Popo brought calypso into chutney,[g] Ras Shorty I took chutney to calypso."

If the truth be told, Shorty, Mighty Composer and I were invited to the studio of TTT[h] in January of 1978 to discuss the implications of the new "Soca" beat which Shorty had introduced to calypso from 1974 to 1977 and which many singers had, by 1978, embraced. I took the opportunity before Shorty went on the television's dais to ask him about the new musical phenomenon that was sweeping the calypso world then. He informed me in no uncertain words that Mr. Ed Watson, who with his band-the Brass Circle-had just completed a tour of Nigeria, had brought back a Nigerian rhythmic beat and had asked him to compose a tune around it. Ed, who possessed a fine ear for music and who was the bandleader and musical director of Sparrow's Original Young Brigade Calypso Tent where Shorty sang, obviously had listened to the music of the Nigerians, particularly their Highlife music.

---

[g] A form of Indian music sung in T&T.
[h] TTT - Trinidad and Tobago Television, a broadcasting, public company in Port-of-Spain, Trinidad.

A few years later, 1978 to be exact, Ed had given the same beat to Kitchener who used it to compose, sing and record "Sugar Bum Bum." Accompanied by Ed Watson and the Brass Circle, it was and still is one of the best musical gems, in terms of sound and arrangement, ever recorded in the Caribbean. [10] Kitchener himself told me that it remained one of his best creations and that it represented for him the most records he ever sold in his entire career. [11] Calypsonians [12] who were at the recording swore that during the session, Kitch was short of a calypso to complete the album and was about to compose one when Ed reminded him of a tune which he had planned to record shortly. Ed played it for Kitch and Kitch loved it so much that there and then he put words to the melody. To Kitchy's percussive beat and haunting lyrics, Ed added his synthesizer and Soca-Bass rhythm making it an instant hit with calypso fans. The beat of "Sugar Bum Bum" together with Ed's harmonic synthesizer changed the overall tone of the long-playing album recording. So impressed with the music and the Soca beat was Kitch, that he called the recorded album "Melodies of the Twenty-first Century."

Shorty felt that the Nigerian beat to which he was introduced by Ed Watson resembled calypso; it reminded him too, of the Indian music he had heard in Lengua, in rural Trinidad. In fact, the Nigerian and Indian beats complemented the 2/2 or cut-time rhythm of calypso.

In addition to the heavy percussive beat of Highlife music, Shorty grew up in the era of soul music in the 1960s. Such music spawned a profusion of styles from black Americans such as Sam Cooke, Otis Redding, Wilson Pickett, Lou Rawls, Smokey Robinson, Curtis Mayfield, Aretha Franklin, Nina Simone, Marvin Gaye, Stevie Wonder and Diana Ross. Moreover, Reggae with Bob Marley at the helm, was leaving the calypso behind internationally, and there was the so-called disco explosion which started innocuously enough with the astounding multi-million sales of George McCrae's "Rock Your Baby" and Carl Douglas's "Kung Fu Fighting" which were in the tradition set by Wilson Pickett's "In The Midnight Hour." Ironically enough too, in a bid to keep some bread on the table, American Jazz musicians had been injecting dance rhythms into their previously largely self-indulgent and introspective modern-jazz stylings. The meeting point of this Jazz and Funk became known as "Jazz-Funk" and men like Herbie Hancock and Freddie Hubbard, and groups like the Crusaders all embraced the new trend. In Britain, the movement grew with many disco-soul bands like Imagination and Linx. Synthesisers played a major role in Jazz-Funk and were picked up on by soul acts and utilized notably well by artists like Stevie Wonder. The 1970s in the U.S. too, produced soul-singing black bards like Teddy Pendergrass, Millie Jackson, Michael Jackson and Randy Crawford; they, with the help of African-American businessmen who invested in booking agencies, recording studios and publishing houses, aided in the internationalization of Soul and started to really make large sums of money from the entertainment industry. Above all, the 1970s produced an ever-increasing diversity of musical styles under the general banner of African-American music.

Shorty therefore, conscious of the rise of African-American music and musicians internationally, and conscious too of the need to internationalize the calypso and help it to spread in the manner of the Reggae, and desirous too, to make more money out of his art, felt that a new rhythm pattern was needed. "The rhythms of Nigeria and Indian-Trinidad could make the thing more danceable," he told me at TTT house. As such, he informed me, Composer and the viewers of television that day that his aim was:

> "to put some Soul into the Calypso…what I am singing-he
> was referring specifically to two tunes "Soul Calypso Music"
> sung in 1974 and "Sweet Music" sung in 1976-is Soul Calypso…

204

I am putting the beginning of the two words Soul and Calypso together...I am adding the 'So' of Soul to the 'Ca' of Calypso to give the thing some soul, some spirit...some life."

In his exemplary work of 1974 termed "Endless Vibrations,"[i] like the American mix of Soul and Funk of the 1970 era, he called for a change in the music to "make it super sweeter." In addition, as if to emphasize the meaning of Soca to his fans in 1974, he composed and sang "Soul Calypso Music." Yet, fearing that Trinidadians might feel that he was selling out the art form by his introduction of "Soul" into the music, in the same year (1974), he therefore reminded them via a calypso entitled "We Thing," that Calypso, Parang, Steelband and Mas were indigenous art forms of the nation. So taken up with creating sweet music embellished with soulful rhythms was Shorty, that in his "Sweet Music" of 1976, he exclaimed:

Ah can't read, Ah can't write music.
But every day, every night I create it.
My system is rhythm....
I make music, sweet music...

At a concert in London in May 2000, neither Defosto, Ella Andell, Crusoe, Baron nor I was able to move the audience as calypsonian Alberto did when he sang Ras Shorty I's hit: "Watch Out My Children." Alberto and I both agreed afterwards that that calypso was not only a timely and timeless composition, but that it had come from the pen of someone inspired by the creator in the same manner as were the biblical writers. A closer look at the calypso reveals not only beautiful well-rhymed lyrics: "sober thinking leads us to righteousness, spiritual bliss," but the lyrics contain that psychological mask that is so common to good calypso. Not once did Ras Shorty I mention the word cocaine and yet the message was so effectively communicated. In the calypso, Ras Shorty assumed the role of the international father-figure pleading with and advising his children to beware of Satan.

---

[i] So called because of the "endless vibes of soul music" he was getting.

Dr. Hollis "Chalkdust" Liverpool

Many singers, especially Lion, Kitch and Sparrow, have over the years assumed that type of international authority in order to admonish their subjects morally and spiritually. That fair evening in May, Alberto and I pondered over Ras Shorty I and agreed that only a man who was truly grounded in spirituality and a faith that made him taste in advance the nutrients of the beatific vision could have composed such a calypso. We theorized too, that had Shorty not experienced the adversity that made him turn from a life of glitter and glamour to one of prayer and dedication to his creator, he could not have composed such a calypso gem.

Black Stalin[j] and I were present at the Jean Pierre Complex in Port-of-Spain in the early 1990s, when Ras Shorty I for the first time sang the calypso "Watch Out My Children." At the end of the first verse, we both watched each other in amazement for we knew that that song was the essence of good calypso, and that it was branded with the stamp of immortality.

Fresh from his victory over his Southern contemporaries such as Composer, Duke and Stalin, Shorty came to Port-of-Spain and joined Sparrow's OYB in 1965 singing songs entitled "Sweet Sixteen," "Must Come Back" and "Begging Competition," in which he triumphantly echoed the pleasures of love and the blissful meanderings of the promiscuous male. Assisted in the writing of his song "Budget" by Duke in 1968,[13] Shorty composed "Country Girl" that year and the two tunes saw him as a finalist in the National Calypso King competition. The reader would therefore note that while Shorty glorified promiscuity in song on the one hand, he sang serious commentaries such as "Budget" in 1968 and "Index of a Nation" in 1969.

In Port-of-Spain in the late 1960s and 1970s, the care-free and nattily-dressed Shorty became a household word among calypso lovers dishing out hits such as "Mouth Is She Business" in 1970, "She Want Cover" in 1971, "The Art of Making Love," "Indrani" and "Nothing At All" in 1973 and "Endless Vibrations," "Soul Calypso Music" and " We Thing" in 1974. Singing "The Art of

---

[j] Stalin in the 1980s changed his name to Black Stalin.

Dr. Hollis "Chalkdust" Liverpool

Making Love" in the Big Yard in 1973, Dr. Eric Williams, the then Prime Minister took offence to Shorty's song and afterwards asked the Chairman of the CDC, Mr. Ivan Williams: "What was that man doing there?" Dr. Williams had taken, it seemed, his daughter and other dignitaries, including the wife of the Prime Minister of Jamaica (his house guest) to the show and took offence to Shorty's strutting his index finger in the air, while demonstrating the art of lovemaking and singing amusingly: "you see this finger, this fat magnificent finger! Always keep it handy, in case of emergency." The CDC, put to shame by Dr. Williams, was tense and flabbergasted, but chairman Ivan Williams, though defending the judges, took the blame. From then on, the CDC took the decision that all calypsonians qualifying for the semi-finals and finals must submit their lyrics in writing to the judges committee. In addition, the body announced that judges would, at the tents, have the right to advise singers on the legal and moral aspects of their lyrics; furthermore, the CDC retained the right to disallow any singer who sang lines that, in the CDC's opinion, bordered on immorality or defamation of a person's character.[14] In true calypso style, Shorty replied to the Prime Minister, deriding him in song in 1974. Today, the competition is run by TUCO and all singers are asked to submit lyrics to that body as part of the rules of participation. In Article 6 of the rules it is stated: "Contestants shall present their lyrics to TUCO, at the date of the first scheduled rehearsal and shall be held liable for any change thereafter."[15] Moreover, in keeping with the rules set by the CDC in 1973, in Article 1 of TUCO's rules, it is stated: "Calypsoes considered by TUCO's designated authority to be indecent, obscene or defamatory will be rejected and the relative contestant notified of the reason for such rejection."[16]

I recall a calypso show in 1968 at St. George's hotel in Brooklyn, New York where the audience, comprised of mainly females, were exuberantly ranting and raving over Shorty and his "Art of Making Love." Back stage afterwards, he was wiping the sweat off his brow when an old man of approximately eighty years or so approached him. The old man asked whether he (Shorty) would take his elderly advice, to which Shorty agreed. The old man then quickly informed him in my presence: "Young man, you sang a nice song...but take my advice...there is no art in making love...what is one woman's meat is another woman's poison." And with that, the old man left leaving Shorty to gaze heaven-wards and ponder. I too, pondered at the wisdom of the aged soul.

When on the one hand in the 1970s, many citizens of Trinidad and Tobago reacted angrily and expressed shock at Shorty's adventurous courage in "Om Shanti," "Indrani" and "The Art of Making Love," as he dared in song to make love to East Indian women while he prayed with them, extolled their inner and outer beauty, and then passed on tidbits to other eager "love men,"[k] on the other hand, young singers like Valentino, Duke, Brigo, Composer, Swallow and I were mesmerized by his creative ability, his "short" height, and his unusual Bob Marley-like voice. Like the Mighty Duke, the late Kitchener and Maestro, his mentors, Shorty used choice words that made for perfect rhymes, yet he never sacrificed rhymes for intelligence and sensible lyrics that captured the hidden, double-entente transcripts of Trinidad and Tobago. For example, in "Mouth is She Business/Don't Chook Yuh Mouth," he warns Dennis, "a makoscious[l] sex pervert," about "always chooking[m] (his) mouth in woman business." He sang:

"All the girls singing the same song:
They like you bad, but they fraid yuh tongue."

In "Love, The High-Falutin' Way" sung in 1975, he derided Trinidadians, who, on returning to Trinidad from their sojourns in England, seek out prostitutes but speak to them in an English accent like "Sir Galahad" thus:

Princes Serene Primus, you are a ruby's enchantment;
A diamond translucent, a pearl of the Orient.

---

[k] Shorty was hailed by many women as a super love maker, and from his performances and manner of dress, he was dubbed by the Press "The Love Man."

[l] A colloquial term for an expert at eavesdropping.

[m] Colloquialism for "pushing."

Dr. Hollis "Chalkdust" Liverpool

Your transcendent flow,
Dynamically glow(ing)
From your pulsating meandering effervescing below,
Has motivated the nucleus of my masculine ego.

As young singers too, Duke, Composer and I were mesmerized by Shorty's ability to accompany his own self on guitar with rare but sweet chords, and to exploit the minor key especially, in a manner that seemed unbelievable, since all musicians know that the minor key at most times is a very restrictive one. Good calypsonians know that the minor key lends itself to melancholy themes, as demonstrated by Sparrow's "Slave" and Merchant's "Umbayayawo." Thus the melodies of Shorty's "Watch out my Children," "Om Shanti," "Whom God Bless," "Soca Fever" and "Endless Vibrations," like Kitchener's "Pan In A Minor," are extremely sweet but rare and outstanding; the application of the major and minor keys superbly intermixed in the melodies create the mood of somber contemplation in all of them.

Sweet, however, are the uses of adversity, which like the toad ugly and venomous, according to Shakespeare, wears yet a precious jewel in his head. In 1977, Shorty embarked on a tour of Canada that not only turned out to be disastrous in terms of the financial ruin it brought him, but the resultant adversity and depression that engulfed him changed his life, his music and his relationship with the master. His financial losses made him realize his powerlessness, his human limitations, and his finitude despite the prosperity and glamour that calypso had provided him.

Calypsonians since the 1930s like Lion, Executor, and Radio used to tour the Caribbean after Carnival. The trend continued with singers like Pretender, Invader, Beginner, Growler, The Duke of Iron and Kitch in the 40s; Melody, Blakie, Small Island Pride, Zebra, Brigo, Superior, Viper and Sparrow in the 50s; Duke, Stalin, Inventor, Shorty, Ella Andell and Striker in the 60s; Funny, Young Creole, Valentino, Skipper and Francine in the 70s, Explainer and Merchant in the 80s, Versatile, David Rudder, Relator and Prowler in the 90s and Sugar Aloes, Crazy and Singing Sandra in the 21st century. The Trinidad Guardian in 1957 described as "Cal-Limbos" a team of calypsonians and Limbo dancers who left for a seven month tour of the Northern Islands. "They included three former calypso kings, "Spoiler," "Sir Galba," and "Mighty Viking," and two others: Mr. Action - "Lord Commander," and "Eisenhower" and limbo dancers "Rocke" and "Merle."[17] The newspaper also wrote that Canadian newspapers described the impact of calypso and calypsonians in Canada in 1957 as "Calypso song knocks the Rock."

> "They were referring to 'Mary Ann,' 1945 Road March, which was one of the hottest tunes last week. Housewives were humming it, teenagers were singing it, and it could be heard on Radio Stations at all hours of the day and night. 'Mary Ann' is at the top of the wave of popularity that calypsoes (sic) have been riding ever since the beginning of the year, a popularity that has put it in a position where it is actually challenging rock 'n' roll. It is significant that Elvis Presley's top tune last week, one entitled "Too Much" could do no better than fifth place in the top ten."[18]

John Grimes, a popular journalist of the 1950s, noted that "after the calypso season, calypsonians are forced to travel abroad because Trinidadians are not interested in their music between carnivals."[19]

These sojourns up the Caribbean chain of islands from Guyana to Jamaica annually have resulted in a more united Caribbean with its several peoples realizing the commonality of the culture traits that exist in the region. They have resulted too, in an explosion of good calypsonians throughout the region and a sharing of ideas for compositions and learning experiences in terms of the music and rendition of the calypso.

It is a well known fact that Trinidadian musicians like Art DeCoteau, Ed Watson, Bert Inniss, Roderick Borde, Cyril Diaz and Frankie Francis have, by their training sessions and assistance rendered to Caribbean regional musicians and singers, raised considerably the standards of calypso and calypso music in the region. All concerned with calypso in the region know that Trinidadian singers like Sparrow, Kitch, Melody, Christo and Zebra-to name a few-and Trinidadian musicians like Art Decoteau, Hendren Boucaud, Roderick Borde, Vasso DeFreitas and Joey Lewis have played a great part in bringing to the forefront of the art outstanding world-class performers like Arrow of Montserrat; Short Shirt and Swallow of Antigua; Blakie, Waddablee and Kwabena of St.Thomas; Prince Galloway and the Mighty Pat of St. Croix; Becket of St. Vincent, Ajamu of Grenada, Lady Guymine, Canary and King Fighter of Guyana; Hunter of Dominica; Socrates of St. Kitts; and Gabby and Plastic Bag of Barbados. Roderick Borde lived in Tortola from the 1970s until he died there in the mid 1990s. He therefore trained the locals of the British Virgin Islands for years, while Art DeCoteau is a household name in Antigua and the U.S. Virgin Islands because of his work there with the local musicians and singers. The fact that today most of the Caribbean islanders hold their carnival and calypso competitions in similar style and structure as those in Trinidad and Tobago, is a tribute to the pioneers of calypso and calypso music like Lion, Sparrow, Shorty and Art DeCoteau. Having conquered the Eastern Caribbean with their calypso music, calypsonians turned their attention to Europe where Beginner in the early 1940s pioneered the movement and were followed in the 1940s and 50s by Kitch, Terror, Young Tiger, The Unknown Soldier and Young Kitchener.

Similarly, with the advent of musicians Lionel Belasco, Sam Manning and Gerald Clarke along with calypsonian Houdini in New York in the late 1920s and early 1930s, calypso and calypso music took root in the United States and paved the way for hundreds of today's singers and musicians who look forward to the concerts there after the Trinidad Carnival is over. As early as 1912, Victor and Columbia Recording Companies put Lovey's Calypso Band on record thereby starting a trend whereby foreign companies began to record the music and make it become internationally known.

Dr. Hollis "Chalkdust" Liverpool

Lovey's band was followed by Lionel Belasco and Julian Whiterose, a chantuelle who made records for Columbia. West Indian vocalists began reaching the studio in the 1920s. One Johnny Walker appeared on the Victor label in 1921. Walker was followed by Phil Madison in 1923; Sam Manning and Wilmouth Houdini began recordings in 1927.[20]

> Wilmoth Houdini was the "Calypso King of New York" from the late 1920s through about 1948. Sam Manning, Phil Madison, and Johnny Walker-his competitiors in New York in the 1920s-were vaudevillians who sang calypso and other popular song forms. Macbeth the Great, Sir Lancelot and the Duke of Iron, New York-based Trinidadians who sang in the 1940s, appealed primarily to the downtown nightclub audiences.[21]

In 1934, Atilla and Lion were facilitated by Portuguese businessman, Eduardo Sa Gomes of Sa Gomes Radio Emporium Company, to go to the United States to make recordings for Decca and the American Record Company. Atilla, Growling Tiger and Beginner in 1935, Lion, Tiger and Radio in 1936 and Lion, Executor, Caresser and Atilla in 1937 began the annual journey of calypsonians to the United States.[22] The trek to the United States and Canada was continued by singers like Sparrow and Melody in the late 50s, Duke and Shorty in the 60s, Explainer and Scrunter in the 70s, Crazy and Francine in the 80s, David Rudder in the 90s and Aloes and Singing Sandra in the 21st century. The annual trek caused calypsonian Relator to sing in the 1990s the following:

> For calypsonians to make a record
> They now have to go abroad.
> It is a fact of life and it's sad
> No records are made here in Trindad.
> The records that are used in the art today
> Are all manufactured in the USA.

It is a sad blow; for Trir
In case you don't know,
We now importing we own calypso.[23]

f Shorty it could be truly said: Prosperity doth best discover ...e, but adversity doth best discover virtue. Shortly after his return from that ill-fated tour of Canada, Shorty turned his life around, grew his hair long in Rasta style, changed his eating and pleasurable, mundane lifestyle and "surrendered to Jesus." Like the biblical Saul who was spiritually transformed into St. Paul, the hand of the Potter was working in Shorty's life. White flowing robes took the place of coloured tight-fitting sexy outfits; Jesus-like garments and leather sandals (often-times he went barefooted) replaced the tight jumper suits lined with tassels, braids and beads; the Piparo[n] wilderness was favoured to the populated Marabella; his wife and many children were embraced instead of Jean and Dinah;[o] the spiritual Ras Shorty I replaced the materialistic Shorty; poverty was seen as virtuous and wealth as immoral and materialistic; Jamoo[p] music replaced Soca and man's creativity was to be used in the service of God who created him to enjoy the fruits of the earth and the happiness of heaven. Of ironic interest is the fact that it was Duke in 1968 who called all of us, contestants in the 1968 Calypso King Competition, to pray for God's blessings before the onset of the show in the Queen's Park Savannah. Duke, while we both reminisced noted: "I remember Shorty hesitatingly agreeing to pray only after I had called him many times and made him bow his head and get into an attitude of prayer…how things and man can change eh boy!"[24]

Jamoo music, though filled with a prayer-like and contemplative appeal, was yet possessed with a rich rhyming scheme, with words of a similar sound within the sentence as well as at the end.

---

[n] An area in forested South Trinidad where Ras Shorty I eventually settled.
[o] Names used in a calypso by Sparrow in 1956 and now associated with prostitution

It characterized too, haunting melodies and choice, intelligent, sensible lyrics from a man who at all times displayed "sober thinking." His calypso, "Watch Out my Children," composed in the Jamoo vein, ought to be communicated to every school child in the world today and to future generations as well.

> My sons and my daughters! To you I plead.
> Watch! Don't get no horrors, but please take heed.
> I know you don't want no sermon, but my admonition
> Is to guard you against all the evils of life
> That create strife and destroy life.
>
> Walk cautiously! Children be alert!
> Cause you have an enemy that's roving the earth.
> I know you're young and restless, but you don't have to be careless,
> Cause sober thinking leads us to righteousness, and happiness, spiritual bliss. So let me tell you this.
> Chorus: Watch out my children!
> Watch out my children!
> It have a fella called Lucifer with a bag o' white powder
> And he don't want to powder yuh face
> But to bring shame and disgrace to the human race.
>
> You are young and your future is ahead of you.
> Right or wrong, sweet or sour, depends on what you do.
> Taking the wrong direction will drain your constitution
> And promote tension, chaos and confusion,
> Then corruption to the inner man.
> And that was not God's plan.

As young singers too, we were hypnotized by the charisma that Ras Shorty I possessed. I was privileged to see that power that was divinely conferred on him openly displayed at Spektakula Forum on Henry Street, Port-of-Spain. At 1 a.m. one morning in 1983, Tommy Joseph, the Emcee, introduced Ras Shorty I and the Love Circle[q] on stage, but the crowd was calling for the traditional

---

[q] The name given to the group made up of Shorty's children. They accompanied him in song.

Dr. Hollis "Chalkdust" Liverpool

calypso instead of the Gospel-like Jamoo music which Ras Shorty I
was singing. It was already late and the crowd preferred then to
dance and sing out loudly, rather than hear the spiritual lyrics of
Ras Shorty I. On this earth, there are few men who can weather that
storm; there are few artistes who can perform amidst that bedlam.
Ras Shorty I in the midst of cat calls and boos began to tinkle his
guitar and to pray aloud: "When I see all my children around me, I
know that the Lord has blessed me," he cried. By this time, with
Ras Shorty I tickling and tinkling his guitar and praying earnestly,
the rowdy crowd of over two thousand souls became quiet. Ras
Shorty I continued:

> "Father, I thank thee for allowing me to know you; I thank
> thee for my children and for the gifts thou has bestowed on
> me; I thank thee for the audience. Forgive them for they
> know not what they do...Ladies and Gentlemen, you here
> are witnesses to the great changes that God has wrought in
> me; you are witnesses to this great event that God has
> caused to happen here this night (it was already morning)
> and you must thank the Lord for your life and the fact that
> you can breathe and can enjoy a calypso concert. Say
> Amen."

The crowd responded with a rather weak "Amen." Ras Shorty I
shouted out: "Say Amen." The now subdued crowd, shocked and
fearful of Ras Shorty's wrath, answered loudly this time, "Amen."
And Ras Shorty I performed for the next half-an-hour to
thunderous applause from the same crowd that previously didn't
want to hear him. Although, in my lifetime, I have seen Cypher,
Sparrow, Duke and Valentino cause, by their stagecraft, voice and
appeal, noisy audiences to calm down, there has never been any
other calypsonian that I know or heard of with the kind of charm,
ability to woo a rowdy audience and personal aura that Ras Shorty I
possessed.

Dr. Hollis "Chalkdust" Liverpool

Kitch used to tell me though of Lion in his heyday in the late 1930s and early 1940s. "No one would enter the cinema until Lion arrived, and when he did, the crowd, still assembled outside, would roar: "Look him! Look him." Then the cinema would be filled "before you say Jack Robinson."[r]

When at the height of his career, Shorty stepped off the Soca stage and embarked on the Jamoo platform, there were many who felt that it was only "a passing cloud."[s] They felt thus because singers like Bomber and Prowler had also done the same in the 1970s, and yet returned to calypso singing after a decade or so. Short Shirt and King Obstinate in Antigua gave up calypso singing in the mid 1990s; King Obstinate was felled by a stroke and turned to the singing of Gospels, using the pseudonym "The Wounded Soldier;" King Short Shirt returned to calypso singing in 1999, but from since then he is only concerned with "conscious lyrics."[25] Calypsonian and policeman, Tambu, read for a degree in the U.S., then gave up calypso in the early 1990s and is now a secondary school music teacher who uses his gifts primarily to woo children into the holy Gospels. Eastlyn Orr retired from the art form in the mid 1990s and is now a full time Gospel singer. Still others like the Mighty Skipper, who sang in the 50s and 60s, turned to the religious ministry in the early1970s. Skipper (Rev. Robert Stafford) is now a Minister of the Cloth in St. Croix, USVI.

In Ras Shorty I's case, however, his great outward show of faith in God made his detractors realize that his changed life and spiritual utterances were indeed "showers from heaven." Even on his death bed when I visited him, he informed me that, unlike other men, he had entrusted his whole life to his maker. "Some men," he said, "give the Lord their baggage of problems, but when they find the Lord is taking too long to help them, they take it back."

---

[r] A colloquial term meaning "in a very short time" as "in the twinkling of an eye."
[s] A local term for a rather short period of time.

Dr. Hollis "Chalkdust" Liverpool

He then proceeded to give me a joke that would make Tommy Joseph proud. "There was this man who fell of a cliff but luckily held on to a protruding tree branch. He looked down on the chasm five thousand (5000) feet below and called aloud on God to help him. Suddenly God answered: Leggo the branch; I am down here." We both laughed and Ras Shorty I thanked God that he could still be used as his servant, even if it was to make others laugh. Mere days before he died, his last words to me were: "Chalkie, Ah tired; Ah going and sleep." I left him with a tranquil-like but satisfied grin on his face as he waded into peaceful slumber. Little did I realize then that, like St. Paul, it was his "desire to depart and be with Christ."

(L to R) Calypsonians Caressar, Young Killer, a Tourist Board Official entertaining Actor Roy Rogers at Piarco International Airport in Trinidad in 1958.

Dr. Hollis "Chalkdust" Liverpool

ENDNOTES

[1] Calypso conversation held at a pub in Newtown. Present were: Duke, Baker, Sniper and I. We were having a drink, having just drawn positions for the finals of the National Calypso King contest at Television House.

[2] Pope, Kelvin (Mighty Duke). Telephone Conversation. Trinidad. May 29th 2003.

[3] Informal conversation with calypsonians in New York, August 1993.

[4] Marshall, Trevor. Personal Conversation. Bank Hall, Barbados. August 1981.

[5] Abraham, Samuel (Brigo). Personal Conversation. St. Thomas. February 1982.

[6] Ramchand, Kenneth. "Tribute to Ras Shorty I." Senate Session of Trinidad and Tobago. Hansard. July 18, 2000.

[7] Ramchand. Kenneth. ditto.

[8] This was the consensus of the calypso audience to whom I lectured in Toronto, Canada, in July 2001.

[9] Ramchand. K. op.cit.

[10] Roberts, Aldwyn (Kitchener). Melodies of the 21st Century. Trinidad, TRC 0006, Charlie's CR 138, 1978.

[11] Roberts, Aldwyn (Kitch). Personal Conversation. Mother's Day Concert, New York. May 1992.

[12] Pope, Kelvin (Mighty Duke). Telephone Conversation. Trinidad, May 27, 2003.

[13] Pope, Kelvin (Mighty Duke). Telephone Conversation. Trinidad, May 28, 2003.

[14] Minutes of the CDC Meetings, March/April 1973. The author at the time represented the Calypsonians' Association on the CDC.

[15] TUCO. "National Calypso King and Queen and Monarch Competitions 2003, Rules of Participation." Article 6, Clause D, p.3.

[16] TUCO. "National calypso King and Queen and Monarch Competitions 2003, Rules of Participation." Article 1, Clause I, p 1.

[17] Trinidad Guardian, March 27, 1957.

[18] Calypsoes Turn Heat On Canada." Trinidad Guardian, March 15, 1957.

[19] Grimes, John. "Trinidad Losing Hold On Calypso Title." Sunday Guardian, February 9, 1958.

[20] Liverpool, Hollis. Kaiso and Society. Trinidad: Juba Publications, 1990. p.25.

[21] Hill, Donald. Calypso Calaloo. Florida: University of Florida Press, 1993. pp. 176-177.

[22] Liverpool, op.cit. pp.25-26.

[23] Liverpool, Hollis. The author's private collection of calypso lyrics.

[24] Pope, Kelvin (Mighty Duke). Telephone Conversation. Trinidad, May 29th 2003.

[25] Emmanuel, Maclean (Short Shirt). Heineken Calypso Show, Lionel Roberts Stadium. St. Thomas, USVI. April 19th 2003.

The Sparks/Wildfire

The March of Dimes behind Pretender
Pics courtesy Irving Rauceo

Dr. Hollis "Chalkdust" Liverpool

Two of Tobago's earliest Calypsonians-Rainbow and Professor

Gene Miles sings Calypso
Picture courtesy–The Express

Dr. Hollis "Chalkdust" Liverpool

Chapter 10

Lord Drake
(Laudric Stephen)

We want peace and love
brotherman.
Peace is the mode man,
that's the code,
And surrender all dem
weapon that is
causing much confusion
If you have on Lady Young Road.
Let peace reign supreme black brother.
Show the world we splendid behaviour.
So when we tramping for Carnival, our
national festival,
Please don't spoil we bacchanal.
Lord Drake. (Original Regal. Trinidad:
DuSu Chalk Associates, 1973). p.25.

In 1973, when I first interviewed Lord Drake, I classified him then as a modern-day kaisonian. Drake, baptized Laudric Stephen, started his calypso career in 1966, and in 1973 he was one of the leading young stars of the calypso world in Trinidad and Tobago. Like Lord Smiley, Drake started off with the Calypso Theatre, but joined the Regal cast founded by Duke, Chalkdust and Superior in 1973.

I was first drawn to him by his humility, he being never a "pushy" character at the Regal, especially when we held auditions. His voice and calypso pseudonym also drew me to him; I found out that he called himself Drake after many persons questioned him about his deep baritone voice that, in the words of many of his admirers, sounded like a male duck. The reader can, I am sure, note his humility from even his alias, for while most calypsonians then associated themselves with beautifully-feathered birds with sweet chirping voices-a la Swallow, Sparrow, Canary-Laudric Stephen preferred to link himself with the slow, raspy-voiced and lowly-esteemed drake.

Most rising stars of 1973 preferred to sing at the Original Young Brigade or at Lord Kitchener's Revue tent, but Drake preferred to take his chances with the Regal where his income was smaller than if he had joined the more popular tents, and where he was exposed to smaller audiences. Yet he felt, he said, "more relaxed and happier under a tent management that understands calypsonians and treat them as humans." Several singers who are, today, stars in the business made their debut at the Regal. The list includes Rootsman, Bopee, Mirror, Diamond, Prince Valiant, Psycho and Snow Cone who later changed his name to King Austin. Several other stars of today's calypso world, at some time between 1973 and 1976, sang at the Regal. The list includes: Young Creole, Lord Nelson, Poser, Companero, Power, Striker, Hawk, Gypsy, Amuser, Valley, Funny, Singing Dianne, Organizer, Rex West, Smiley, Penguin, Explainer and Composer.

In the Regal Calypso Tent Brochure for 1973, an excerpt from the foreword reads as follows:

> Tent managers, since they were the financiers, talked down and yelled at singers whenever they felt like doing so. They would fix the programme according to their whim and fancy, and hired and fired singers at will. It was not uncommon to see a singer grounded because his song may be attacking some member of society or some political party with which the manager is friendly, or perhaps the song is taking the wind out of the sails of some bigger singer in the tent.[1]

It was for that reason that Regal was formed. Calypso tents were big business then and managers aimed to procure for themselves as big a share as possible, yet cared very little for the human relations side of the industry. Indeed, the managers hardly took into account the varying personalities of their singing employees; they saw themselves as bureaucratic-line and staff supervisors who, in their greed, robbed the public of their gold. They trampled upon the talents of the singers, sometimes mercilessly extracting the culture and skills which those calypsonians possessed, in return for a few pieces of silver.

In 1957, for example, the editor of the Trinidad Chronicle writing of the Young Killer stated: "Things did not go too smoothly (for him). Many nights they kept him off the show and gave him only a few dollars."[2] In 1959, Calypsonians Brynner, Director, Pretender, Spider and Protector complained to the newspapers and to the then chairman of the CDC, Mr. B.W. Celestain, stating that the manager of the Young Brigade on Park Street, Mr. Henry (Spike) Clarke, had refused to pay them their correct wages. Moreover, they informed the press that they could do nothing because the manager "had his men around him and a cutlass lying on the table." They complained too, of the restrictions to which they were exposed: "if the singers didn't come in a suit, they couldn't sing…Spike had received $1,000 from the CDC and did not pay them any money at all."[3] All such ill-treatment of singers in the 1970s caused Drake to come over to the Regal on Wrightson Road, Port-of-Spain, where Mr. Prince Jorsling superbly managed the tent.

One of the calypso tent happenings that caused Drake to sing calypso was the tent chorus; he was always fascinated with it. The idea of having tent choristers started off with Railway Douglas who brought the stickfighters and jamettes into the tent to back up the main singers. Over the years during the first half of the 20th century, calypsonians mainly doubled up as chorus singers.

The first "true-true chorus group" according to Drake was the "March of Dimes" quartet which, according to Christo[4] was founded by Conrad "Laddie" Prescott in 1937. They were then known as the McClean Brothers. The group's style of harmonizing was influenced by the "Mills Brothers," one of the leading singing groups in the United States of that era, and they sang at weddings and other social functions.

They consisted then of Prescott, Errol McClean, Al Thomas and Lewis Clarke. In 1957, the editor of the <u>Trinidad Chronicle</u> noted of them:

> "Following their regular performances over the station (Radio Trinidad), they were flooded with engagements, and sang at private parties, night spots, cinemas and once did a nine month engagement at the Macqueripe Officers Club, at the United States Naval Base, Chaguaramas."[5]

When tenor Lewis Clarke died in the early 1950s, Christopher Laidlow was taken as a replacement.

As the Mc Clean Brothers, the group got its first big break internationally to sing at the March of Dimes Festival in the U.S.; the Carnival Queen of that year and other local entertainers were part of the entourage. The festival was in aid of polio victims and Laidlow had composed for the group a special calypso for the occasion: "Little children, keep your fingers crossed! Have faith in the bigger boss..." The kaiso made the group and Christopher Laidlow so famous that Laidlow left, on his return to Trinidad, and went solo as Lord Christo, the calypsonian. The group then changed its name to the March of Dimes Quartet and brought in Willy Haynes[a] and later Nap Hepburn to fill Christo's place. Nap was then singing with the Star Stylers but joined the more prosperous March of Dimes. Through Nap Hepburn's father, Syl Taylor,[b] the group was offered a contract to sing at the Young Brigade Calypso Tent at Good Samaritan Hall on Duke Street, Port-of-Spain, in 1956. In the late 1950s, female singer Marjorie Johnson[c] joined the group.

Other groups that started singing with calypsonians include the

---

[a] Willie Haynes left for England soon after.
[b] Syl Taylor was the manager of the tent and continued in that post for many years until the 1980s when he died.
[c] Marjorie and Nap are the only members of the group still alive; Laddie died around year 2001.

"Firesticks" formed by Laddie Prescott when the March of Dimes was on the wane; the "Regenerations Now," a trio, in the mid 1970s at the Regal, comprising Paul Noel, Clifton Lewis and Carlton Duray;[d] the "Spark"[e] who joined the Calypso Revue in 1970 at Legion Hall, P.O.S., sang until 1975 when the Revue functioned at Queen's Park East, and later changed its name to "Wildfire;" the "Earthworms" who joined Kitch's tent in 1976; the "Sensations" who joined the Revue in 1978; the "Sprinkling of Love"[f] who with Laddie Prescott accompanied singers at Spektakula in 1980; the "Sparkles" seen at Sparrow's Young Brigade in Petit Valley in 1985; and "Ruby[g] and the Roots" who accompanied singers at the Calypso Theatre onward from 1986. Over the years too, Patsy Holder, the longest chorister alive, has become a household word in the business. Introduced into calypso by the Mighty Duke, Ms. Holder, well-known for her ability to harmonize, has been accompanying calypsonians since 1973 and sang with Regal, Maljo[h] and Spektakula Calypso tents.

Drake, although he liked the calypsoes of old, such as those sung by Destroyer, Growler, Beginner and Spoiler, firmly believes that the singers of the 1970s were far better than singers of any other era. He was intrigued too, by the antics and songs of Trinidad's first East Indian calypso singer who called himself "Indian Prince." "Indian Prince" was born in 1922 and by the 1950 era, he sang calypsoes with the Senior Brigade in Port-of-Spain, where, because of his antics, he was described as "the hot boy."[6] Indian Prince started his career in Princes Town, the same place as Spoiler. He then moved to San Fernando at the Southern Brigade tent and in 1954, he came to sing in Port-of-Spain. David Renwick, a noted journalist of the era, described him as "a benign pussy-cat" who "kept the crowd rocking at the Senior Brigade with his "Disaster In A Shango Tent." In the calypso,

---

[d] Duray migrated to Canada in 1977; Since then Noel and Lewis have held the group together.

[e] The group started in 1964 and comprised Oliver Chapman, Lennox James, and Terry Moore.

[f] Dale Coombs, Akida Frontin and Wendy Griffin were the original members.

[g] Her real name was Ruby Radix. She sang as a chorus woman for years and died in 2001.

[h] From French/Patois "Mal Yeux" meaning "Bad Eyes" but pronounced in Trinidad "MalJo" and "Malju."

Dr. Hollis "Chalkdust" Liverpool

223

the Prince said that he gave himself fatigue. One of the verses was:

> Hear the sweet refrain
> In a Shango[i] dance down in La Romain.
> Trouble for the Prince again
> In a Shango dance down at La Romain.
> They say they never see the audacity
> Wey this Indian fellow come to do by we?
> Since when Indian get so creolise,
> As if he come by we fete to criticize.[7]

Other outstanding East Indian singers who joined the calypso bandwagon include the "Mighty Clipper"[j] who was famous for his smutty songs at Sparrow's OYB and who died in the early 1990s; the "Mighty Indian" who was a regular at OYB during the 1980s and early 1990s; the "Mighty Rajah" who sang with the Regal tent, OYB and The Kingdom of The Wizards tent in the 1970s and 80s; "The Shah" who was a regular at Spektakula Forum in the 1980s and who has since died; "Hindu Prince" from Tabaquite[k] who joined Victory tent in the 1970s, sang at Spektakula in the 80s and is still holding his own; "Drupatee" who made a name for herself in the 1980s; and "Rikki Jai" of current chutney and calypso fame.

Drake is of the opinion that modern society[l] doesn't seem to understand the meaning of calypso or its purpose, or else not only would there be more youths identifying themselves with the art, but a wider section of the society would be influenced by it. He agrees with Duke that calypso "is a feeling which comes from deep within; a tale of joy or one of suffering; it is an editorial in song of the life that we undergo."[8] He said: "people come to the tents to hear events of the day but they can take pattern from what the calypsonian sings." In other words, Drake knows that calypsonians have a message, moral, philosophical and sometimes religious; such songs can help to create a better citizenry or a better way of life. According to him, there have been calypsoes composed on

---

[i] The Orisa faith in Trinidad is called sometimes by their God "Shango."
[j] He was a barber by profession and kept his hair clipped very low.
[k] An area in Central Trinidad.
[l] The reader ought to remember that I interviewed him in 1974/5.

Dr. Hollis "Chalkdust" Liverpool

every possible topic; they exhort people to practice and inculcate the virtues inherent in them. There have been calypsoes calling upon the nation's citizens to have greater respect for themselves, for their fellow men, and "wear their colour" in a dignified manner.[9] There have been calypsoes showing the nation the way to prosperity, to peace and to justice.[m] Yet Drake feels that if people are to love the calypso as an art form, if they are to grasp fully the message it contains, if they are to understand their roots and ancestry through it, then it must start with the primary school children. As such, the calypso, for Drake, must be on the curriculum of every school child. "Let him read it, understand it, and then let him reject or accept it." With children in mind therefore, Drake tries to make all his compositions factual, non-smutty and moralistic so that the child gains some value on hearing them.

In terms of the historical roots of the calypso, Drake is of the firm opinion that the calypso came to the Caribbean by way of African enslavement and feels that Lion was wrong to associate the art form with France.[n] He opines that Lion might have felt that way because of the presence of so many French Creoles on the island during the 18th and 19th centuries, and the fact that the early calypso was sung in French Patois. Drake may be quite correct, for a feature article in the Trinidad Guardian in 1962 noted thus:

> The calypso is African in origin, conception and rhythm. And all attempts to link it with French culture are plain humbug. The only relation between the calypso and France is that West Indian recognition of the song form could be traced, or maybe was only traced back to the time of the French. More hedonistic than the Spanish, the French were tolerant of vocal expression in the slaves, and that brought the calypso into the open. But the only resemblance that the Calypso ever bore to French culture was that it was once expressed in Patois, the corruption of the language of the estate workers.[10]

---

[m] See Sniper's "Productivity."
[n] See Rafael De Leon's Calypso from France to Trinidad (Trinidad: The Author, 1988).

Dr. Hollis "Chalkdust" Liverpool

It is a historical truism that one of the reasons why carnival and calypso prevailed despite the fact that Whites and Elites tried to wipe out such cultural practices in the 19th century, was due to the number of French Creoles living on the island. The Free Coloureds-French Creoles, locally born Whites and Mulattoes[o] loved the cultural traits displayed by the Africans who were able to carry out their Africanisms[p] within the shelter of the Free Coloured majority. Between 1814 and 1817, 3,823 Free Coloureds were given permission to stay in Trinidad. By 1822, out of a population of 39,974 in Trinidad, there were four times more Free Coloureds than Whites. By 1832, census returns show there were 16,302 of them as against 3,683 Whites, while by 1834, toward the end of enslavement for Africans, the number of Free Coloureds rose again to 18,724 as against 3,632 Whites. What all this further meant was a social monopoly of fetes by the Free Coloureds who also deeply resented any political interference with carnival and calypso by Whites. Since Free Coloureds too, were subject to discrimination, they saw carnival and calypso as a form of passive resistance and a barrier against the imposition of White and Elite values upon the rest of society.[11]

Like John Grimes, an outstanding journalist of the 1960s, Drake noted that the singers in the 18th and 19th centuries used satire and humour to hide, as it were, their political views from the Whites.[12] As such, they couched the lyrics in humourous tones to escape the whip of the slave masters during enslavement, and the wrath of their white, colonial oppressors during the Post-Emancipation era. Drake felt too, that it was that aspect of the culture of the early Africans that has caused Trinidadians to be so humourous, and able to view serious concerns with humour. Small wonder that the author in the early 1980s sang a calypso entitled "Learn to Laugh" in which he informed listeners that when they were hurt over political concerns that they saw affecting them, they

---

[o] Mixtures of Whites and Africans.

[p] Those elements of culture found in the New World that are traceable to an African origin.

Dr. Hollis "Chalkdust" Liverpool

should simply learn to laugh. Again Drake may be quite correct, for the notable journalist John Grimes commented thus:

> It was this circumstance (the ability of the enslaved to create humour) more than any other which gave birth to the calypso, picong[q] and the unique humour of the Trinidadian; which inspires his native philosophy to find humour in the most trying and vexing situations. It is this aspect which makes the Trinidad calypso unique, even though it emanates from an older culture.[13]

As the calypsonians of the late nineteenth century battled with big English words and high-sounding phrases, and as they went from tent to tent in the twentieth century to practice the carnival leggos and road marches, there emerged the practice of giving picong to one another. These picong battles not only brought out the best lyrical verses in the oratorical style, but it laid the foundation for wit and humour which later became the weapons of these singing troubadours, as they taunted their fellow artistes and entertained their guests. Hear how the learned Attila who later became Deputy Mayor of Port-of-Spain taunted his victim:

> I admire your ambition, you'd like to sing,
> But you'll never be a kaiso king.
> To reach such a height without blemish or spot
> You must study Shakespeare, Byron, Milton and Scott.
> But I'm afraid I'm casting pearls before swine,
> For you'll never inculcate such thoughts divine.
> You really got a good intention,
> But poor education - sans humanite.[14]

Picong too, saw calypsonians wandering into the world of fantasy and imagination, into a world of mock battles, into a world of war like the Batonnier,[r] Pierrot and Carnival Robbers, and delving

---

[q] A term used in Trinidad for making fun of a person. It came from the French term "piquant" meaning sharp/biting.
[r] From the French word "baton," meaning a stickfight masquerader.

Dr. Hollis "Chalkdust" Liverpool

into the English vocabulary to colour their world with big words in an attempt to show themselves not only educated, but masters of the English language. In the nineteenth century especially, the majority of carnival characters were bent on picong and humour, and the calypsonian to a large extent, provided the atmosphere for such a humourous tendency within the population, by his quick wit.

To a large extent, Trinidad humour is derived from the calypsonian's humour which today is seen in the calypsonian's political analyses, satire, oration and verbal battles. Take, for example, Funny in 1973 singing "Soul Chick," with his numerous double entendres[s] wood, hammer, rip, screw, etc. Having sung it, one could have heard a driver on Frederick Street, next day, telling another clever driver: "How you could drive so?" Even the Bomb newspaper in 1973-in making fun of Karl Hudson Phillips, a former Attorney General of Trinidad and Tobago who had been rejected by Dr. Eric Williams, then Prime Minister of Trinidad and Tobago-dressed Karl as a pregnant bride with the caption: How you could expect so!"[15]

Humour too, is transmitted through the performance of the calypsonian, using double entente[t] and puns but acting out on stage the clear meaning. Spoiler was humourous and imaginative, and patrons in the 1940s and 50s especially, came to the tent to be entertained, above all, with humour. Spoiler was the greatest in that field in his day. Over the years there have been many humourists. To name a few, I recall: Viper, Wonder, Young Creole, Melody, Unknown, Dougla, Beginner, Kitchener, King Fighter, Rex West, Rex East, Jackson, Cypher, Duke, Bill Trotman, Crusoe Kid, Relator and Power. Viper used to tell me, in the early days when I started to sing, that if you wanted to make a good calypso, make sure that it contained two characteristics: first, ensure that children like it; second, make it humourous.[16]

---

[s] From the French "entendre" meaning "to hear." Thus words used with a double meaning.
[t] Double meaning.

Dr. Hollis "Chalkdust" Liverpool

Calypso humour comes out of the folk culture, but it is sharpened, packaged, and given a public hearing, then returns for us as common language, with common meaning available to all the people of Trinidad and Tobago, and indeed the Caribbean; available too, to the Press and politicians. Thus revelers and women hunters have been heard to say, like Shadow: "I come out to play;" the People's National Movement supporters echo with Sparrow: "we like it so;" and oral sex is rationalized using Sparrow's dictum: "Sixty Million Frenchmen Could Not Be Wrong."

The calypsonian has made fun of the upper class, the tourist, the politician, the Yankee, the immigrant and even, to a lesser extent, the lower class attitudes and values. Humour reflects the positive effect which accompanies triumph and the feeling of superiority. Humour explores sexual and aggressive themes and Freudian psychoanalytic theory of humour points directly to many of the salient features of the calypso.

The calypso then, over the years, has contributed immensely into making in Trinidad a way of life where as Dougla says: "a man will curse his friend to show how glad he is to meet him." [17] In Trinidad, through the calypso, no idea, event, emotion or person can rise above the common denominator: humour. It can brutalize you if you are weak and humble you if you are strong. Thus George Chambers, once the Prime Minister of Trinidad and Tobago, was ridiculed by calypsonian Plainclothes as "Done See" (he meant of course "duncy"), and Pharaoh taunted the colonial Governor: "The Governor tall, tall; The Governor peeping over the wall." No one escapes, as the calypso eases the tension of a confrontation and heightens the enjoyment of a happy time.

Drake noted that as a boy he spoke to many elderly people, two of whom were calypsonians Executor and Attila the Hun. From them he learnt that despite the fact that calypsonians in the 18th and 19th centuries sang out in opposition to the colonial elite, the calypso was not suppressed because the earliest singers reserved for their own ears their more pungent and satirical humour describing their masters their love affairs and general characteristics. In addition, when they attacked or when they gave full reign to their imagination in heaping opprobrium on members of the upper class, they usually had the backing of powerful French Creoles, whom the newspaper described as "some powerful patrons."[18] Both Drake and John Grimes noted that guys like Executor lifted the calypso out of its "paternalistic dungeon" by singing out on events that affected all. For example, Executor, whose contemporaries were the Duke of Albany, Douglas, Baldavia and the Radiant Nightingale, claimed that after singing out on the evils of the Government in "The Burning of the Red House" during the Water Riots of 1903, the calypso became the "voice of the masses."[19] It was seen as an art form that dared to expose and claim redress for wrongs done in the highest echelons of the society. Executor, who was a master of the Extempo calypso, sang outstanding songs like the "Death of Queen Victoria" in 1901 and the "Loss of Sir Murchison Fletcher." Drake was quick to point out Executor's idea of the calypso which Executor himself defined in song:

> From abolition to '98
> Calypso was still sung in its crude state.
> From French to English it was then translated
> By Norman LeBlanc who became celebrated.
> Then it was rendered grammatically
> In oration, poetry and history - sans humanite.[u]

From his conversations with Attila, Drake found out that Attila's strong fort was his ability, like Executor, to improvise. Attila was educated, compared with his contemporaries, and became, in time, a member of the Legislative Council and the City Council of Port-of-Spain. Besides political themes, Attila also chose "backyard" topics such as "Man Santapee Bad Bad, Woman Santapee More Than Bad."

---

[u] Quoted also in The Trinidad Guardian, March 4, 1962.

Dr. Hollis "Chalkdust" Liverpool

Drake noted that with the advent of the Americans during World War 11, "wit and philosophy, even skillfully-veiled sex themes were sacrificed for the bawdy, the salacious and the smutty." Possibly the best remembered song of that period is "Rum and Coca Cola" which assured its composer, Lord Invader, a place among the truly greats in calypso. That calypso, according to Drake, opened new horizons for calypsonians, who until then had not fully appreciated the economic possibilities of the calypso. Ambitions became alive and every singer dreamed of composing a tune which would be a hit on the American market. But years were to pass by before Melody's "Mama Look a Boo Boo" attained the same heights. Drake pointed out that while Invader and Melody gained international standing and wealth from their songs which were re-recorded and sung by the Andrews Sisters and Harry Belafonte respectively, they both died, coincidentally, amid circumstances that reeked of poverty. Truly, Drake is correct for of the period, Errol Hill wrote:

> World War 11 and the American presence in Trinidad did much to popularize the calypso on the international market. Prior to the war, the calypso had a following among West Indian communities in the United States and a small segment of converted Americans. It was hardly recognized in England, almost unheard of in Europe, and totally absent in other parts of the world. But as American troops in Trinidad were reassigned to stations elsewhere, they took calypso recordings with them and helped to spread knowledge and appreciation of the song-form world wide. Whereas previously calypsonians were limited to a yearly trek to the United States for recording and public performances in night clubs, after the war they traveled to all parts of the world including Europe, Africa, and Australia to give concerts, while their recordings were played as far afield as India and Japan. [20]

Before the end of the Second World War, according to Drake, Kitch was the undisputed king of calypso in Trinidad. His "Donkey Race at Siparee," "Tie-Tongue Mopsy," and "Mount Olga" were challenged but not surpassed by Killer's "Stickman and Priest" and "Brigidip." Spoiler too, according to Drake, was on the scene; he was indeed humourous and imaginative. His "Rum Bacchanal" is a collector's gem.

> Rum bacchanal! Hear rum confusion!
> Vat 19 call Mount Gay a small island (repeat).
> Mount Gay say you're fresh, you can't call me such;
> He run and call Scott's liquor, Liberty and Top Notch.
> Ah felt so shame to see four Barbadians
> Want to stand up and fight one Trinidadian.
> Chorus: So Mountain Dew jump in the brew
> Waypah - You fight up with Vat, you fight me too.
> Be careful how you hitting mi partner
> With mi razor in mi hand, Ah going to spoil yuh character.
>
> Vat 19 said: boys don't worry with me,
> I've got backings like fire in La Trinity.
> Black Label, Fifty Fifty, yes Black and Gold,
> Carupano, White Star, Cannings Three Year Old,
> Dolly's Windmill, Puncheon and Coconut Liquor,
> Siegert's Bouquet, V.O. Forres Park, and Canecutter,
> Providence and White Lily rum
> Only waiting to release the Atomic Bomb. [21]

Drake feels too, that not enough is known by the people on the geographical facts of the country. Perhaps it was for this reason that Drake, in a calypso sung in 1970, tried to educate the children about "the wonders of our homeland." In the calypso, Drake spoke of an Englishman who was asked by the Immigration Authorities to leave the country, but refused; his refusal to leave was on account of the beautiful beaches, the sandy coves and green-covered mountain tops which he had encountered, and, above all, "the mystery of our pulsating rhythms of calypso and carnival."

Drake as a young singer had foresight in that he was aware that hundreds of calypsoes have gone down the drain unrecorded during the past two centuries. To stem the tide, he believes that more recording facilities should be opened to today's singers. "Just imagine," he says, "what a great archive and a rich collection this country would have possessed, if all the songs of Mentor, Muncy Daley, Attila, Executor and Lion were available to today's listener or to the university student intent on research." Although these cannot be had, "no effort is being made at governmental level," he says, to preserve today's crop of calypsoes.[v] In fact, up to 1974, Drake's songs were never recorded.

Most persons, though, are unaware of the hardships that impeded the young singer like Drake in the recording field of the 1970s. One must realize that the business then was being run by money-grabbing financiers and capitalists who recorded only persons with the ability and selling power to bring profits to them. Recordings then were so expensive that few recorded. To produce a long-playing calypso recording of approximately eight tunes, in the 1970s, cost in the vicinity of eighty thousand T&T dollars ($80,000). For Drake then, a National Recording Company, to assist all singers, is a must.

Drake feels that calypso "will outlast soul in years to come, if taken to the schools." Yet he believes that the local slangs and idioms used by singers are hindrances in the way of progress. "We must sing," he says, "for people both local and foreign to understand. We must aim at capturing the foreign market." There are many people who hold the same belief. Well do I remember famed journalist Eric Roach writing in the <u>Trinidad Guardian</u> in 1968 stating: "Chalkdust's calypsoes are not worth a green fig outside the Gulf of Paria."[22]

---

[v] On August 13, 1999, Government under the auspices of the NCC, inaugurated the Carnival Institute to carry out, inter alia, the documentation of Carnival. The Institute, however, became still-born after a year for a number of reasons, lack of funding being one.

Dr. Hollis "Chalkdust" Liverpool

In terms of documentation, Drake is of the opinion that the calypso singers who were part of any event held for the first time should be duly documented. For example, **Document No.1:** The Young Brigade Calypso Tent moved from 108 St. Vincent Street to Dirty Jim's Club on South Quay in 1954 and comprised singers Superior, Albany, Eisenhower, King Iere, Viking and Small Island Pride. **Document No. 2:** When Princess Margaret, the sister of the Queen of England, visited our shores in 1955, a command performance of calypso was held in her honour; six calypsonians were selected. They were: Panther who sang "Welcome Princess Margaret;" Melody, who sang "Much Binding in the March;" Sir Galba, who intoned about "The Queen at Montego Bay;" Spitfire, with his "Dance Hall Distressers;" Dictator who informed the Princess about "Trinidad, the Land of Calypsoes; and Viper who sang "Oh, Princess Margaret." Of all the songs to mark the visit of the Princess, Panther's own stood out, as everybody was singing the chorus:

> "Oh Princess Margaret!
> In the atmosphere you can feel it.
> Everyone here is rather glad,
> To welcome your Highness to Trinidad."[23]

Document No. 3: In 1956, when Sparrow won the Calypso King Competition with the well-known calypso "Jean and Dinah," the other finalists in that historic contest were: Eisenhower, singing: "From British Currency to Decimals;" Cypher, singing "Defining Love;" Small Island Pride, singing "Arguments to Federation;" Syncopater, recalling "The Events of last Year;" and Lord Melody with "Hurricane Janet."

Document No. 4: The Original Young Brigade started in 1959 at the Good Samaritan Hall, 106 Duke Street in Port-of-Spain, when, in the same year, the Young Brigade shifted its location from that site to the Waldorf Club on Park Street under the management of Mr. Henry Clarke. The cast of the OYB included Sparrow, with "You Can't Get away From the Tax;" and "Sparrow Aint Dead;" Melody with "Pedlars in Town;" Christo; Zebra with "Jamaica and the Federation;" King Fighter; Viking; Commander with "One Cannot Please People;" Coffee; Power; Cobra; Young Killer; Chang kai-Chek; and Nap Hepburn whose group, the March of Dimes, provided the chorus. Mr. Cyril Diaz,[w] who, it is said, wrote music for the entire cast (and, according to Striker, was the first to do so) provided the musical back-up.[24]

Document No.5: Continuing his list of "firsts" in terms of documentation, the Big Bamboo Calypso Tent opened its doors to the public in 1960 at 53, Park Street, P.O.S., with calypsonian Skipper as (M.C.) emcee and Phil Britto supplying the musical accompaniment. Skipper sang "The Big Bamboo," Nasty Frenchmen" and "South of the Border." Other singers included: Inventor with "What Yuh Born to be Yuh Must Be; Creator[x] with "A Mother's Love" and "Long Time Lovers;" Conqueror, singing "This is a Dog Eat Dog World;" Warrior; Eisenhower, singing "Mouth and Belly;" Young Sparrow, with "Do's and Don'ts for Carnival;" Spitfire with "Indians of Nowadays" and "Long Time Better than Now;" Young Growler; Crooner and Chicky Chong.

Document No. 6: The first National Independence Calypso Competition took place on August 15, 1962; it was won by Lord Brynner. The other placings in order of merit were: Sparrow, Nap Hepburn, Pretender, Dougla, Striker, Power, Chang Kai-Chek, Bomber, Hawk, and Christo. The second competition was held in 1972 to mark the 10th year of Independence; the competition was won by Chalkdust singing "We are Ten years Old." Composer, Pretender, Dougla and Lion were some of the other contestants in 1972.

---

[w] According to Striker, Cyril Diaz wrote music for the cast of the Young Brigade in 1955 at the Dirty Jim Club, South Quay, Port-of-Spain. Diaz played Tenor sax, Phil Britto played Alto sax, Sonny Bain was on the drums, Clifford and Red Popo on guitar, and Spoof on the Bass.

[x] Rumour had it that Creator died a few years ago. On investigation, a telephone call to Jamaica at the time of writing informed the author that Creator is very much alive.

Dr. Hollis "Chalkdust" Liverpool

235

Document No. 7: 1962 saw the birth of two new tents. They were: The Independence Brigade Tent at Unity Hall, Chacon street, P.O.S. featuring, Unknown, Young Killer, Striker, Robin, Viper, Popo, Slammer (from Barbados), Pretender, Professor, Panther, Terror, Magic and Wrangler, and **(Document No. 8)** the French Line tent on 8, Abercromby Street, featuring Baker, Clipper, Young Creole, Impressor, Pancho, Crooner, King Solomon, Scaramouche, Young Syncopator, Sad Sack, Gibraltar, Rambler, Surpriser and Harmony. Bently Jack (Watap) supplied the music. Kitchener joined the Independence Brigade then managed by Mr. Rudolph Spann in 1963. The tent was held then on Duke Street and calypsonian Viking was really the one who was responsible for Kitchy's return from England where he had resided for sixteen years. Viking bought Kitchy's ticket after Kitch accepted his advice to return home.[25]

Document No. 9: In 1964, as if to mark their debut into the homes of Trinidadians and Tobagonians, TTT[y] held a calypso contest for the first time. It was won by Lord Brynner. Brynner was followed by the Roaring Lion and Dougla respectively.

Document No.10: Drake remembered the special theatrical play put on in the tent by the boys of the OYB in 1964; it was entitled "Stella Wedding" from a calypso sung by Lord Nelson that year. It starred Sparrow as the parson and Nelson as the old man who was in love with Stella. Bill Trotman played Stella; Robin played the young groom who was marrying Stella; Christo was the chief bridesmaid and Brigo and Mystery were the other bridesmaids in the play that explained in song and drama the woes of the old man who was overcome with tears, when he saw Stella his girl friend being wedded to a younger man.

---

[y] It stands for Trinidad and Tobago Television, a broadcasting company in Trinidad..

Historically, the Calypso Drama/ theatrical play started as early as 1933 when Attila and Lion sang a duet to woo the fans away from the Silky Millionaires tent of Railway Douglas, Radio, Beginner and Inveigler. The success of the duet caused Lion and Attila to compose and sing many more on themes such as "Gombo Lai Lai"[z] and "Asteroid."[26] They also recorded many songs in duet style including "I Will String Along With You," "Louis-Schmeling Fight," and "Modern Times." Donald Hill's research showed however, that as early as 1929, Attila, Munsee Daly, Executor and Lord Inventor were involved in a calypso skit in San Fernando, South Trinidad. The skit was backed by Capt. A. A. Cipriani and "other upper-class Trinidadians." He noted too, that that "show was a precursor of the calypso drama" which he said began with the staging of the "Divorce Case" in 1933.[27]

> Calypso Duets gave birth to Calypso trios, such as the Keskidee Trio of Attila, Beginner and the Growling Tiger, who recorded nine tunes between March 15th, and March 22nd 1935. These were 'Don't Let Me Mother Know,' 'Dingolay,' 'Marian Leggo Me Man' which was an adaptation of the kalinda 'Fire Brigade Water the Road;' 'Congo Bara' (which also supplied the melody for the chorus of 'Nettie Nettie'); 'Trinidad My Home;' 'Go Down The Valley' (probably a Shouter/Baptist hymn); 'War,' (an exercise in 'Sans Humanite' picong); 'Shango' and 'Sa Gomes Emporiums' (a song eulogizing the Portuguese businessman through whose initiative most of the recording of calypsoes was done).[28]

Although Beginner as early as 1931[aa] dramatized the calypso in the tent,[29] and Railway Douglas, according to Iere, dramatized many in the tent in 1921 and thereafter,[30] Calypso Duets[bb] did give rise to Calypso Trios and these in turn gave rise to Calypso Dramas.

---

[z] Gombo Lai Lai was a famous town-character who went around using big words a la Ms. Malaprop.
[aa] According to Rohlehr, the Crystal Palace tent held a show in Arima. It belonged to Douglas.
[bb] In 1934, Lion and Attila dramatized, via a duet, the first beauty competition held in Trinidad in 1933. They were in their own way objecting to the fact that despite the beauty of African women, a white girl was chosen as the winner.

Dr. Hollis "Chalkdust" Liverpool

These dramas underscore the calypsonians' ability to act onstage, for all calypso aficionados know that all good calypsonians can act; the calypso itself is about drama on stage for the singer has to use his physical assets to paint pictures that will allow the audience to understand the lyrical story. The calypsonian uses his hands, his face, his clothing and his dancing to tell the musical story. As such, many of these calypso dramas were carried out with little rehearsals, save the calypsonian's ability to communicate. Errol Hill has pointed out that, from 1933 to 1966, there have been nineteen such dramas.[31] **Document No.11:** In 1933, Douglas, Attila, Executor, Lion and Inveigler carried out the first calypso drama; it was entitled the "Divorce of the Huggins Family" and was staged at the Railroad Millionaires tent on 44 Nelson Street, and at Attila's Salada Millionaires Tent on 47, Henry Street.[32] Attila in his book noted that there were other dramas namely: "The Civil Servant and the Obeah man" and "The Wooing of Olga" which were carried out by Douglas, Lion, Executor, Radio and he himself in the 1930s.[33] In 1934, in response to the Shouters' Prohibition Ordinance of 1917, a Calypso Drama on the theme was staged by the calypsonians in Port-of-Spain.[34]

Document No. 12: In keeping then with the tradition of staging calypso dramas, the calypsonians at the OYB in 1965 re-staged the "trial of Mano Benjamin,"[cc] a notorious criminal who was found guilty of sexually abusing and imprisoning two sisters in his home. Sparrow acted as the judge, Bill Trotman acted the part of Dulcie who was blinded by Mano played by Lord Bitterbush. In the skit, Lord Caruso was the policeman who prosecuted Mano, while Christo represented the Jury.

[cc] Found guilty of abuse, the Judge called him "a beast in human form."

Dr. Hollis "Chalkdust" Liverpool

Document No. 13: In 1966, at the SWWTU[dd] Hall, the OYB's members staged a calypso drama entitled "Nine Years Honeymoon." It starred Bill Trotman as the Bride, Lord Nelson as the Groom, Sparrow as the Reverend Minister, Fighter as the Policeman, Christo as the Judge while the audience acted as the Jury. In 1967, Bill Trotman at the OYB staged a calypso drama entitled " One Man Commission of Pitchoil Enquiry," while the tent dramatized in song and dance Sparrow's "Governor's Ball," **(Document No. 14)** starring Blakie as Mr. Prospect and Bill Trotman as the mad woman who jumped the wall and gate-crashed the Governor's ball. So successful were these dramas that the crowd looked forward to them as part of the night's entertainment. Accordingly, OYB in 1968 staged the "Hospital Baby Kidnap" recalling the event when a woman stole a baby from the General Hospital in Port-of-Spain that year, and in 1970 the tent's theatrical skit was entitled "Racial Discrimination."

Document No. 15: In 1976, the year of a national election, the management of the Regal Calypso Tent put on an election skit depicting in calypso song all the party leaders and their manifestos. Written by Chalkdust, the theatrical drama witnessed calypsonian Alligator singing the praises of Dr. Ivan Perot, a party leader; Composer, dramatizing in song Mr. Arnold Thomasos, the Speaker of the House of Representatives; Organizer, showing the wiles of Mr. George Weekes, trade unionist and politician; Shah, acting out in song and body movement the character of Mr. Vernon Jamadar, the leader of the DLP; Young Creole, displaying the activities and plans of politician Mr. Alloy Lequay; Superior singing as Mr. ANR Robinson; Penguin acting as Mr. Roy Richardson; Smiley representing Dr. James Millette; Vallee putting forth the views of Lloyd Best; Power singing the views of Ashford Sinanan and Chalkdust intoning the humour of Eric Williams. Accompanied by Boyie Mitchell's orchestra and the Regenerations Now supplying chorus, all the singers dressed in a manner imitative of the characters

---

[dd] The letters stand for "Seamen and Waterfront Workers' Trade Union."

Dr. Hollis "Chalkdust" Liverpool

they represented. The drama was so well received that in 1977, another political skit was staged by the tent members of Regal.

Document No. 16: Kitch returned to Trinidad in 1964 and, for the first time, he headed Calypso Revue; it took place at Queen's Hall and starred-besides Kitch-Melody, Brynner, Nap Hepburn, Blakie, Bomber, Power, Conqueror, Pretender, Zebra, Fighter, Superior, Cypher, Spider, Sniper, Calypso Rose, and Creole. Roaring Lion was a guest at times and Frankie Francis and his nine piece orchestra supplied the music.

Document No. 17: In 1965, the first "Buy Local Competition" was held. It was staged by the PNM in the Queen's Park Savannah, and aimed at getting the populace to support local industries, rather than allow the country to lose, through importation, much-needed foreign exchange. Of 57 singers auditioned, twelve were selected for the Final. They were: Roaring Lion, Cisco who later became known as King Wellington, Citrus, Duke, Laro, Pretender, Skipper, Tiny Terror, Unknown, Viper, Striker and Cliff Lezama. The contest was won by Striker, followed by Duke and Skipper. That year, a National Junior Calypso Monarch contest was staged for the first time; it was won by Willard Harris, Lord Relator, who went on to become one of the nation's foremost calypsonians.

In keeping with the need to document "firsts" in calypso history and development, Drake spoke of the cast of the first Calypso Theatre **(Document No.18)** that was started by George Goddard with the assistance of the CDC in 1966. It represented a big break in calypso as, for the first time, the Government became involved in the running of a calypso tent and singers, who otherwise could not have sung in a commercially-run tent, got the opportunity to do so. The tent was held at 100, St. Vincent Street with music supplied by John Buddy Williams. The cast comprised Leveler who reached the final of the Calypso King contest that year, Lord Funny, Harmony, Reporter, Penman, Wrangler, Spitfire, Viper, Rainbow, Gibraltar, Unknown, Lord and Lady Iere, Barow, Scraper, Sad Sack, Observer, Young Invader, Tiny Terror, King Solomon and Viking.

Document No. 19: In 1970, for the first time, Blakie headed a calypso tent. It was established at the Port Services Club on Wrightson Road and was called "Victory." The tent made waves in terms of patronage, to the extent that at times on weekends, management had to put on two shows and these were usually sold out. The tent was financed by lawyer Theodore Guerra and managed by Mr. Earl Patterson, the well-known masquerader. Backed by the March of Dimes, the singers were accompanied by Roderick Borde and his orchestra. Blakie, Shadow, Brigo, Power, Funny, Composer, Lester, Pretender, Terror, Francine, Princess, Hindu Prince, Valentino and Poser comprised the cast. This was the year when Lord Inventor sang and accompanied himself on a pan at Kitchy's Revue. He was in fact, the first person ever to do so and the calypso dealt with the fact that he, having arrived at Piarco had no passport to prove that he was a Trinidadian; he had forgotten it in St. Thomas where he resided. He therefore pulled out his pan and played telling the Immigration Officer: "Look mi passport right here." Mr. Guerra in 1972 also sponsored a new tent at the corner of Abercromby Street and Independence Square; it was headed by the Mighty Duke and featured singers Chalkdust, Creole, Zebra, Inventor, Contender and Gypsy to name a few.

Document No. 20: In 1973, the Regal Calypso Tent opened its doors for the first time at Legion Hall, Lower Richmond Street, Port-of-Spain. It was a revolution in calypso tent history, for the tent was managed by the singers themselves. Headed by Duke, Superior and Chalkdust, the tent's cast comprised the following: Johnny Calypso, Lord Coffee, Psycho, Lord Smiley, Funny, Roamer, Young Creole, Lecturer, Gypsy, Striker, Bopee, Black Angel, Vallee and Lord Drake.

Document No. 21: In 1976, a new tent by the name of the "Professionals" was formed. Housed at 150 Frederick Street opposite the prison, financed mainly by Brutus from New York, Duke, Shorty and Wellington, the cast comprised the Mighty Duke, Wellington, Young Eagle, Contender, Gypsy, Tallish, Calypso Height, Lord Shorty, Brigo, Funny, Calypso Jane, Lion, AllRounder, Rio, Indian Prince, Count Robin, Rajah, Adviser, Cardinal, Becket from St. Vincent and poet Cheryl Byron.

241

Document No. 22: Another new tent termed "The Kingdom of the Wizards" started in 1978. It was owned and managed by Mr. William Munroe who erected building to house the tent and future calypso concerts on the Upper Henry Street site. The building later became the home of Spektakula Forum until year 2001, when the members of Spektakula's cast held court at the Jean Pierre Complex. The Kingdom of the Wizards was headed by Shadow and comprised singers: Funny, Stalin, Valentino, Brigo, Singing Francine, Gypsy, Smiley, Count Robin, Squibby, Cro Cro, Rio, Warrior, Almanac, Calypso Height, Emba and Lord Fluke. **Document No. 23:** In 1979, the tent was taken over by the Martineau Brothers and though it was still named The "Kingdom of the Wizards," it might be fair to say that it was in fact the first year of Spektakula Forum which has now become a household word in the establishment and development of calypso tents in Trinidad. With music supplied by Earl Rodney and Friends and with the Regenerations Now giving the singers chorus support, Black Stalin, Chalkdust, Melody, Short Shirt, Valentino, Merchant, Relator, Francine, Kele Zanda, Squibby, Composer, Canary from Guyana, Unknown, Power, Warrior, Double Feature, Contender, Almanac and Commentor comprised the cast.

Document No. 24: That very year another new tent termed the Master's Den was formed. The shows took place at NUGFW Hall on Frederick Street. Gypsy, Shadow, Brigo, Blakie, Psycho, Cro Cro, Rio, and Delamo-to name the main persons-were the members of the cast. **Document No. 25:** Spektakula Forum officially opened in 1980 at 111-115 Henry Street, POS. Roy Cape and his TNT Rainbow band supplied the music. The year saw the advent of "comedians" as "emcees," for Errol "Stork" St. Hill and Tommy Joseph, comedians all, were appointed to chair the proceedings as emcees at the Masters' Den and Spektakula respectively. The historical cast at the first opening of Spektakula Forum included Lord Relator, Black Stalin, Lord Valentino, Singing Francine, the Mighty Arrow of Montserrat, Explainer, Merchant, Chalkdust, Shah, Rajah, Eagle, Fighter, Lord Smiley, Traveller, Psycho, Fluke, Grabbler, Struggler, Brother Idi, Commentator and Hindu Prince.

I thanked Drake for all his documentary knowledge, congratulated him and wished him well, for there are few calypsonians, excepting Duke, Composer, Sparrow and Lord Blakie in St. Thomas, who see the need for proper documentation of the art form. Drake realized that there is need for an institute that will house the feats carried out by calypsonians so that future generations will understand better the art and its history and development.

Finally, Drake, having lived through the Black Power Confrontations with the Government and the Elite in 1970, was concerned with how calypsonians saw the uprising of mainly African young men seeking justice and trying to change the economic and political systems. "There were," he said, "over twenty calypsoes on the disturbances, and few, if any, have ever been made public or even recorded." Again, he stressed the need for a National Recording Company.

Drake recalled that the "Black Power Movement had affected everyone, to the extent that even Gene Miles sang calypso." The name Gene Miles, more than any other woman in Trinidad and Tobago, had become identified with protest. Though, because of her light complexion and the fancy clothes she wore, she was looked upon as a member of the upper class, she boasted that her father had cracked open the Caura Dam Racket, [ee] and she had exposed the illegal Gas Station Scheme of the 1960s. [ff] Because of her exposure, she fell into the bad books of the Government who dismissed her from the Public Service on the grounds that she had left her post without due leave or permission. Gene contended that she had only taken leave that she had rightfully accrued and that Ms. Muriel Donawa, the Government spokesperson in Parliament, had lied on her. Grieved, she took to the streets and to alcohol and died amidst unfortunate circumstances in the 70s. Before she died, I

[ee] A racket involved in the building of the Caura Dam, a water trapment area in North Trinidad.

[ff] Specially chosen but unqualified persons were able to obtain licenses to open gas stations.

Dr. Hollis "Chalkdust" Liverpool

I would visit her from time to time, when she was a patient at the hospital, and she would pour out her inner soul to me. Gene was so hurt that in 1970, she used the opportunity, following the Black Power Confrontations, to take her grievance to the calypso tent and thus sang at the Revue. The Express newspaper recorded her entry into the calypso tent thus:

> Over the years she has shown an outspokeness which was once thought to be the special privilege of the calypsonian. Now Gene has decided to use yet another channel to promote her criticisms: the calypso stage. This calypso season found her in Lord Kitchener's 'Calypso Revue' tent. The former civil servant is now calypsonian, singing about the 'Gas Station Racket' in which she herself played such an essential part. Like Chalkdust, Gene, newcomer that she is, belongs to the old school of calypsonians: sure of herself, hard-hitting even when attacking people in high places with topics that most would regard as taboo. But then Gene, as she has so often said, 'doesn't really care a damn.'[35]

Of the Gas Station Racket, Gene Miles sang:

> Ah was born right here
> And Ah grow right here.
> So to sing out loud
> I aint have no fear.
> He was found guilty
> And yet they set him free.
> Tell me where is the justice in T&T.[36]

History has shown that the Black Power Confrontations of the 1970s occurred, because the people, faced with high unemployment, inflationary prices, institutional racism and discrimination of the poor by the Elite, were angry with the authorities who seemed to be complacent in the midst of all their suffering. Moreover, the elitist Whites and French Creoles were prospering while the lower and middle classes suffered from pecuniary strangulation.

This caused the author in his calypso "Answer to Black Power" to ask: "Why must the small minority control us economically?" Chalkdust went on to state that "the answer to Black Power was …to fill every hole, nook and cranny" with members of the lower classes who must now take charge of vital economic areas like "sugar and oil," and that foreign ownership "must now over." The words of one chorus of the calypso are:

> Doctor, the answer to solve Black Power
> Is to tax the rich some more
> And build houses for the blind, the lame and the poor.
> Doctor, the answer to solve Black Power
> Houses for everyone we must ensure.
> Vital areas like sugar and oil
> Must be run by sons of our soil.
> Why must the small white minority
> Control us economically?
> Make sure that our black majority
> Fill up every hole, nook and cranny;
> That's the answer for Black Power. [37]

Drake said that he had loved Pretender's contribution to the Black Power debate. Pretender spoke of the oppression that Africans have had to face "ever since time began," and Preedie summed up the cause of the confrontation simply: "You can't keep pushing Black people around." Valentino, dubbed "The People's Calypsonian" after 1970, was of the view that the strikes, the loss of life and the destruction of property were regrettable. The people wanted change and not "revolution." Valentino sang:

> You talk bout power, Doctor!
> Is you have power.
> Ah know when you act,
> It would have been a horse of a different colour.
> You gave them an inch; they take a whole yard.
> And when you had them under yuh clinch, people say you bad.

But when I heard you address the nation,
I knew what was your intention.
But some of the powers you exercise,
Unfortunately, I must criticize.

Chorus: Because we didn't want dem trigger-happy police;
We only wanted to demonstrate in peace;
Yet you held my people and charge them
for sedition.
We was marching for equality,
Black unity and Black dignity;
Dr. Williams! No! We didn't want no revolution.

You must be aware that the Black
consciousness is here.
I further declare is time that we get an equal share.
Is Black blood, Black sweat and Black tears,
but is White profits;
Cause all through the years, is the White
man reaping the benefits.
But now we are coming down from the shelves,
And we (are) getting to know ourselves.
So let us hail Geddes Granger,gg
For bringing all Black people together.

Chorus: Because the fight was against racial prejudice,
The Imperialist, the Capitalist,
Yet some ignorant people talking
'bout Communism.
We didn't want all this set of burning down
And the smashing of all them stores in town;
Dr. Williams! We didn't want no revolution. [39]

---

gg The leader of the National Joint Action Committee, the body that was in the
forefront of the struggle. Geddes in 1970, changed his name to Makandaal
Daaga, who himself fought for the liberation of Africans in Trinidad in 1837.

Dr. Hollis "Chalkdust" Liverpool

A few calypsonians like Black Stalin saw the confrontation as part of a world uprising and awakening of black people. Stalin therefore urged the Africans in Trinidad to "get up, get up" in his calypso entitled "Time." In his other lyrical work on the Confrontation entitled "National Reconstruction," Stalin sang:

> "What happening to the blacks in America
> Is the same in the West Indies and South Africa.
> So for once black people getting together.[40]

Short Shirt from Antigua sang at the Revue in 1971 and saw the problem, like Black Stalin, in terms of the global war being staged by Black people. He sang:

> Some people may say the problems are for lands afar
> Places like England, United States and Canada.
> But brother let me sock it to you again
> That once you're black, you are in trouble just the same.
> In this world, your future could be dimmed
> Because of the colour of your skin.
> King Shortie say: May God forgive.
> This world is ours to live in, as the others live.[41]

Duke saw Black Power differently. He felt that the faces that led the country were all black already. "The Government in power black and that's a fact." Therefore what was needed, according to Duke, was black economic power to take care of the inequalities reigning in the society. In the traditional minor key, Duke sang beautifully:

> Ah know they'll get vex and want to fight me down
> But the term Black Power used here is wrong.
> Ah making it clear Ah don't care who vex,
> But Black Power here is out of context.

Cause 90 per cent of the people black;
The Government in power and that's a glaring fact.
But you take Uncle Sam ideology,
And try to implant it on this society. [42]

While many singers, including the author and Lord Kitchener, sang "on the imposition of the curfew and its effect on spousal relationships," [43] Lord Kitchener produced a gem of a calypso on the confrontation entitled "No Freedom." Kitch proved that, contrary to what some believe, he was not a "Yes-man," [hh] even though he supported openly the ruling party at the time. By speaking out against the actions of his own party, Kitch showed the mettle of which "true-true" calypsonians are made. "True-true calypsonians," Pretender used to say "never take sides in any dispute or bacchanal." [44] Like the historian, it's the only way one can comment fairly and justly, if the singer's mission is the attainment of truth. Errol Hill thus wrote:

> Kitchener produced one of the hardest hitting calypsoes on the revolt...Kitch denounced the summary jailing without trial of the movement's leaders and asked where is the vaunted freedom in this independent country of ours. Written in short, strongly syncopated lines that are the trade mark of the Road March King, and rendered with energetic vitality, the calypso stands as an angry indictment of dictatorial rule. Here is part of the lyric:

Ah glad for Geddes Granger;
Ah glad for Weekes also.
Ah glad for all dem detainees; Ah so glad they let them go.

They captured them one morning;
They tell them is no bail.
They innocently push the people straight in the Royal Jail.

[hh] A term used for one who always subordinates himself to his superiors.

Chorus: Oh! What a country!
Oh! What an awful sin!
How come they could be jailing people so
without a hearing!
Where is our freedom?
Somebody put a hand.
Oh Gorm, the Vengeance of Moko[ii] go
surely fall on this land.

We criticize Rhodesia,
And Alabama too;
I'm sure you would never dream that
this could happen to you.
We pull down South Africa;
We bad talk every place;
We spit into the skies and now it fall right
back in we face.

Well sometime in the fifties,
You could hear them say:
This Colonialism is a blight and must go away.
But since we independent,
What they do for we?
They introduce the I.R.A.[jj] and the State of Emergency.[45]

Drake singled out Pretender, Chalkdust and Kitchener as being the three greatest bards of the art form. Kitchener, in his opinion, has the "best melodious tunes and sensible compositions." Moreover, Kitch had "memory like a wounded parrot and blended his tunes with the old time touch." To him, "Chalkdust is the social critic who brings the events of the day into the tent," while Pretender is "the greatest" he being "always able to sing a good calypso and extempo in the same tune." While there are thousands who will agree with Drake's chosen trio, there are tens of thousands who certainly feel that the name Sparrow must be linked with any aspect of calypso.

Drake left me a wiser man, and I realized, from speaking to him, that the calypso is in good hands, for he proved that many of our young people understand the art and its importance to human development.

[ii] A popular term in Trinidad for a curse.
[jj] Industrial Relations Act.
Dr. Hollis "Chalkdust" Liverpool

249

ENDNOTES

1 Foreword of <u>Original Regal; Calypso Hits 1973</u>. (Trinidad: DuSuChalk Associates, 1973), p.3.

2 <u>Trinidad Chronicle</u>, January 31, 1957.

3 <u>Trinidad Chronicle</u>, February 13, 1959. 1.

4 Laidlow, Christopher (Christo). Personal Interview. P.O.S., August 1973.

5 <u>Trinidad Chronicle</u>, January 27, 1957.

6 Renwick, David. "The Original Indian Prince." <u>Trinidad Chronicle</u>, January 24, 1959. 6.

7 Renwick, David. ditto.

8 Pope, Kelvin (Mighty Duke). "What is Calypso?" (1968), The Author's Collection of Calypso Lyrics.

9 Pope, Kelvin (Duke), "Black is Beautiful." Calypso Theater, Old Fire Brigade Building, Abercromby Street, P.O.S., 1968.

10 Grimes, John. "From Slave Chant to Hit Parade." <u>Trinidad Guardian</u>, March 4, 1962.

11 Liverpool, Hollis. <u>Rituals of Power and Rebellion: The Carnival Tradition in Trinidad and Tobago, 1763 - 1962</u> (Chicago: Frontline Distribution Int'l., 2001), 138 - 139.

12 Grimes. op. cit.

13 Grimes, ditto.

14 Quevedo, Raymond. <u>Attila's Kaiso: A Short History of Trinidad Calypso</u> (POS: UWI, Extra Mural Dept., 1983), 93.

15 <u>The Bomb</u>, Friday, December 7, 1973.

16 Lewis, Roderick (Viper). Personal Conversation, P.O. S., March 1968.

17 Ali, Clayton (Dougla). Lyric from Independence Calypso King Competition, Queen's Park Savannah, P.O.S., August 1976.

18 Grimes, ditto.

19 Grimes, ditto.

20 Hill, Errol. "Calypso and War" in <u>Papers: Seminar On The Calypso</u>, Volume 1, UWI, St. Augustine, Trinidad (January 6 -10, 1986).

21 Quevedo, Raymond (Attila). <u>The Growth and Improvement of Calypso</u> (Trinidad: The Author, 1947), 37.

22 Roach, Eric. <u>Trinidad Guardian</u>, March 1968.

23 Liverpool, Hollis. The Author's Collection of Calypso Lyrics.

[24] Oblington, Percy (Striker). The True History of Calypso. (Trinidad: The Author, 2000), 10.

[25] Springer, Victor (Viking). Personal Interview. P.O.S., August 1972.

[26] Quevedo, Raymond (Attila). Attila's Kaiso (Trinidad: UWI, Extra-Mural Dept., 1983), 47-47.

[27] Hill, Donald. Calypso Calaloo (Florida: University Press of Florida, 1993), 147-148.

[28] Rohlehr, Gordon. Calypso in Pre-Independence Trinidad. (Trinidad: The Author, 1990), 135.

[29] Rohlehr, op.cit., 135.

[30] Thomas, Randolph (Iere). Personal Interview with Iere, UWI., August 1973.

[31] Hill, Errol. The Trinidad Carnival: Mandate for A National Theatre (Austin: University of Texas Press, 1972), 80.

[32] Rohlehr, op. cit. 136-137.

[33] Quevedo, op.cit., 46-48.

[34] Rohlehr, 138.

[35] "Calypso is Dying - but who cares?" Express, Monday, January 5, 1970. 10-11.

[36] Pope, Kelvin (Duke). Telephone Conversation, July 2, 2003.

[37] Liverpool, Hollis (Chalkdust). "Answer to Black Power," Calypso Theatre, 1971.

[38] Farrell, Aldric (Pretender). Calypso Revue, 1971.

[39] Liverpool, Hollis. From the Author's Collection of Calypso Lyrics.

[40] Calliste, Leroy (Stalin). "National Reconstruction" Calypso Revue, 1971.

[41] Emmanuel, McClean (Short Shirt). "Black Like Me." Calypso Revue, 1971.

[42] Pope, Kelvin (Duke). Telephone Conversation, (11.12 a.m.) June 25, 2003.

[43] Hill, Errol. "Calypso and War." op. cit.

[44] Farrell, Aldric (Pretender). Personal Conversations, 1973 - 2000.

[45] Roberts Aldwyn (Kitch). "No Freedom." Calypso Revue, 1971; Hill Errol, op. cit.

Conclusion

In looking at the development of calypso through the mouths of the singers themselves, I have sought to gain a truer picture of the calypsonian, his attitudes, his undying love for the art and the hardships he encountered and still encounter today. I have sought to give readers a clearer and more realistic picture of the development of this indigenous trait of ours. I have sought to show readers and interesting persons that one can only understand the calypsonian's mode of living, by studying the social structure that has bred and fashioned him or her. I have sought to show readers the contributions made by the singers to society, to the development of the art form, and consequently, to human development as well. I have sought to show that there is much more to a calypso than the music or the lyric which it contains. I have sought, above all, to show that the elder calypsonians have much to tell in terms of the social history of our nation; they are tools and wells of information that teachers ought to use in the education of our children.

The reader, I hope, will have a clearer picture of how the upper-uppers and wealthy classes frowned upon the art as being crude, devilish, orgiastic and immoral. We know now that not withstanding all the lip-service paid to the creative ability of the calypsonians and their achieved status, some people yet classify them as social lepers. We have seen the calypsonians' fight to better themselves both culturally and financially, and gain for themselves thereby, a higher place on the hierarchical ladder of respectability and social acceptance. In addition, the calypsonian's history and conditions surrounding his toil make us able to compare tents and styles of living of yesteryear, with those of today. The reader will note the movement from bamboo constructed, coconut covered, flambeau-lit tents, competing in the hastily contrived nightly contests for the few dollars thrown into a hat by the affluent patrons who went slumming, to spacious neon-lit halls, with bureaucratically organized managerial systems.

Dr. Hollis "Chalkdust" Liverpool

The research brought out three outstanding points that need further perusal. Firstly, elder calypsonians should be and can be of great use to this nation of ours, if their memories, their talents, skills and their experiences are made use of in primary, secondary and tertiary schools, at Adult Education classes, and at the learning environment promoted by Village Councils and Community Centres. Most of the elder singers, especially, live in abject poverty and government and the private sector can assist them financially by having them thus employed. At least it would be a way of making up for the callous disregard that a society paid them for their contribution. Secondly, there is need for a Calypso Archive containing tapes, records, books, recordings and pamphlets that will underscore the development and progress of the calypso. Such documentation, including the life histories of the calypsonians, will be made accessible to the public in general, and to students and lovers of the art in particular, by way of a noteworthy building and landscape that will serve to house all aspects of the carnival of Trinidad and Tobago. Thirdly, a foundation or grant ought to be set up, either at Governmental or private level, so as to provide researchers with the tools and resources for further study of our social past. This study, will, I am sure, not only make our youths more appreciative of their cultural traits, not only help in erasing the many false values that they now hold, not only move them to take a greater pride in their culture, heritage and themselves, but in doing so, the social history of our country will, at last, be written. To these perspectives, my research has forced and motivated me to dedicate myself.

Dr. Hollis "Chalkdust" Liverpool

The 1970 Black Power Confrontation: Daaga Leads

Bill Trotman in a dramatical play at OYB

INDEX

Inventor, Senior (Henry Forbes) 30, 63; Inventor (Lloyd Merchant) 159, 186, 208, 234, 240; Modern Inventor 9, 23, 31
Inveighler 30, 31, 236, 237
Italy 70

Kaiso 24, 44, 55, 56, 57, 96, 99, 111, 114, 118, 179, 221
Kalenda 2, 34, 58, 136
Keate, Governor 26, 53
Keane, Tom 5
Kele Zanda (singer) 241
Khan, Harold 91
Khan, Johny 34, 82
Khan, Amral Sultan 28, 62
Killer 7, 22, 91, 104, 140, 231
Kimling Restaurant 115
King Albany 1
King Frankie 5
King George VI, 60
King Mike 5
King Iere 67, 80
Kitchener, Lord 34, 65, 66, 71, 72, 83, 96, 99, 103, 104, 108, 109, 111, 116, 134, 137, 145, 147, 161, 164, 169, 179, 180, 192, 194a, 197, 198, 199, 202, 204, 208, 210, 215, 235, 239, 243, 247, 248; Kitchener as the Road March Winner 139 -140; Kitchener Thorpe 28; Young Kitchener 210
Klassic Rouso 172
Krehbiel, Henry Edward 59
Kwabena 210

Lacou Harpe 103
Lady B 188, 190, 192
Lady Bird 189
Lady Chaconia 189
Lady Countess 189
Lady Filly 189
Lady Guymine 210
Lady Iere 82, 85, 89, 185, 188, 190, 192, 239

Without the contributions of our sponsors namely:

The Ministry of Community
Development and Gender Affairs,
Angostura Limited,
The National Lotteries Control Board,
The Royal Bank Of Trinidad and
Tobago,
Republic Bank of T&T Ltd.,
Mr. Irving Rauceo,
Mr. Peter Albert of Maser Ltd.
Rhand Credit Union Co-operative
Society,
Trinidad and Tobago National
Petroleum Marketing Co. Ltd.,
The Office Centre Ltd. of Dominica W.I.
&
The National Carnival Commission

It would not have been possible to
publish this book.

Digital Artwork and Printing by Maser Ltd.